GRAHAM
HENRY

GRAHAM HENRY

FINAL WORD

BOB HOWITT

HarperSport
An Imprint of HarperCollins*Publishers*

Dedication

To all the players from schoolboy and club level
through to the World Cup-winning All Blacks who
have helped make my job as a rugby coach, across
four decades, such a stimulating and rewarding one.
Thanks for the memories, guys.

— Sir Graham Henry

HarperSport
An imprint of HarperCollins*Publishers*
77–85 FulhamPalace Road
Hammersmith, London W6 8JB

www.harpercollins.co.uk

First published by HarperCollins*Publishers* (New Zealand) Limited 2012

This edition published by HarperSport 2013

1 3 5 7 9 10 8 6 4 2

Typeset by Springfield West

© Graham Henry 2012

Graham Henry asserts the moral right to
be identified as the author of this work

A catalogue record of this book is
available fom the British Library

ISBN 978-0-00-751467-0

Printed and bound in Great Britain by
Clays Ltd, St Ives plc

MIX
Paper from
responsible sources
FSC **FSC C007454**

FSC™ is a non-profit international organisation established to promote
the responsible management of the world's forests. Products carrying the
FSC label are independently certified to assure consumers that they come
from forests that are managed to meet the social, economic and
ecological needs of present and future generations,
and other controlled sources.

Find out more about HarperCollins and the environment at
www.harpercollins.co.uk/green

Foreword by Sir John Graham

From World Cup-losing coach to knighted winner, from disaster to triumph over the years, the Graham Henry story is a remarkable one of 37 years of coaching and dedication to rugby in New Zealand and the UK.

As one of his third- and sixth-form teachers at Christchurch Boys' High School, I know that he was no star scholar, yet his persistence gained him University Entrance.

He played First XV rugby and First XI cricket — a gritty young sportsman, but not a natural one. Determination has always been part of his character and even then he had that dour southern desire to succeed.

It was during my years as his headmaster at Auckland Grammar School that I observed Graham's outstanding work ethic: he ran the school hostel, coached the First XV, carried a full teaching load — and studied and earned a degree. He'd discovered the value of hard work and understood that, for him in particular, nothing would be achieved without total effort.

His eventual destiny was still many years ahead and, in fact, unthought of. By 1982, he was deputy headmaster of Kelston Boys' High School and by 1986 the school's headmaster, a remarkably quick climb up the educational ladder.

His rugby coaching, too, had continued to prosper. He was learning his rugby trade at secondary school and senior club level and constantly developing outstanding teams. His rugby ambitions were blossoming. He won the Auckland coaching position in 1992 on merit and thus began a tumultuous rugby coaching career of 21 years at senior levels of the game.

For the next four years, until 1995, he successfully combined leading a major boys' school along with coaching the Auckland rugby team. These years honed his coaching skills and slowly improved his man-management ability.

Graham was careful in his approach to players, often distant, and he was sometimes seen as being unapproachable; he was certainly careful and wary of a growing, intrusive media. But he worked tirelessly at developing his coaching skills.

He was growing as a coach and developing a deep knowledge of how the game should and could be played. His players were won over by this passion for a quality winning performance.

He won four NPC championships, but the pressure of being both a school headmaster and a dedicated coach was all-consuming and logically one should have taken a back seat in time and commitment — an impossible dilemma for Graham Henry the workaholic!

Fate then intervened with the game becoming professional in late 1995. By the end of 1996 he had become a professional rugby coach. Call it luck or destiny, the opportunity came at exactly the right time in his life and career.

Graham had developed a number of positive qualities: he was a hard worker and put in the hours, he had a passion for the game, and he was ambitious and determined to succeed. He was also a risk taker, a gambler. But he could never have imagined the challenges he would face over the next 16 years.

Graham's Auckland Blues won the 1996 and 1997 new Super 12 competition, these successes adding to his growing confidence and ability. But his decisions weren't always sound; restless ambition cropped up and perhaps a growing ego.

Wales showed a genuine interest in him. Graham was keen and naively thought that the NZRU would support him in extending his coaching experience, despite them having blocked an earlier English approach. But the Union's reaction was swift and clear: pursuing this Welsh proposal would mean any All Black coaching possibilities would disappear.

This was patently a stupid reaction; already three well-known coaches were coaching international sides. This treatment raised Graham's determination to follow through in his ambitions, to coach at the highest level.

He left for Wales amid controversy to face a foreign rugby environment. The next few years required all his resilience, tenacity, determination and coaching ability.

In 12 months, the New Zealand coach had convinced Wales and its people that they could win at rugby again.

But then came a speed wobble! Wales exited at the quarter-final stage of the World Cup and in the 2000 Six Nations tournament the team suffered major defeats against France and England, the first signs perhaps that Wales's stand-out successes were at an end.

Graham always expected to win. Losses were unacceptable and he suffered when they occurred. Answer? Try something different. This, too, was a feature of his coaching. So he persuaded Steve Hansen to join him to improve the Welsh forward performance; this coaching combination clearly a portent for the future.

Then another major decision: incredibly, he was asked to coach the British and Irish Lions. Coach Wales and the Lions? Impossible!

It was a seminal time in Graham's career. He faced a totally different rugby environment from any he had experienced — players from four nations to mould into a united team, and a complex coaching and management group.

The tour, probably predictably, ended with a lost series, a fractured team and Graham shattered by the whole experience. It was his first major failure as a coach.

Back in Wales, where he should have stayed in the first place, he faced serious criticism from the Welsh players who had played a minor role on tour. Then the Welsh side's performances convinced him he should resign. Steve Hansen took over and Graham returned to New Zealand. A more dramatic conclusion to the overseas experience would be hard to imagine.

After stints in Japan and assisting Auckland and the Blues, his big opportunity came when the All Blacks lost the World Cup in 2003 and John Mitchell's job was on the line.

The remarkable Henry coaching saga continued when he convinced the NZRU he could and should coach the All Blacks, which had been his aim over the past 28 tumultuous years. The next eight were to be equally dramatic and often controversial.

The years 2004 to 2007 saw mostly outstanding All Black perform-ances. The disaster at Cardiff followed. Then that gutsy decision to reapply for the All Black coaching job.

Four years later came that dramatic one-point win over France and a World Cup victory in Auckland. There followed an outpouring of emotion and elation throughout the country and a knighthood for the Cup-winning coach.

The peak of the rugby coaching experience had been reached through a combination of resilience, ambition, hard work, rugby nous, constantly improved people management, some important, successful choices of personnel, a burning desire to win while playing attractive rugby, some good fortune along the way, and the experience gained from 37 years of coaching at all levels of the game.

He learned good lessons from his few failures and finished his coaching career as the most successful coach in New Zealand's rugby history.

What next? Graham has the experience, the knowledge and the passion for rugby to perhaps consider looking at solving the two great ills in the modern game: the complexities of the rules, particularly around the second phase, and the scrum and the resultant inconsistency of the referees in trying to interpret these rules.

Better this than a bits-and-pieces man, helping everything and everyone, from Marmite to rugby league, Argentineans and Olympians.

What next for GWH?

Sir John Graham KNZM CBE

Contents

Ted's welcome

A lot happened in my 40 years as a rugby coach and I thought it would be appropriate to share the highs and lows. It's been an amazing journey and as I began recounting it to Bob Howitt, I sometimes wondered how I managed to survive — there must have been a touch of madness!

The public see the finished product: the All Blacks performing on the field, mostly with a high percentage of success, but occasionally stumbling, sometimes inexplicably, such as during the 2007 World Cup in Cardiff. But so much goes on behind the scenes that can't be talked about there and then.

The circumstances of our loss to France in 2007 deserve to be told. It's something I've kept under wraps until now but I believe it should be shared.

The French have a lovely saying that out of despair comes energy. Well, playing out of their skins that day in Cardiff, the French caused us unbelievable anguish, but Wayne Smith, Steve Hansen and I, plus Richie and the boys who backed up in 2011, learnt from that disaster. And thanks to the NZRU's display of confidence in us, we were able to turn those lessons to our advantage and win the Webb Ellis Cup four years on.

To win a World Cup takes a massive amount of focus, effort and planning to ensure that the right strategies are selected and executed correctly. You also need world-class players, and we were certainly blessed in that regard.

You also need dual management, both old and young. Players will handle the challenge if it is *their* challenge. The power of player leadership, and the player leadership group that was established, represents one of the most important messages in the book. It wasn't just the All Black management preparing the team for the 2011 World Cup, it was the management plus the players — seven very special players, in particular.

We knew our players had to be mentally stronger than they were in 2007 and we prepared this time for worst-case scenarios. And just as well, because such scenarios don't come much worse than Dan Carter falling in a crumpled heap at training, having snapped his adductor longus tendon off the bone at training prior to the finals.

The 2011 World Cup was a magnificent occasion for New Zealand and the fact the All Blacks were able to celebrate it with victory was both enormously satisfying and a huge relief for all involved.

We wanted to defeat France as decisively in the final as we had in pool play — although the final chapter wouldn't have made for such a riveting read if we'd waltzed away to an easy victory. Never will I forget the agony I endured in the coaches' box in those final 30 minutes, as Steve and Wayne and I were trying to get the players to change tactics — and they were ignoring us! But of course, they were right and we were wrong.

A lot of people have asked me what I would be doing now if the All Blacks had lost the final by a point instead of winning by the smallest margin possible. Who knows? Who cares? We won and that's all that matters! Four years after the most excruciating time of my life, I had found peace and a feeling of enormous pride in a group of talented New Zealanders.

It all makes for a gripping yarn. I hope you enjoy it.

GH

1

Young Ted

It's funny how things have a way of working themselves out. And why you must never abandon hope. Or believe that what is happening will never change.

No-one exemplifies that better than Graham Henry. When he first attended Christchurch Boys' High School back in 1961 he struggled with the entrance tests. He's not sure why. He was probably more focused on some sports event. He certainly didn't appreciate how significant it was to score well in the paper before him, which was effectively an IQ test.

Graham's mother and father, Allen and Ann, experienced the Depression of the 1930s and two world wars; in fact, Allen flew Catalina flying boats in the Pacific during the Second World War. They were the sort of people, of strong and sound principles, who never purchased anything unless they could afford it. They naturally hoped that Graham would follow to some extent in the footsteps of their eldest son, Brian, who was extremely bright. Brian was an exemplary student who had breezed through the entrance test to take his place in a top class and was now cruising towards a BCom and a sterling career in banking.

Graham's muddled effort with the entrance test resulted in him being placed in the 3C2 class. It didn't get any worse than that: the approximately 250 first-year students were spread, in clusters of 20 to 25, across seven classes. The seventh and bottom of these classes was 3C2.

Graham was embarrassed. His parents were dismayed — where had they gone wrong? How could a son of theirs possibly finish up in the bottom class? Oh well, he's a good sportsman, at least he's got something going for him!

Graham's ego, it has to be said, took a serious battering at the realization he was in the humblest third-form class. He didn't regard himself as a dullard, but he'd certainly cocked up the entrance test horrendously, and, in the sporting context he related to, he would have to apply himself and win promotion.

He soon buddied up with a classmate called Stu Hunt. Stu's father, Bob, had played as an opening batsman for both Canterbury and Otago at cricket and was, at the time, a teacher at Christ's College, coincidentally Christchurch Boys' High School's greatest rival. Poor Stu had botched the entrance test also and was equally dismayed to find himself in the bottom class.

Graham and Stu had played together in the Canterbury primary school representative cricket team and they shared a love of sport and a determination to succeed. Unlike most of their classmates, they applied themselves more diligently than normal to tests and exams throughout the year — and finished first and second in the class. They would not only earn promotion to a higher fourth-form class for 1961, but both would also go on to become secondary school teachers, Graham even attaining the position of headmaster. Although for Graham, it has to be said, there would be further academic challenges ahead.

It was Graham Henry the sportsman who most prospered while at Christchurch Boys' High. By 1964, his final year at college, he commanded a position in both the rugby First XV (as a first-five) and the cricket First XI (as a wicketkeeper-batsman), earning blues for both sports.

The rugby team enjoyed a vintage season, taking out the collegiate championship by winning all 19 of its matches. Interestingly, though, not one member of the side went on to become an All Black and only a couple earned selection for Canterbury.

How different it was with the cricket team, which was perhaps the best school XI in the country. Such was the strength of the side that it competed in the Canterbury 2A men's competition, at the second level, and won the title.

The team included Robert Anderson, Dayle Hadlee, Alan Hounsell and David Trist, all of whom would play for New Zealand, plus Cran Bull, Chris Baker and Graham, who would represent Canterbury. Also in the team were John Christensen, who went on to win a gold medal in hockey at the 1976 Olympics, and Martin Hadlee. Three of the Hadlee boys — Barry, Dayle and the legendary Richard — followed in the footsteps of their father, Sir Walter, and played for New Zealand.

The cricket XI's boast that it was the best college team in New Zealand was put to the test whenever it took on Auckland Grammar, a college that abounded in cricketing celebrities at the time. Players like Mark Burgess, Hedley Howarth, Terry Jarvis, Ross Dykes, John Millener, Rex Hooton and the incomparable Grahame Thorne graced the side. In reality, Grammar shared the unofficial 'best college team' title.

Graham played his first game for the First XI when he was just a fourth former. The game was against Auckland Grammar, on a trip north. He was billeted by Thorne, who startled him the first evening by offering him a beer … his very first beer. Things were different 50 years ago. Graham was too embarrassed to refuse.

Graham became a difficult, rather arrogant student as he progressed at Boys' High. He had a low tolerance for teachers he considered were not up to scratch. Into this category fell his fifth-form maths teacher, only five of whose students passed School Certificate maths although almost every student in the class, Graham included, passed School Certificate.

When Graham realized this same teacher was taking him for biology the next year, he was not impressed.

'Excuse me, sir,' asked Graham, 'last year almost all the students in our class passed School Certificate, but only five students passed mathematics. What do you think was the reason for that?'

The teacher was not amused. This was not the first example of young Henry's impudence and, not unexpectedly, the following year G. Henry did not become a prefect. Given that he was in both the rugby First XV and the cricket First XI — the only student so honoured that year — his appointment should have been automatic.

His sixth-form history teacher, however, was John Graham, a man who would have a massive influence on Graham's career. One Friday afternoon, the discussion wandered away from history to the weekend's rugby international … which it was inclined to do during the final periods on a Friday.

Graham interrupted his tutor, who was in full flight, saying, 'Sir, I want to get accredited this year, so could we please stick to the subject!'

The difference this time was that the question was asked with total respect for the teacher. Unfortunately in those days Graham was not wise enough to know when to keep his mouth shut. He wonders whether things have changed!

Not only did the individual who would become a headmaster miss out on a prefect's badge, but he would also be caned on his final day at school — unbelievable as that may sound. It happened because the day before, when Graham should have been returning text books to the school book shop, he was representing the First XI in its annual cricket game against Auckland Grammar. Graham did his bit, top scoring with 78.

And that's how he came to miss the final assembly — because he was diligently taking his books back. Unfortunately, he was 'spotted' by the gifted but eccentric music teacher Clifton Cook, who took a dim view of Graham's choice of priorities and reported him to the deputy headmaster.

The deputy headmaster considered Graham's actions serious enough to justify the cane.

Graham protested. 'I don't consider my returning books grounds for being caned, sir.'

'Hmm,' replied the deputy headmaster, who after a few moments' deliberation sent him to the headmaster, Charles Cordwell.

The headmaster was sympathetic to Graham's situation but wasn't prepared to bend on what he regarded as an important matter of principle: he had to support his staff.

'I have to give you the cane,' he said, whereupon he delivered two light taps on Graham's rump.

News of the caning shot around the school like wildfire and a lot of the teachers were upset. Graham had a profile in the school even if he wasn't a prefect. It seemed scarcely believable that a senior pupil and one of the school's outstanding sportsmen would be caned for such a seemingly trivial offence.

Graham considered the caning a gross injustice, especially given the circumstances. He hadn't had the opportunity to return his books because he'd been representing the school in the annual fixture against Auckland Grammar, the 'big' game of the year. However, he departed the college with lots of fond memories and with a wide range of experiences which would prove valuable as his career developed.

Seven years after the caning, he would return to Christchurch Boys' High.

Although Graham would make an indelible impression on his country through rugby, rather surprisingly he created his first ripples on the national sporting scene as a cricketer … in unusual circumstances.

At the time when Graham was energetically keeping wickets for the Boys' High First XI, the Canterbury selector was Mac Anderson, and he would regularly pop in to watch the team because his son Robert batted at No. 4. Although he never commented on Graham's talents, it was obvious he rated him.

And so, when Canterbury's vastly experienced international keeper John Ward broke his thumb during Graham's first year out of college, the player selected to replace Ward was Graham Henry.

Being selected for Canterbury was daunting enough, but Graham was positively alarmed when he realized the three speedsters he would be keeping to were Gary Bartlett, one of the fastest bowlers in the world, Dick Motz and Bruce Taylor. All would enjoy distinguished first-class careers; collectively, they would claim 235 test wickets.

It was a fearsome learning experience for young Henry, who felt battered and bruised from diving around retrieving Bartlett's thunderbolts. On one occasion he was knocked flat by a ball that reared nastily and struck him in the chest. Graham lay stunned until Bartlett advanced down the pitch. 'Get up, you little prick,' Bartlett barked at him, 'and take the next one!'

They were exciting times and Graham enjoyed his season of representative play. He was never going to survive in the side once Ward, one of the game's most accomplished glovemen, returned but while he was there he secured most of the catches that came his way, effected the occasional stumping, and generally justified selector Anderson's faith in him.

It was an experience he would recall on occasions when he became an influential representative (rugby) selector himself. Should he risk an untried young player he considered had the potential to succeed? Why not? Someone took a huge gamble on him and they all survived.

While Graham's sporting career flourished, again academically he was a disaster. Sport was his consuming passion but he remembered his parents' profoundly sensible advice that sport would never provide him with a living — 'sport will never keep you!' — (Yeah right, as the Tui billboard would say). They kept reminding him of the value of a complete education.

So, operating on everyone else's advice and ignoring his own instincts, Graham enrolled at the University of Canterbury in pursuit of an arts degree, tackling some of the subjects he was weakest at. It was an experiment doomed to fail. He didn't pass a single paper, unlike his brother, Brian, who was powering ahead towards his BCom degree. Meanwhile the third member of the family, Carol, seven years Graham's junior, was becoming a talented musician who would go on to win several provincial awards with her piano playing.

Having flunked university, Graham allowed himself to be convinced that, even without a degree, an excellent future lay ahead working for the National Bank. Chalk up another disaster. After six months he was bored out of his tree. Without knowing what his true vocation was, he most certainly knew it wasn't functioning as a teller or would-be accountant/manager in a bank.

He resigned and went to work for Firestone, the tyre people, as a serviceman, working all sorts of odd shifts. For the first time since leaving Boys' High, he actually knew what he was doing. It wasn't a career move, merely a stepping stone towards the next important stage of his life. The job paid big money, money that would allow Graham to move south to Dunedin and enrol at the University of Otago in pursuit of the physical education diploma he knew was his calling.

Graham's life, and state of mind, underwent a most remarkable transformation. Instead of forcing himself to concentrate on classical literature and equally obscure subjects, he found himself completely immersed in his studies. This was what he'd been put on Earth for. He'd always been a lover of sport and team culture and from a surprisingly young age he'd had urges to coach. So working towards a diploma in physical education was perfect for him because the coaching of sports teams was a natural extension of those studies.

The diploma involved such subjects as exercise physiology, sports psychology, biomechanics, nutrition and fitness training, all of which prepared him ideally for the rugby coaching that would soon become such a major part of his existence and eventually take over his whole life.

Although it's not something he has ever bragged about, he always felt the physical education diploma gave him an important advantage over the average rugby coach who might have trained in marketing, economics, medicine or whatever.

After the futility of his studies at Canterbury University, he found it enormously gratifying to graduate in Dunedin; indeed, he would never fail a paper again. He regarded it all as part of the great learning experience and considered he was a better person for what he had endured. His advice to aspiring young people when the time comes to make decisions regarding their futures: Heed other people's advice by all means, but make your own decisions, based on your own knowledge and instincts. Know yourself!

So much of Graham's training and preparation of rugby teams relates to those days in Dunedin. He'd always been interested in the scientific side of sport — physiology, psychology, skill development and fitness — and therefore had a sound understanding on how it related to the preparation of sports teams.

Right from the start, Graham possessed a special ability to manage people in groups. He saw running a rugby team as an extension of his training as a teacher of education, in that the organization of training sessions equated to a lesson plan in the classroom. Build the knowledge on firm foundations, which in turn relates to how you perform in the next test or the game coming up that weekend. He found his background in education invaluable once he became a serious rugby coach.

But it wasn't all sport and study in Dunedin — there was also time for a little romance. For there was another Christchurch student working her way through the phys-ed diploma at Otago University in the late 1960s, another sports nut: Raewyn Cochrane.

Raewyn grew up in a rugby-mad household. There were other topics of conversation, but when winter rolled around nothing competed with rugby. Alan Cochrane, Raewyn's father, was so obsessed with rugby that he christened his first son Calvin Fraser Cochrane so his initials of CFC matched those of the Christchurch Football Club, of which Alan would become a life member.

Alan Cochrane had played a few games for Canterbury during the war years and both Raewyn's brothers, Calvin and Bruce, would emerge as talented players. Calvin made 18 appearances as a robust loose forward for the Red and Blacks and was an All Black trialist, while Bruce won selection for the New Zealand Juniors.

With all this rugby madness happening around her, Raewyn's mother, Jeannie, maintained a good, balanced approach to life. She went back to work to ensure there was enough money for her children to complete their education. Tragically, when he was only 50, Raewyn's father died from bowel cancer.

For three years from 1967, Raewyn flatted in Dunedin while working her way through her phys-ed diploma, and this brought her into regular contact with this Graham Henry bloke. He was into rugby and cricket while Raewyn's interests were netball, basketball and athletics, particularly sprinting.

Initially, Raewyn wasn't impressed with Graham, but because their studies brought them into contact so regularly, they eventually became good friends ... such good friends that they married in 1970, the year after graduating. Graham was 23; Raewyn, 21.

Graham made a modest impact as a competitor during his stay in Dunedin. He secured a place in the University of Otago cricket team that was the dominating side in the Otago club championship in the late 1960s. Graham's team-mates included Rudi Webster, a fast bowler who'd represented the West Indies; Murray Webb, Murray Parker and John Mitchell, who all won New Zealand selection; and Lindsay Green, Ray Hutchison, Stu Edward and Ata Matatumua, who all played for Otago.

Graham's old mate Stu Hunt, from 3C2, was also in the team, which was on paper probably the strongest club side in New Zealand. In the final of the Otago club championship, University beat Grange outright in a day, an astonishing result.

Murray Parker and his wife-to-be Verna James, an Otago netball rep and fellow physical education student, became Graham and Raewyn's best man and bridesmaid, and vice versa.

Graham won a fleeting selection for the Otago Plunket Shield team, without managing to displace Barry Milburn as the wicketkeeper. He was utilized as an opening batsman in a game against Canterbury, but with scores of none and two, didn't demand further selection.

He played rugby for Union in 1967 before switching to Otago University for the next two seasons, so he could play with his mates in the University C team which competed in the top senior club competition.

In his final year at Otago University, in 1969, he chaired the New Zealand Universities winter tournament committee which co-ordinated the event for hundreds of university students, men and women, from throughout the country. It was a reflection, perhaps, of his desire to step outside his comfort zone, take on major challenges and not be afraid of hard work, qualities that would distinguish him in the years ahead.

Once graduated, Graham returned to Christchurch to attend Teachers College, eventually winning a teaching appointment at Christchurch Boys' High School, the same institution where he'd been caned on his final day at secondary school.

And nothing had changed: built on tradition, the school still recognized seniority ahead of ability when it came to the appointment of sports coaches. When Graham indicated interest in taking charge of a team, the master in charge of cricket offered him the under-14 sevens, i.e. the seventh-best (and bottom) team of players aged under 14. It was 3C2 all over again!

Graham bristled. 'I'm not going to waste my time with the seventh-best team,' he informed the master.

'You're the latest teacher appointed to the school — you have to start at the bottom.'

'If you're going to apply that logic, I'm afraid I won't be available.'

'Why do you think you deserve to be placed in charge of a higher team?'

'Well, having played representative cricket for both Canterbury and Otago, I believe that gives me some important qualifications that most, in fact probably all, of the other candidates lack.'

'Hmmm,' said the master, 'let me think about that.'

The following day he contacted Graham to advise him he had been appointed coach of the under-14 firsts!

If that was Graham's first appointment as a cricket coach, the origins of his rugby coaching — something he is often asked about — are more obscure and relate to his time with the High School Old Boys club in Christchurch, where he played first-five for the senior team, taking over as captain for one season.

He worked with a good mate, Vance Bishop — the fullback in the senior team — to prepare a colts team for an end-of-season competition. He didn't see it as the start of anything big and, in fact, cannot remember how successful the team was. Graham was in his mid-20s, utterly enthusiastic and wholly consumed by sport. Just being involved was satisfaction enough.

2

Graham and Graham

The scholastic and sporting careers of John Graham and Graham Henry were starting to intersect. John Graham, who had played 53 matches for the All Blacks from 1958 and even captained them in a series against the Wallabies, was coach of the High School Old Boys team for the 1971 and 1972 seasons. He had taught Graham at Christchurch Boys' High, subsequently moving across to Linwood High School as the head of history and social studies.

When John Graham was preparing to depart Christchurch to take up the prestigious appointment of headmaster at Auckland Grammar School in 1973, he asked Graham one day whether he would be interested in heading north should a suitable position become available.

'Yes,' replied Graham, putting the matter out of his mind immediately. He didn't expect anything would come of the conversation.

So when John Graham phoned him a few months later, he was quite blown away.

'Graham, would you be interested in a post at Auckland Grammar teaching physical education?'

'I certainly would.'

'Then the position is yours. When can you start?'

'I'll get back to you on that,' said Graham, not knowing how his young wife would take the announcement that would result in them having to quit their home and their home town for Auckland.

Graham and Raewyn had recently bought a house in Linwood,

costing $10,300. Raewyn's parents had never owned a house of their own; the commitment to a piece of real estate had represented a major happening, and had been especially exciting for Raewyn.

Now here was Graham suggesting they sell it and move north.

'What do you think?' he asked Raewyn.

Raewyn, in tears but supportive as ever, replied, 'If you want to do it, I guess it's a good opportunity ... so OK.'

The good news was that the Henrys made almost a 100 per cent profit when they sold their house. The bad news was that establishing themselves in Auckland was a real challenge. They existed initially in a terrible flat, Auckland turned on one of its wettest winters — the rain was unrelenting — and Raewyn wrote off their car attempting a U-turn in a narrow street, failing to notice that another car was bearing down upon her. The car was badly damaged but Raewyn escaped uninjured.

Graham would soon find his Physical Education Diploma restrictive, the diploma having become a degree course in 1970, the year after he'd qualified. If he was to progress in education, he needed a degree qualification. So while working full time at Auckland Grammar School, continuing to play rugby and cricket and even managing some coaching responsibilities, he diligently applied himself to extramural study at Massey University. This placed an enormously challenging workload on him, which he handled, eventually being rewarded with a BEd degree, which led to promotion at Auckland Grammar School and ultimately a headmaster's appointment.

Graham found working under John Graham totally refreshing. At Christchurch Boys' High, you had to wait until someone died before you would be considered for promotion. At Auckland Grammar, if John Graham felt you had ability, he gave you the opportunity to express it.

Under his guidance, teachers prospered. From those who were teaching at Auckland Grammar in Graham's time, at least half a dozen went on to become distinguished headmasters — Dave Syms at Palmerston North Boys' High, Steve Watt at Kelston Boys' High, Steve Cole at St Paul's Collegiate, Ken Rapson at Mt Roskill Grammar, Greg Taylor at Mt Albert Grammar School, plus

Graham himself. And there were many others who went on to win important appointments. It was a reflection of how these young teachers relished their responsibilities and learnt from the 'master' how to impose high standards for their pupils both in and outside the classroom.

In 1974 Graham joined the University Rugby Club. It turned out to be a most enjoyable and successful year, unexpectedly. He imagined the club would find a position for him in one of the social teams but when the senior team's first-five broke his leg, there weren't too many players about with senior experience in the No. 10 jersey.

The backline was almost of Dad's Army status. It featured three Peters brothers, Winston (who would make an indelible mark in politics), Ron and Wayne, Dave Palmer (who would die in the Erebus plane crash), Gary Weinberg, and Grahame Thorne, who at 28, though somewhat rotund, was still commanding headlines.

The pack featured such seasoned performers as Dennis Thorn, Greg Denholm, Dave Syms, Mac Fatialofa and Ken Baguley. The team was coached by Bob Graham, John's brother.

After starting the season with no expectations whatsoever, University finished strongly, so strongly the team caught the Auckland Rugby Union by surprise. There were no semi-final/final situations in those days and University was allocated its final game, against Manukau, on Eden Park No. 2. Suburbs, the front runner, was drawn to play Ponsonby in the feature match on Eden Park No. 1.

Here's how the *New Zealand Herald* recorded the odd-ball conclusion to the competition:

> The Auckland Rugby Union's hopes for a thrill-packed last-second decision on the Gallaher Shield quietly ebbed away at Eden Park on Saturday. Only 200 people watched University deal to Manukau on the back ground while Suburbs saw its championship hopes blown away by Ponsonby. Had Suburbs won, there would have been a midweek play-off at Eden Park. It was an affecting moment as University marched across to the No. 1 field to get the trophy, the players hoisting captain Dave Syms on to their shoulders in celebration.

The season's delights didn't end there. In his first significant role as a rugby coach, Graham was appointed to prepare the Auckland Grammar 3A team in association with Nev McMillan, the school's history master, who would achieve renown in later years as an author of such significant works as *Men in Black* and *The Encyclopedia of New Zealand Rugby*.

Messrs Henry and McMillan soon recognized that they possessed a backline of exceptional talent and pace. At first-five was Nicky Allen, who would become an All Black in 1980; in the midfield was John Collinson, who would go on to play 38 games for Auckland; and on the wings were Gary Henley-Smith and Peter Beguely, who would become nationally ranked as track sprinters.

With the team oozing such talent, it wasn't difficult for the coaches to formulate a game plan. At every opportunity, the ball was worked to the wingers, who spent most of the season racing away to score tries. Grammar's 3A team won the competition undefeated.

Modesty wasn't one of Graham's natural traits in those days. John Graham would write of him many years later that he was 'a restless, driven soul, never fully satisfied with his lot, and that became one of his personal strengths. He was not prepared to just let things happen, rather he set himself targets, went for them and having reached them, set himself new challenges.'

After one imposing year in Auckland, Graham was indeed ready for a fresh challenge. He approached John Graham and told him he wanted to coach the First XV.

He had one important factor on his side. While his team had been running riot in the 3A competition, Auckland Grammar's once proud First XV was experiencing a forlorn season. Not only had the team lost several traditional fixtures, it had gone down to New Plymouth Boys' High by an embarrassingly large score.

Graham knew that John Graham, accustomed to success as a Canterbury and New Zealand player, wouldn't be happy with those results because rugby is vitally important to schools like Auckland Grammar and forms an integral part of the school.

John Graham received Graham's submissions without comment but when 1975 rolled around Derek Stubbs, the head of physics who had prepared the First XV the previous year, and Graham were named as joint coaches. They would form a harmonious and successful partnership; indeed, Auckland Grammar would breeze through 1975 and 1976 undefeated. Graham Henry's reign as a successful rugby coach, which would stretch over 36 years, was under way.

Graham soon demonstrated that as a rugby coach he was a lateral thinker. He had been enormously impressed by the 1971 British Lions, who he considers revolutionized back play in New Zealand, and also by Waikato's progressive coach George Simpkin, who introduced a daring flat backline concept to representative play. Graham picked up on this and adapted it for his Auckland Grammar team. He was utilizing the rare talents of Allen, Collinson, Henley-Smith and Beguely, whom he brought through with him from the champion 3A side.

He had both five-eighths and the centre standing together, flat, and expediting the ball to the flying wingers. Bearing in mind that Henley-Smith would set a New Zealand junior sprint record of 10.4 seconds in 1977 and go on to win the national sprint title twice and that Beguely was almost as fast, it wasn't surprising that the team ran in tries by the bucketload.

Beguely isn't a name that will mean much to most New Zealand rugby followers, but Graham identifies him as the best winger he ever coached. He was a big player with blistering pace, who could step anyone, the standout individual in a team of vast talent. Unfortunately, a stress fracture of the back cut short his rugby career.

John Drake, who would share in New Zealand's World Cup triumph in 1987, captained the side in 1976. Interestingly, one player who didn't make the team that year because, in his own words, he was 'fat and lazy' and didn't possess any burning desire to play rugby, was Gary Whetton. Gary and his twin brother, Alan, wouldn't feature in the First XV until 1977, when they were seventh formers.

In the six years the Auckland Grammar First XV was coached by Graham, only six matches were lost, and four of those happened in

1977. But it's for another reason Graham most vividly remembers that year. Well, there were two other reasons actually, one much more painful than the other. While playing club cricket for Cornwall he snapped his Achilles tendon and spent months in a plaster cast, getting around on crutches.

His more positive experience came when one of the boys in the hostel at Auckland Grammar, where Graham was the house master, suggested he visit the bottom ground to check out a third former who was playing for the sixth-grade team and who, from all reports, was raising eyebrows.

Graham looked in and found this fellow in the No. 10 jersey kicking goals from the sideline out of the mud. He could run and chip-kick; in fact, there didn't seem to be much he couldn't do. In challenging conditions, he was absolutely brilliant. Graham inquired of his name. Grant Fox, he was told.

Late in 1977 when Auckland Grammar undertook a tour of Fiji, Graham included a few young players. Grant Fox, then a fourth former, was among them.

The team played a match against the Fijian outer islands in which every member of the opposition fronted up in bare feet. So the Auckland Grammar players removed their boots, which didn't stop young Fox, who was troubled by a sore hamstring, from kicking a penalty goal from halfway.

Despite Fox's youth and inexperience, he was selected for the 'test' match against Combined Suva Schools, in which he performed outstandingly on one leg and was effectively the difference between the two teams. An ugly brawl caused the match to be abandoned 10 minutes early, which Fox didn't mind one bit because he was carrying a serious injury.

Upon his return to Auckland, Graham took Fox to see a sports medicine specialist who expressed grave concern at the extent of the injury. Fox had torn the muscle tendon off the bone. The specialist gloomily told Fox he would never play rugby again.

That wasn't the assessment either Graham or young Fox wanted to hear, so Graham sought a second opinion. He next referred his prodigy to Graeme Hayhow, a physiotherapist who had worked closely with sports teams including the New Zealand cricket team and the America's Cup yachting squad.

Hayhow conceded that it was a serious injury but believed he could put it right. On his instructions, Graham and Fox set up a pulley system at the foot of his hostel bed and throughout the summer he applied himself to strengthening the muscle, lifting weights with the troubled leg. So diligently did Fox apply himself, he not only resumed rugby action the next season but went on to accumulate an incredible 4106 points (1067 of those for the All Blacks) in a celebrated first-class career.

Fox related to Graham right from the start because they had the same analytical approach to rugby. Both were meticulous planners and researchers who believed in playing to their team's strengths and away from the opposition's.

The chances of two rugby luminaries like Graham and Fox finishing up in the same school hostel at the same time are slim indeed, but fate pitched them together. They would not only mould the Auckland Grammar First XV into the nation's most formidable collegiate team — it won 41 matches in succession — but they would do the same with the Auckland NPC team.

Fox spent three years as the kingpin of the Auckland Grammar First XV. He and Graham effectively lived together because Fox boarded at the hostel at which Graham was the master. They spent endless hours talking sport, mostly rugby and mostly tactics.

Much of the coaching philosophy Graham would apply when he became coach of Auckland and subsequently coach of the Blues, once rugby turned professional, was formulated in those years at Auckland Grammar, and a good percentage of it in animated after-hours discussions with Fox.

As he developed as a coach, Graham came to appreciate that it was important to be innovative. He knew he had to think outside the square. Auckland Grammar, and later Auckland, won a lot of games because of his originality.

John Graham noted early in the piece that Graham genuinely coached a team. He did not just train it, which is what made him special. In spite of his pursuit for excellence in his players, he gave them space to be themselves, which kept them fresh and keen to perform.

In Graham's final year coaching Auckland Grammar, the leading try-scorer was a fellow by the name of Martin Crowe, who'd had the audacity to score a double century in a two-day cricket game against Christchurch Boys' High School. A strapping lad, he played on the wing and benefited considerably from Fox's genius at first-five. Fox devised countless clever moves down the right-hand blindside that invariably left Crowe with an unopposed run to the goal line. He was a champion finisher, although half the time all he had to do was catch the ball and fall over the line.

They were stimulating times — it was nothing to have 10,000 spectators ringing the field for Grammar's annual clash with King's College.

Graham always believed a team should train the way it intended to play. So his Auckland Grammar team rehearsed fundamentals and moves until the players understood them perfectly, but always underpinned by an attitude with edge.

Alan Faull, an Auckland Grammar teacher who became manager of the First XV, recalls that Graham was a professional in an amateur rugby era. He out-thought other teams. One school put out a newsletter with suggestions on how to beat Grammar: 'They've got brains but we've got brawn.' That, says Faull, was exactly how Graham would have perceived it himself. It didn't matter if his team conceded height and weight — he'd work on achieving quick ruck ball to get his wingers racing away.

Besides being uncommonly gifted at analysing opponents and devising match-winning tactics, Graham was utterly committed to winning and hated losing. 'If Auckland Grammar was to play in Wellington, he wouldn't accept travel by bus or train; he would insist his team flew to the venue. Because his teams always produced the goods, no-one ever objected!'

Graham was to the rugby players of Auckland Grammar what John Graham was to the staff. Those under them were automatically motivated. Neither wasted praise on individuals for achieving what they were expected to. 'Well done' was as much as players would get out of Graham or staff out of John Graham.

After six years' coaching Auckland Grammar — in only one of those years did the side fail to win the championship — Graham was ready for a fresh challenge. He approached John Graham.

'I'm getting bored, DJ,' he told him.

'What have you got in mind?'

'Well, ultimately, I'd like to coach at provincial level, but I'm not sure running a college team will qualify me for that. I need to serve an apprenticeship at senior club level.'

'Thanks for what you've achieved with our First XV — good luck for the future.'

So with John Graham's blessing, Graham offered his services to the Grammar Old Boys club for the 1981 season, a natural step from Auckland Grammar. The decision makers there plainly didn't have the same appreciation of Graham's coaching talents as Graham himself did.

'We'd like to offer you the fifth-grade team,' they told him.

'I don't want to coach the fifth-grade team,' he retorted. 'I want to coach the seniors.'

'You're only in your early thirties. We feel you're too young to be coaching at senior level.'

'Well, thank you for that assessment. I'll see you around.'

Big mistake, Grammar. The team hadn't won the Gallaher Shield, Auckland club rugby's premier trophy, since 1972. And it hasn't won it since. But three years after Grammar rejected Graham's offer, University triumphed. The coach was Graham Henry.

Deflated by the Grammar rejection, Graham promptly offered his coaching talents to the University club in Merton Road. Not without some opposition, he was appointed to coach the senior team. He noted that the Gallaher Shield hadn't found its way into the University clubrooms since he'd worn the No. 10 jersey in 1974.

Coming from Auckland Grammar, where the pupils were so malleable and basically did what the coach demanded of them, Graham was in for a culture shock at Merton Road. He'd forgotten that university students and graduates tended to operate from their own agendas.

For Graham's first training run, only six players turned up. Graham sought to introduce a degree more urgency by phoning around but quickly concluded he was dealing with extremely laid-back individuals, players like Greg Denholm who around capping time once turned up for a match in a dinner suit, having come straight from the ball!

As an aspiring coach, Graham expected all his players to be serious. At University, though, he found he was dealing with an eclectic bunch for most of whom rugby was an entertaining pastime.

Fortunately, Graham had talked Grant Fox into staying in Auckland and had convinced him University was the club to play for. It had been Fox's intention to return to his home town of Te Puke and get involved in the family kiwifruit business, but he found Graham's sales pitch hard to resist.

Graham eventually converted his rag-tag group of players into a competent team, one that rebounded from a 30-point thrashing at the start of the season to finish second in the championship, behind Ponsonby.

Over the next couple of seasons, Graham moulded University into a formidable team, one that should have won the championship in 1983 — losing the final game to Ponsonby when Fox, of all people, experienced a rare horror day goal-kicking — before breaking through in 1984.

The *New Zealand Herald* waxed lyrical over University's disciplined performance in 1984, which came after the team had been accused of over-robust play:

When the chips were down, the University team from hooker to fullback were models of angelic innocence. Rugby was the name of the game and so well did University play that Ponsonby (downed 19–3) was a beaten side from the first minutes. Amid the celebrations, coach Graham Henry, who inspired his team to 20 wins from 21 games, was entitled to his moment of glory. But Henry calmly put the credit back on the players. 'The side had been subjected to some pretty cruel criticism,' he said. 'Now I hope the players will be given some credit.'

Graham took a major career step in 1982, winning a position as deputy headmaster of Kelston Boys' High School in West Auckland. The following year, with his agenda already full, he accepted the position as New Zealand secondary schools coach.

In any normal season that wouldn't have been burdensome, but late in 1984 the New Zealand schools team embarked on an historic first tour of the UK, playing 12 matches, including internationals against Ireland at Lansdowne Road, Scotland at Murrayfield, England at Twickenham and, in the only game lost, Wales at Cardiff Arms Park.

Graham's team was chock full of talented footballers, players like Daryl Halligan, Jon Preston, Matthew Cooper, Stephen Bachop, Rhys Ellison, Duane Monkley, Robin Brooke and Steve Gordon, and Graham got them playing exciting attacking rugby, running the legs off most opponents. However, the Welsh climate brought about their undoing: heavy rain negated the team's expansive game and the tourists lost 12–9.

While Graham enjoyed his association with the school team, it was plain he had over-committed himself. By the time he returned from the UK tour, he was exhausted. He was still coaching the University club team, functioning as a deputy headmaster, and trying to be a worthwhile husband and father. Around that point he nearly fell off the rails. He relinquished his role with the national schools team and rounded out his senior club coaching with University in 1985.

By 1986, he was ready for a fresh challenge and with John Hart being promoted to the All Black selection panel, having brilliantly converted Auckland from easy-beats into the nation's champion side, he decided to have a crack at the Auckland coach's job.

There were two other contenders — Maurice Trapp, who had Bryan Williams as his assistant, and long-time Auckland B coach Barrie Herring.

The Auckland Rugby Union management committee of the time comprised 27 delegates, all of whom had a vote. After the first ballot, there were nine votes for Trapp, nine for Herring and nine for Henry.

The chairman, Malcolm Dick, instructed delegates to reconsider their options and vote again. After the second ballot, there were nine votes for Trapp, nine for Herring and nine for Henry!

'Well,' said chairman Dick, 'we're not leaving here until we make an appointment. Someone is going to have to change his vote.'

Someone did, and after the third ballot Maurice Trapp was declared the new selector-coach of Auckland.

Graham wasn't too disappointed and in hindsight considers the outcome was a blessing in disguise. He had just been appointed headmaster of Kelston Boys' High (following the death of Jim Paton) and he concedes he was much better qualified for the coaching role when he succeeded Trapp four years on. And, besides, he'd won a sweet appointment, anyway, being given charge of the Auckland Colts.

The Colts represented a stimulating challenge for Graham, and their philosophy became that whatever the Auckland A team could do, they could do better. If Auckland scored 60, the Colts would try to hit 70.

In Graham's time in charge of the Colts, they played 50 matches and won 49, including demolishing a useful Waikato Colts team 112–4. Mind you, the team fair oozed talent, Graham being able to call on players of the calibre of Matthew Ridge, Inga Tuigamala, Craig Innes, Pat Lam, Eroni Clarke, Olo Brown, Craig Dowd, Robin Brooke and Mark Carter and others.

The Ranfurly Shield was Auckland's property when Maurice Trapp and Bryan Williams took charge of the team in 1987. When 1991 rolled around, the shield was still in Auckland's possession and that previous year Trapp and Williams's team won 19 matches out of 19. But Graham didn't leave it at that. In his opinion, although the team lost just one game in 1991 (to Otago — a result that cost it the NPC), Auckland was in decline. Graham observed what he deemed to be worrying signs and he didn't know whether the union's administrators were aware of them.

So Graham prepared detailed reports and comments, about which he was later embarrassed, and submitted them to the decision makers at the ARU. The message he was delivering was that Auckland urgently needed a new direction. Although the team was still largely successful, Graham could see that it was no longer operating with the same awesome physical power and skill as previously.

He observed that the older forwards were controlling the pattern more and more and it was becoming a less athletic game. He believed the team urgently required a fresh direction.

Trapp chose not to stand for coach in 1992, but Graham's appointment was anything but automatic, with more than a few of the ARU committee supporting the perennial challenger for the position, 'Tank' Herring. Herring was a dinkum Aucklander whereas Graham was seen by some as 'a schoolteacher from Canterbury'. Was that who they wanted coaching their representative team?

Fortunately, there were sufficient members of the committee aware of the exceptional record Graham had fashioned with Auckland Grammar, New Zealand Schools and Auckland Colts, and he won the appointment.

When Graham takes over a rugby team, the first thing he does is build a management team of well-qualified individuals. He looks for strong characters, people he respects, people who when necessary are able to add value to the team. He doesn't appreciate yes-men.

He asked John Graham, a man who had credentials etched in gold, to be his assistant coach. Graham knew he could trust him totally and that he had no hidden agendas. His manager became Rex Davy, a real estate company owner whom Graham had got to know and appreciate during the Development team's tour of Argentina in 1989. Davy's greatest strength was that he got on with everybody … even people from Canterbury! He could relate equally to the janitor and the Queen. The fitness trainer was Jim Blair, who'd been involved with Auckland teams since the 1980s and who had revolutionized rugby conditioning in New Zealand. George Duncan, another Auckland Development team tour member, became the muscle therapist, beginning an association that would last fully 20 years.

Remarkably, these four gentlemen would meet twice a year for lunch, a tradition that lasts to this day, although there have been justified apologies when some of them, like Graham, have been away on overseas assignments. At their luncheons, they make sure all is right in the world!

The first year was a challenging one for Graham because he knew a major overhaul of the team was essential. Graham always rated the team above the individuals, and still does, which meant he was going to have to jettison some high-profile heroes, one of the most difficult tasks in coaching. He had total respect for the players he was replacing, but time takes its toll and the younger players he gave opportunities to usually went on to enhance the team.

Auckland had taken out some insurance for the future by sending the Development team to Argentina. It had been Graham's initiative and he got to coach the team. Now he was preparing to promote several of those players to the A team at the expense of established All Blacks.

Four who were relegated to largely support roles in 1992 were winger Terry Wright, midfielder Bernie McCahill, blindside flanker Alan Whetton and prop Steve McDowell, who collectively claimed more than 450 appearances for Auckland.

Graham was finally able to apply his strategies and philosophies at representative level. He believed environment was everything in a rugby team. Without it, you couldn't expect players to perform to their potential.

Graham has always prepared his teams to be creative and enjoy their rugby, to take on the opposition with pace and skill. Such rugby is only possible with a lot of rehearsing.

The teams Graham coached have always had a wealth of moves to call on; some might say too many. Grant Fox was a factor here. In their days together at Auckland Grammar, the two of them had spent endless hours discussing tactics and plotting manoeuvres. Fox never participated in a competition game without methodically preparing a sheet of moves that he would distribute among the players. It was a practice Graham continued.

Preparation was all important in Graham's mind if you wanted to succeed as a rugby coach, or a coach of any sport, for that matter. He did his homework, which was burdensome before the advent of professionalism because he had to dovetail rugby coaching with his role as headmaster of Kelston Boys' High; this often meant studying videos and preparing training schedules through till 2 o'clock in the morning.

In 1992 Auckland played 17 matches spread across six months from March to September, and for each of the most important games, Graham methodically prepared specific schedules.

Although Graham's team lost three times, it dealt a 62–7 hiding to Ireland — Graham would never lose to a touring team in his time with Auckland — retained the Ranfurly Shield, and finished runner-up to Queensland in the Super 6 championship.

The most significant loss was to Waikato in the final of the revamped NPC competition. Play-offs were introduced for the first time, and the weekend before, Auckland had seen neighbour North Harbour off in an epic Ranfurly Shield defence. Seven points down at half-time, it had taken a mighty effort from the pack and some masterly play by Fox to get home in front of a capacity crowd at Eden Park. The players had put so much into that defence of the Shield, at the end of a long season, that they weren't able to refocus seven days later and Waikato won the NPC handsomely.

It was a sobering setback for Graham, although he and his men in blue and white would rebound so powerfully they would win the next four NPCs on the trot. Graham, need it be repeated, hated losing and this one felt like a death in the family … the first NPC grand final, and Auckland had blown it.

Waikato would cause Graham misery the next season as well, finally lifting the Ranfurly Shield after an incredible 62 defences. Graham had realized that interest in the shield had diminished after eight seasons in the Queen city. The hype that traditionally accompanied the famous old 'log' no longer existed. The players had to hype themselves.

So when Waikato, on the back of a stunning performance from first-five Ian Foster, lifted the shield late in 1993, Graham was on the one hand almost relieved; he knew it would do more for Waikato and New Zealand rugby away from Auckland where it had been in residence for eight years. But the fiercely competitive G. Henry who hated losing was despondent.

The morning after the shield defeat, Graham was to attend his son Andrew's prize-giving at the Cornwall club.

'I don't think I can front up after losing the Ranfurly Shield,' he said to Raewyn. 'How will they react?'

'Don't be ridiculous, it's not the end of the world. Andrew's all ready to go.'

Graham yielded to his wife's pragmatism and headed for the Cornwall club with his son. To his surprise, and delight, not one person commented on the shield game. The world hadn't come to an end!

A week later, Auckland beat King Country by a record 97–3 and went on to win the NPC. Having lost the shield, Graham felt the NPC success was important for his survival. He knew there were administrators eager to have him replaced. But they couldn't sack a successful coach.

Auckland's golden shield era was recognized by the Auckland Rugby Union at a dinner. Every player who had participated in the 61 defences from 1985 to 1993 received an invitation, and their wives and partners were involved also. It was a marvellous celebration. There were two speakers: John Hart, who'd won it, and Maurice Trapp, who'd kept it. But Graham Henry, who'd lost it, wasn't required to say anything, which upset some of Graham's closest supporters.

The ultimate for any sporting coach is to maintain a favourable public image while achieving success. This can be facilitated by getting onside with the media. Through his early seasons with Auckland, Graham struggled to manage that, purely because of the astonishing workload he was handling.

Besides coaching Auckland, he was holding down a huge job at Kelston, which had a roll of 1250 and a staff of 100. On the home front, Raewyn was teaching at Baradene College and coaching netball at school and club level, while their two eldest children, Matthew and Catherine, were at secondary school and young Andrew was still at primary school.

Graham was therefore regularly rushing between Kelston and Eden Park before trying to work in some quality time with his family before working through to 1 a.m. or 2 a.m. most nights to keep on top of both jobs.

Graham regularly reminded his teachers and students that in life there is no substitute for hard work. It was a tenet he certainly applied. When the mid-year reports went out to Kelston Boys' High School's 1250 students, each one included a message diligently handwritten by headmaster Henry; something meaningful, not just 'try harder next term'.

With the advent of professional rugby, Graham was able to concentrate on his coaching role, which allowed him to relax and give more time to the players and the media. But in those hectic amateur rugby days from 1992 to 1995, Graham was perceived as a grumpy bastard, rather arrogant, seldom available to engage the media. For Graham, it was a matter of survival. Without insulating himself, he could never have done both jobs.

The *New Zealand Herald*, normally the most conservative of publications, carried a feature in 1994 written by Peter Calder in which he highlighted Graham's apparent lack of sensitivity. Calder wrote:

> Henry has left more than a few bruised egos in his wake as he's climbed to the top of Auckland rugby. On-the-record comments are hard to come by when it comes to his past and some make it plain they belong to the school of thought that if you can't think of something nice to say about somebody, you say nothing. Few dispute Henry's knowledge of the game, few defend his personal style, which they find abrasive and often dismissive. In Henry's first year, the A team failed to make the finals of the NPC. Last year it rectified that but went into the championship having lost the Ranfurly Shield to Waikato. It was an unprepossessing start to Henry's spell as coach and seasoned observers suggest he will have to produce better results if he wants to hold on to the job when it comes up for grabs in November.

Not only did Graham hold on to the job, but he was also fashioning a superb record with Auckland, which would win four consecutive NPC championship titles from 1993 to 1996, beat the British Lions, and win the Ranfurly Shield back from Canterbury. While this was going on, Kelston Boys' High School, where Graham was headmaster, made its mark both academically and in sport. One year the school had two students in the top 10 in New Zealand in Bursary, while on the sport fields Kelston became national champions in rugby, soccer, basketball and touch football. It was, without question, one of the top schools in the country.

If there were still doubters about Graham's ability to prepare his team for vital fixtures, they were surely swept away when Auckland challenged Canterbury for the Ranfurly Shield at Lancaster Park in 1995.

Canterbury had won the 'log' from Waikato the previous season and had impressively resisted half a dozen challenges that season, sweeping aside Marlborough 79–nil, Waikato 58–30 and Wellington 66–17. While Auckland was plainly a formidable opponent, most pundits favoured Canterbury to win.

In what became a bizarre spectacle, Graham's team dealt the greatest hiding to the holder in the 92-history of the Ranfurly Shield, winning 35–nil!

Auckland's victory represented a masterpiece of planning by Graham. He prepared his team to play rugby chess, which completely befuddled Canterbury. Auckland did things that afternoon it never attempted again, like consistently kicking the ball dead, thus forcing Canterbury to take 22 drop-outs from which Auckland regathered possession. Graham's tactics undoubtedly influenced the lawmakers, because now if you kick the ball across the dead-ball line, it's a scrum back from where you kicked the ball.

Canterbury, boasting such celebrated All Blacks as Andrew Mehrtens, Justin Marshall, Mark Mayerhofler, Todd Blackadder, Mike Brewer, Richard Loe, Con Barrell and Mark Hammett, never saw which way Auckland went.

Three weeks after the demolition of Canterbury, Auckland wrapped up the NPC, in controversial circumstances, courtesy of a penalty try awarded against Otago by referee Colin Hawke. The penalty try outraged the Otago fans, and most of New Zealand, and wasn't the way Graham wanted to win the championship. He believed that penalty try, and all the hype that surrounded it, would come back to haunt him — and it did in the 1998 Super 12 final when Paddy O'Brien declined to award a penalty try but kept resetting scrums.

The most stunning development for Graham in 1995, indeed for the game generally, was the announcement out of Johannesburg on the eve of the Rugby World Cup final that rugby was embracing professionalism. Rupert Murdoch's News Ltd was pouring $US550 million into the game and from the next season a Super 12 competition, embracing teams from New Zealand, South Africa and Australia, would be launched.

The announcement came as a hell of a shock to Graham and obviously had serious ramifications for coaches like him. He had been an amateur rugby coach for 21 years, since his days at Auckland Grammar School. All that was about to change.

It was Marguerite Seager, Graham's secretary at Kelston Boys' High School, who always championed him as a principal and rugby coach, who first suggested he should contemplate becoming a full-time rugby coach.

'It would be perfect for you,' she said.

'But I enjoy my job here at Kelston,' replied Graham. 'It's a very important job, more important than coaching a rugby team. It would be hard to just abandon it.'

'Yes, but now you can command a full-time salary as a rugby coach. It's perfect for you.'

'You may be right.'

3

The pro scene

It would have been easy for Graham to have yielded to temptation and become a full-time professional coach the instant rugby went professional in 1995, but he didn't relinquish his headmaster's role at Kelston Boys' High until late in 1996. He was reluctant to abandon the educational duties that had been so much part of his life, even after negotiating handsome contracts with the New Zealand and Auckland Rugby Unions. He remained Kelston's headmaster while the inaugural Super 12 was played out, being in charge of the newly constituted Blues franchise, and also continued as coach of the Auckland NPC team.

He didn't find it easy parting company with Kelston Boys' High School, having spent 25 years in education. He valued his headmaster's job highly and took great satisfaction from the school's achievements. Many of the students claimed English as a second language and were from lower socio-economic strata, and a lot of them didn't find school all that stimulating. It was vastly different from Auckland Grammar School where there were a lot of intelligent boys competing against each other. Yet the Kelston examination results were usually positive.

Kelston punched well above its weight in sport. It won the national First XV rugby title on a number of occasions, and in 1998, when Graham was into his third year as a professional rugby coach, it claimed the world schools tournament in Zimbabwe, a stunning achievement.

Graham had adopted many of the attitudes and philosophies of John Graham who'd always given teachers the opportunity to develop their talents and abilities, and that was also how Graham operated. Several of those under him at Kelston went on to become head-masters in their own right.

But rugby was now his master. He was a full-time professional coach. How marvellous. He couldn't believe that as a sports coach he was commanding a greater salary than when he was in charge of 100 staff and 1250 pupils, but that obviously was the way of the world.

The new Super 12 franchises, particularly the northernmost ones, were a source of controversy. Because Auckland and North Harbour were flush with All Blacks, the NZRFU, in its wisdom, decided to split them. Auckland was teamed up with Counties Manukau, which presented the Blues with the country's two most dynamic wingers Jonah Lomu and Joeli Vidiri, while poor old North Harbour was lumped in with Waikato, a rugby 'marriage' that was never going to work. Geographically, it was illogical and it took three years to fix.

Graham just loved his new role. Suddenly, he had enough time to analyse videos and develop strategies in preparation for the game coming up. Previously, the only time in his hectic schedule when he could work videos in was usually around midnight.

Because the professionalizing of rugby was rushed through — to prevent a privatized takeover of the sport by an organization called the World Rugby Corporation — the Super 12 competition that launched the game's new era was imperfect. Each of the dozen franchises (five from New Zealand, four from South Africa and three from Australia) had to play 11 high-pressure matches in three countries in 10 weeks. The organizers didn't get it right, expecting travelling teams to play midweek matches. The Blues, for example, took on Transvaal in Johannesburg on a Tuesday night and had to regroup for a critical match against Natal in Durban four days later.

New Zealand created five fresh franchises for the inaugural competition whereas South Africa put forward its four highest-ranking Currie Cup teams and Australia fielded its two obvious state teams, New South Wales and Queensland, plus a hybrid team based in Canberra, by name of the Brumbies, that picked up many of the individuals unwanted by the other two franchises. Coached by Rod Macqueen, it became the surprise package, finishing fifth and knocking over the Queensland Reds and four of the New Zealand teams along the way.

The Canterbury Crusaders, who would become the titans of Super rugby, finished a lonely last that first season, winning just two matches.

Graham's Auckland Blues triumphed, producing some sensationally effective rugby in the play-offs after a couple of major setbacks along the way — they'd been smashed 51–13 by the Queensland Reds in the Brisbane heat and were outgunned by Transvaal, the then bottom team, at Johannesburg's Ellis Park. The only other game they lost was to the Brumbies in Canberra.

The loss to Transvaal really irked Graham. Normally he reserved his comments and criticisms for the next team session but after his team's woeful performance in Johannesburg he was confronting players that evening demanding to know why the team had performed so poorly.

He was mightily upset because it meant that if the Blues didn't now win their last contest, against the formidable Natal Sharks in Durban, they would miss out on a home semi-final. Worse than that, they would have to remain in South Africa for another week and play Northern Transvaal in Pretoria.

Because victory against a Natal team bedecked with Springboks and coached by Ian McIntosh was essential, Graham set about preparing a critical game plan. After studying a number of tapes of Natal's games, he realized that the Blues would have to change how they had been playing if they were to combat the Sharks. Graham knew he had to get the players to buy into his strategies. Fortunately, he had a group who had confidence that his daring theories would work.

His radical plan, outlined on a blackboard at a small club south of Durban, involved nullifying Natal's two most potent weapons — fly-half Henry Honiball and the lineout pairing of Mark Andrews and Steve Atherton.

Honiball ran a lot and his team consistently drove off lineout takes.

The Blues therefore had to neutralize both of these strengths. And there were a few raised eyebrows when Graham suggested the Blues would not jump at the lineout on Natal's throw in any position on the field, instead committing every forward to stopping their drive. It's a common ploy now, but it was undoubtedly revolutionary in 1996.

The second part of the plan involved flankers Michael Jones and Andrew Blowers. Blowers went straight for Honiball, ensuring he didn't breach the advantage line, while Jones, utilizing his freakish anticipatory skills, knocked over whomever Honiball passed to. Usually this involved an inside pass. This put a serious dent in the major components of Natal's game plan — the drive from the lineout and the team's ability to consistently bridge the advantage line.

The Blues also stacked their three loose forwards at the front of the lineout on their own throw, with the jumpers at the back, and consistently threw to Michael Jones, confusing the enemy.

The Blues didn't spend much time practising these innovative plans because they were worried the locals might be spying on them. Most of the planning was done on the blackboard and walked through on the gymnasium floor.

Notwithstanding Graham's master plan, Natal hung in doggedly before a late try by Eroni Clarke clinched victory, 30–23. Graham had never known a happier dressing room. The players were elated because they knew they had implemented a game plan to perfection to overcome one of the most formidable provincial sides in the world.

Victory in Durban ensured the semi-final (against Northern Transvaal) would now be played at Eden Park, not in Pretoria, which gave the Blues a massive advantage. Experiencing a full house at Eden Park, something which only intermittently occurred even for test matches, and having all New Zealand cheering for Auckland created the perfect environment for a top-notch performance. The team received countless messages of goodwill from around the country. As the only New Zealand team to qualify for the play-offs, the country was firmly behind the Blues.

The ultimate buzz for Graham as a coach came when his team hit 'The Zone', the perfect union rugby players periodically achieve when truly sensational things happen, almost by instinct. In those times, the score can rocket ahead in multiples of five or seven, and opponents are left thoroughly demoralized. Teams engage The Zone only when the players are not only physically and tactically prepared but when their mental attitude is 100 per cent. The greatest worry for a coach was having his team at a peak physically but struggling mentally.

For Graham, having his team embrace The Zone was why he coached, to achieve those priceless moments when the 15 players on the field functioned with complete precision. It made all the planning, scheming, soggy nights at training, criticisms and anxieties worthwhile.

A classic example of a Graham Henry team hitting The Zone occurred in Oamaru in 1993 when Auckland took the Ranfurly Shield on tour. Admittedly, it was against a humble opponent, North Otago, but after conceding the first try, Auckland went on to win 139–5, running in 23 tries.

The Blues would hit The Zone in both the 1996 Super 12 semi-final, in which Northern Transvaal was demolished 48–11, and the final, won just as convincingly, 45–21, against Natal. Eight tries were scored against Northern Transvaal, six against Natal.

Such was the regard Northern Transvaal had for Jonah Lomu, it deployed its crack scrum-half Joost van der Westhuizen to the wing to try to defuse him. The experiment was a rank failure. Lomu was unstoppable and van der Westhuizen reverted to his specialist scrum-half position at half-time.

The Blues' other winger, Joeli Vidiri, irked his coach by indulging in some bizarre behaviour. He was about to touch down by the corner flag when he glanced infield and saw Robin Brooke pointing to the goalposts.

Vidiri threw a long pass infield to Brooke and said, 'Score it yourself!'

Brooke accepted the bonus try, which naturally was converted. 'Thank you, bro,' he said to Vidiri.

Graham wasn't so charitable. 'An absolutely bloody ridiculous thing to do,' he said to his winger later.

At the press conference, a journalist light-heartedly asked Graham if the move had a name.

'Yes ... stupidity!'

While criticizing the almost reckless play of Vidiri, Graham privately recognized that it was a further example that his players were in The Zone, possessed of a total confidence to express all their exceptional skills.

Mighty Jonah Lomu was the standout player of the final and not just because he stood up Natal's world-class fullback André Joubert in scoring a try, and caused the defence problems every time he handled the ball. Jonah was also involved in a wicked piece of originality. When the Blues summoned him into a lineout, it was obvious where the ball would be thrown. Well, that's what the Natalians thought, but Sean Fitzpatrick caught them napping by throwing short to halfback Junior Tonu'u, who flicked the ball straight back to Fitzpatrick. He burst down the sideline, setting up a try for Andrew Blowers.

The attendances for the semi-final and final were 42,000 and 46,000, respectively, vividly illustrating how professionalism had won back support for rugby. The year before, Auckland had played its home games before a largely empty stadium. That was the year the Warriors launched and Auckland's floating sports population preferred to attend Ericsson Stadium.

One of the great strengths of the Blues, particularly in 1996 and 1997 when Zinzan Brooke (the Blues captain) and Sean Fitzpatrick (the All Black captain) were involved, was their ability to improvise, to change tactics on the field. Graham always regarded it as paramount to have this flexibility because although a coach could outline the options open to his team, it fell back on the individuals out in the middle to have the nous to know which tactical plan was going to succeed.

Brooke, Fitzpatrick, Robin Brooke, Michael Jones, Carlos Spencer, Lee Stensness, Eroni Clarke, Junior Tonu'u and others were all individuals who were always thinking 'how can we improve' while they were playing.

Graham concluded early in his coaching career that what wins most games involving teams of comparable strength is the ability to stop the opposition playing their game. It hurts them psychologically to have their game shut down.

He found Australians so naturally confident and cocky they

appeared personally affronted if his team could disrupt their battle plan. The Aussie attitude and self-belief won them a lot of test matches when they weren't necessarily the better team, simply because they out-psyched the opposition. But Graham found this brazen attitude that could be their greatest strength could also become a weakness and one he, as a coach, always enjoyed challenging.

A classic example came in the 1997 Super 12 match against the ACT Brumbies. Superbly coached by Rod Macqueen, the Brumbies had been tearing opponents apart in Canberra, with much of their play masterminded from fly-half by David Knox. A super passer of the ball, with subtle options, Knox operated flat and embarrassed many opponents. He was the catalyst for dangerous attackers like Stephen Larkham and Joe Roff.

Before arriving at Pukekohe, the Brumbies had put 49 points on the Crusaders, 38 on Northern Transvaal and 50 on Free State.

Graham spent a lot of time analysing videos of those games before formulating a game plan that would depower Knox. The video study of the Brumbies backline yielded a bonus — a defensive weakness that could be probed at centre.

After defending against a Knox stand-in for a serious length of time in training, Michael Jones, Mark Carter and Zinzan Brooke executed the defensive game plan to perfection and completely closed down the Brumbies' backline operations, causing the Brumbies to become totally frustrated. And while shutting the Brumbies down, the Blues prospered themselves by penetrating the midfield with almost ridiculous ease, eventually winning the game 41–29, after leading 41–10.

In the next game, the Gauteng Lions, having obviously studied the Blues' performance against the Brumbies, concluded the way to succeed was to stand up flat and knock the Blues' backs over.

If the Blues had persisted with their initial game plan, they would have been in trouble. That's when Zinzan Brooke took charge. This was one of the finest examples of his marvellous leadership skills.

'Stuff this,' he said to his players, 'they're making a meal out of us. We're switching to "pick up and go". See how they handle that!'

The Transvaalers, who were leading at the time, had no answer to the Blues' altered game plan and eventually lost 63–22.

The Blues wrapped up their second Super 12 title by defeating the ACT Brumbies 23–7 at Eden Park in a contest that was rather spoiled by two hours of heavy rain prior to kick-off. The saturated surface didn't lend itself to running rugby and certainly negated the Brumbies' game plan. An intercept try by Michael Jones was the clincher.

In their 13 matches in 1996, the Blues had scored 70 tries, an average of 5.3 a game, and in 1997, when they were undefeated, they scored another 66 tries, the average dropping fractionally to 5.

Graham's spectacular sequence of successes in his dual roles with the Blues and Auckland finally came to a halt in the semi-finals of the NPC in 1997 when Canterbury edged out Auckland 21–15 in a tense encounter in which no tries were scored. Andrew Mehrtens's boot won the day.

Graham, unaccustomed to defeat at the business end of champion-ships, accepted that Canterbury, coached by Robbie Deans, probably deserved to win. He was disappointed, though, that both his captain, Zinzan Brooke, and the referee, Paddy O'Brien, lost their cool. At one stage during the second half, Brooke had hollered at Paddy, 'Come on, come on, you're a f… joke!' and O'Brien had barked back at him, 'We'll see who's right!'

O'Brien would later say in his biography that Brooke spat the dummy big time that night at Lancaster Park. 'Things weren't going his way and he got completely out of control. His behaviour cost Auckland the game.'

If it did, Brooke was still massively in credit with Auckland because there had been countless occasions since his debut as a 21-year-old in 1986 when he had helped his team win courtesy of his leadership, try-scoring and sheer talent.

Graham found the 1997 representative season hard going: Sean Fitzpatrick was carrying a knee injury that would ultimately end his career, Michael Jones had undergone major knee reconstruction again, while Zinzan Brooke, now 32, was considering a tempting offer to go and play for the London Harlequins and this distracted him. On top of which teams like Canterbury, Waikato, Counties Manukau and Otago were getting stronger.

Canterbury went on to win the NPC crown in 1997, crushing Counties Manukau 44–13 in the final. The previous four championships had all been claimed by Auckland under Graham's guidance.

While the Auckland players, administrators and fans were all on good terms with themselves, it was obvious there were many others around New Zealand who considered the game would be better served if the major championship titles were shared around. At an NZRU meeting in Wellington, which Graham attended, it was suggested he should give serious consideration to taking over the coaching of the Highlanders after they finished last in the Super 12 competition in 1997. It was made abundantly clear that the game's administrators, and certainly the marketing people, believed Auckland's continued domination was not a good thing.

Graham took on board the concerns echoing out of Wellington. He was prepared to consider the move south, reasoning that a fresh challenge had appeal, although he came away from the meeting with a feeling of unease. If the administrators were feeling this way and wanted the spoils shared around, were the referees of like mind? Graham remembers thinking that perhaps there should be neutral referees for NPC finals and even for Super 12 play-offs when two New Zealand teams were involved.

Appealing as the offer to coach the Highlanders was — and probably Otago in the NPC as well — logistically it was never going to work out: Raewyn had commitments as a teacher and as coach of the Auckland representative netball team, while their son had important exams looming. Graham was only prepared to move to Dunedin on the condition the whole family went with him. Then, around the time Graham was determining that a move south was improbable, the Auckland Rugby Union, through the initiative of its CEO Peter Scutts, tabled an offer making it thoroughly worthwhile for Graham to stay put.

So when 1998 rolled around, Graham was once again in charge of the Blues and Auckland, in addition to which he had been appointed coach of the New Zealand A team, with Frank Oliver his assistant.

Graham's contract with Auckland was signed and sealed but his contract with the NZRU was not because there were several items which, on the advice of his lawyer David Jones — his adviser on contractual matters — had been referred back to the national body. Many months later, when Graham entered into negotiations with the Welsh Rugby Union, the contract had still not been returned to him.

The Super 12 had become the Auckland Blues Show and that seemed likely to continue in 1998 as Graham's team, minus Zinzan Brooke who had gone off to play in the UK and Sean Fitzpatrick who had finally succumbed to his damaged knee, defeated the Otago Highlanders in a breathtaking semi-final (won 37–31) to advance to a third straight final. With the New Zealand franchises dominating the competition, the Blues would do battle with the Canterbury Crusaders, prepared by Wayne Smith, in the final. In the absence of Brooke and Fitzpatrick, Michael Jones had taken over as captain of the Blues.

The prospects of the Blues contesting another final seemed bleak after Graham's team crashed to defeat against the Coastal Sharks in Durban in the opening game of the campaign, then, a week later, found themselves 37–11 down against a Springbok-laden Golden Cats team at Ellis Park, Johannesburg. In the grandstand, Graham was squirming and wondering how much worse it could get!

But in what ranks as the greatest, and most unbelievable, comeback in his career, the Blues scored 27 points in the last half hour to win 38–37, clinching the game with a penalty try, bravely awarded by Australian referee Wayne Erickson.

The final, on Eden Park, followed a predictable pattern and with the Blues ahead 10–3 well into the second half and with their scrum awesomely in control, there could surely be only one outcome.

The turning point came with the seven or eight five-metre scrums the Crusaders survived without conceding a penalty try. Although the Crusaders' scrum kept collapsing, referee Paddy O'Brien courageously declined to take the ultimate option.

Like many of the Auckland fans, Graham was astounded no penalty try was awarded. He wondered whether Paddy's actions were subconsciously related to the penalty try Colin Hawke had controversially awarded Auckland in the NPC final against Otago a few season earlier.

without a penalty try the Crusaders were able to hang
       ⁔mately, through a late try by James Kerr, ironically an
     ⁔-based player contracted to the Crusaders out of the draft,
       most unexpected victory.

Fe⁔ present that afternoon, when captain Todd Blackadder was
paying tribute to Nelson Bays, Marlborough, Buller, West Coast, Mid
Canterbury and South Canterbury (the unions that with Canterbury
make up the Crusaders franchise), could have expected that the Red
and Blacks would go on to become the Goliath of the competition.
The Super rugby competition would expand to 14 teams in 2006 and
15 in 2012, and the Crusaders would win again in 1999, 2000, 2002,
2005, 2006 and 2008.

In the wash-up, there was some criticism of Graham for not making
more extensive use of his reserves bench. Reason was, because
his team was controlling the game, he didn't believe changes were
necessary.

The first overseas union to approach Graham was England, at
the conclusion of the 1997 Super 12. He fielded a call from Don
Rutherford, England's director of rugby, who simply asked if Graham
would be interested in coaching overseas. Graham said he could be.

Rutherford subsequently flew into Auckland and took Graham out
to dinner. He explained that they were interested in having him work
with the under-21 and England A squads as well as having input into
the national team, eventually taking over as coach.

Rutherford's visit and the fact England was targeting the Blues
coach suddenly became common knowledge. Not only was it not
favourably received by the NZRU's top administrators, but the news
broke at a most inopportune time in Sydney, where England was
preparing to play Australia. Coach Jack Rowell was not impressed
to hear his coaching director was 'Down Under' interviewing a likely
successor.

NZRU chairman, Rob Fisher, and CEO, David Moffett, subsequently spent time in the UK and, in discussions with England's
leading administrators, quashed any suggestions of Graham coaching
there. Moffett told Graham personally what they'd done, so Graham

had to presume that avenue was sealed off.

However, the England experience proved valuable when Wales came calling a year later. By now, Graham had learnt that the smartest way to handle proceedings was to say nothing … to deny everything.

Ironically, the first point of contact was from a Welsh journalist, Andy Howells of the *Western Mail* in Cardiff, around the time the 1998 Super 12 was winding up. He asked Graham if he had been approached about coaching the Welsh national team. When Graham replied no, he was assured he soon would be.

So when Terry Cobner, Wales's director of rugby, phoned, Graham wasn't caught by surprise. He said yes, he was interested, if there was a full business package offered. He stressed he wanted negotiations kept under wraps, and Cobner gave him that assurance. At that point, Graham understood the offer was to coach Wales through to the 1999 Rugby World Cup or perhaps on to the Five Nations (to become the Six Nations) in 2000.

Graham explained he had a signed contract with Auckland but was optimistic they would be supportive of any move. He hadn't concluded his contractual arrangements with the NZRU but, naively, didn't believe they would be obstructive.

Graham viewed the whole issue much more simplistically than those individuals running New Zealand rugby. While the All Blacks were the team he most wanted to coach, obviously with John Hart contracted through to the end of the 1999 World Cup, there was no short-term opportunity for him to coach them.

Here was a passionate rugby nation, a traditional rival of New Zealand's, struggling. The NZRU had been on about developing the game globally and Graham saw this as a marvellous opportunity that would benefit both nations. He genuinely saw it as an extension of his role with the NZRU.

Well, in that regard, Graham was the only one in step. He first broached the issue with Bill Wallace, New Zealand's director of rugby services, who was lukewarm in the extreme.

Graham next talked to David Moffett, the chief executive officer. If Graham had told him he was about to blow up the NZRU offices, he wouldn't have got a more volatile reaction. Slotting an alarming number of expletives into exceptionally few sentences, Moffett vividly conveyed to Graham his opposition to the idea.

Moffett's chief concern seemed to be that Graham would be leaking New Zealand rugby secrets to another country. Graham attempted to promote a case to the contrary, but from Moffett the message was clear: Go to Wales, or even negotiate with them, and you will never coach at national level in New Zealand again.

Graham was shocked and demoralized by the reactions of both Wallace and Moffett. He had coached in New Zealand for 23 years, most of that time as an amateur, guided Auckland to countless NPC titles and the Blues to two Super 12 triumphs, and now he was being told if he as much as talked to the Welsh he would never coach the All Blacks; indeed, he would never coach in New Zealand again.

He was ready for a fresh challenge, which obviously wasn't going to be the All Blacks — although Graham wasn't to know that the All Blacks would come so spectacularly unstuck in 1998 that John Hart came close to being sacked. It was decision time.

Graham weighed up the options. John Hart had waited eight years to win the All Black coaching appointment. No-one could give any assurance Graham's wait would be any shorter — or even that he would ever coach the All Blacks.

Graham chose to apply the bird in the hand strategy. The NZRU hadn't settled on the terms of his contract after almost a year of negotiating. Meanwhile, Wales was genuine about contracting him as its national coach, and Graham was genuine in wanting the job, which he finally conveyed to Terry Cobner.

He made Cobner aware he would be *persona non grata* with the NZRU if he went anywhere near Cardiff, so a meeting was arranged in Sydney immediately after the New Zealand A team's game against Tonga in Wanganui (a game Graham's team won 60–7, a fortnight after upsetting England in Hamilton).

Representing Wales at the meeting at the Sydney Hilton Hotel were the chair of the Welsh union Glanmor Griffiths, the secretary Dennis Gethin, and Terry Cobner. Graham was largely there to listen but one condition upon which he was insistent was that if he took over the national team he had to have an input into the whole structure of Welsh rugby and the various competitions that were being run. He considered they were a mess, with the nation's best players involved in competitions that were never going to adequately prepare them for international rugby.

Graham was completely upfront with the Welsh, who appreciated he would be making huge sacrifices in moving to the other side of the world, not least sacrificing the opportunity to coach the All Blacks. Graham outlined the package that would secure him. 'You guarantee it, I'll come,' he told his Welsh audience. 'There will be no stuffing around; no further conditions.'

Graham understood the Welsh wanted him through to the conclusion of the Five (or Six) Nations tournament in 2000, and was shocked in Sydney to realize he was being offered a five-year contract that would span two World Cups. He would belong to Wales till 2003.

Oh well, the NZRU having made it plain that once he aligned himself with Wales he would never coach the All Blacks, he decided he might as well go the whole hog and sign for five years.

For several weeks after the Sydney meeting, faxes were flowing between Auckland and Cardiff.

Life became uncomfortable because the Welsh press were saying Graham was the leading contender to win the coaching appointment, and so Graham was fielding countless calls from media around the world wanting to know what was going on. Graham answered all of them by saying he didn't know.

When journalists approached the NZRU on the issue, they were told Graham was contracted till the end of 1999, which, of course, he wasn't. When rumours that he was not contracted leaked out, which was obviously a source of embarrassment, it was claimed by the NZRU that as Graham had been banking the union's cheques for the coaching duties he had carried out, that was tantamount to him having signed the contract. Yeah right, as the Tui billboard would say!

London's *Sunday Times* on 19 July carried a story, which instantly came to the attention of the NZRU. It said Wales would name Graham as the successor to Kevin Bowring within the week, at a reputed salary of £250,000 a year for five years. Vernon Pugh, the boss of Welsh rugby, was supposedly flying to Auckland to sort out the details that very weekend.

With Graham's name featuring in news bulletins daily, the NZRU naturally became anxious, knowing it did not in fact have its man contracted. On 22 July, Bill Wallace, director of rugby services, faxed Graham: 'We accept that submitting a final contract document has been delayed for a variety of reasons. We are naturally happy to talk through the detail of the document, but in the meantime we regard you as contractually bound to the NZRU. We are concerned about the recent publicity regarding Wales and have informed the Wales RFU that you are contractually bound, to ensure it is aware of your contractual commitments to us.'

Graham saw red when he read the letter. The NZRU had resorted to 'Big Brother' tactics the previous year to spike his negotiations with England and now it was trying to do the same with Wales.

Graham replied to the NZRU:

There is little point in dwelling on the question of income. Given my letters and conversations with you over the last year, you are well aware that I do not accept the income you offered. You cannot on the one hand say that I am bound but on the other say that you are not bound. NZRU has in the past attempted to spike approaches made to me from overseas. If you do not advise the Welsh RFU immediately that I am not contracted, I will have no choice but to seek legal advice on my rights against All Black Promotions Ltd and NZRU. I look forward to your confirmation that you have advised the Welsh RFU accordingly. Having regard to your conduct, I have no further interest in continuing discussions with you at the present time.

Graham's arrangement with Auckland was completely different because he did have a signed contract. However, he had kept CEO Geoff Hipkins advised of events from the moment Wales first approached him, and Hipkins said he would not stand in his way and would be supportive of whatever move Graham made.

Graham was perplexed, therefore, when Hipkins telephoned to say the board members wanted to talk to him. Graham talked to his legal and contractual adviser, David Jones, who suggested that he should accompany Graham to the meeting. Graham's reaction was along the 'she'll be right' line. 'I've got guarantees from Hipkins and [Reuben] O'Neill [Auckland Rugby Union chairman],' he assured Jones. 'Everything will be OK.'

Yeah right. Graham's political naivety was exposed when he fronted the Auckland board, explained what was happening, and requested a release from his contact. They heard him out, after which he left.

Later that day, Hipkins telephoned Graham spelling out the three conditions on which Auckland would release him from his contract: that he must coach Wales and nobody else, that he would relinquish the two grandstand seats and car-park space at Eden Park which had been granted him for life — and that he had to pay the ARU a $250,000 release fee.

This came as a massive bombshell to Graham. Suddenly, the union wanted a quarter of a million dollars from the individual who had coached their representative teams for five seasons for nothing. For the past 18 months he had received a generous but not exorbitant salary. Now they wanted him to pay $250,000. As for taking away the lifetime seats and car park, that represented sheer petulance. Incidentally, they have never been reinstated!

Graham had gone through two months of negotiation during which he had kept Auckland's CEO fully briefed. Now suddenly there was a massive impediment to his resigning.

Graham had completed his financial negotiations with the Welsh and wasn't prepared to go back to them to ask for more. So anything Auckland demanded would have to come out of his own pocket.

Working with David Jones, and writing with no little passion, Graham penned the following letter to Geoff Hipkins:

Dear Geoff,

Two months ago you agreed to release me from my ARU contract. Apart from our understanding that I would keep you briefed … that release was unqualified. Specifically, the release was not qualified by the requirement of board approval.

I was astonished then that the board has now purported to impose terms on my release, in particular to demand compensation of $250,000. If you now suggest you did not have the authority to give me the release, that is a matter between you and the board. My position is clear — you had the authority to give me the release as the CEO of Auckland.

The demand for compensation is opportunistic and wrong. The demand for compensation appears to be predicated on your assumption that the Welsh RFU will pay what you have demanded. This assumption is completely wrong.

Since my negotiations with Wales have finished ... there is no way I can go back and impose another condition.

Without prejudice to my position, I am prepared to consider paying compensation up to the sum of $100,000 on terms of payment to be agreed if after a period of one year you can show me that the ARU has suffered losses which can be attributed to my departure.

After some unofficial discussion with Graham's mates, John Graham and Rex Davy, the board agreed to reduce the amount of compensation to $150,000, payable over three years. It still meant $50,000 came out of Graham's Welsh salary each year until 2001 to help the Auckland union's coffers.

Graham couldn't comprehend the ARU board's meanness. What had prompted them to behave this way? Was it jealousy of his lucrative deal with Wales? After 13 years coaching Auckland representative teams, 10 as an amateur, the outcome was unbelievably mean-spirited. Had no-one noticed the numbers that flocked to Eden Park every time Auckland and the Blues secured home semi-finals and finals? What would those contests alone have meant in tangible terms to the ARU? No wonder Auckland rugby constantly underachieved, Graham thought.

In the end, Graham even paid for his own farewell, staging it at the Henry homestead in Epsom while Raewyn was away at the netball nationals. A male-only show, he invited all his mates along. The chairman and CEO of the Auckland Rugby Union were not among them!

The NZRU had the final say, releasing a most extraordinary press statement on 25 July. Here's how it appeared in the *New Zealand Herald*:

> Should Graham Henry be appointed national coach of Wales, he will never be given the All Black job.
>
> In a move which looks to be the direct result of the current Henry furore, the NZRU announced a new policy which precludes any New Zealand coach who has been in charge of another national team from getting on to the All Black staff.
>
> The decision is immediate but not retrospective, so therefore it will not affect John Mitchell (assistant coach of England), Warren Gatland (national coach of Ireland) or Brad Johnstone (national coach of Fiji).
>
> 'We are simply protecting our investment in coaches,' said CEO David Moffett, 'in the same way we protect our investment in players.'

Graham couldn't believe the stance being taken by the NZRU. He saw the decision as lacking logic, thought, sensitivity and maturity. 'I'm sure they'll change it when they have time to consider it — it doesn't correlate with the global objectives of the union,' he told a journalist. 'Most professional companies in New Zealand prefer to employ individuals with overseas experience. But if you seek that experience as a rugby coach in New Zealand now, you are penalized to the point of being banned for life from association with the All Blacks. Isn't that simply an unenforceable restraint of trade? There's one law for the corporate world, another for rugby.'

It was plainly a knee-jerk reaction from the board who saw this fella Henry as not doing what he was told. *We'll put him in his place.*

Thanks to the brilliant negotiating skills of David Jones, the deal between Graham and the Welsh Rugby Union was finally concluded late in July. The decision to commit himself to five years with Wales had not been taken lightly. Graham had talked the move through with several of his close mates, individuals whose opinions he respected, and they'd all said go.

Graham revealed his exciting new challenge at a press conference at the Centra Hotel in Auckland. Graham wondered whether anybody would bother to turn up. In the event, more than 50 journalists packed the room.

He'd sought the guidance of talkback host Murray Deaker about how he should go about things. Murray's advice was to share the announcement with all media, when Murray could have saved the 'scoop' for himself. 'They will respect you and your decision more,' he said.

Then, becoming the coach himself, Deaker added, 'These are professional journalists whose attention you must capture from the start. Don't waffle. Hit 'em straight between the eyes.'

Graham heeded the instructions implicitly.

'I'm off to Wales and I'm going tonight,' was his opening line, after which he explained that the Welsh coaching role represented a dream opportunity to coach internationally through until 2003, spanning not one but two Rugby World Cups.

'My heart told me to stay but my head said go. I could have finished up a grumpy old man in 18 months because I might have missed out coaching the national team in both countries. One reason I've accepted the offer is because there are only two nations in the world where rugby is the national game — Wales and New Zealand. Both are totally passionate about the game.'

The Welsh team was coming off a shattering 13–96 hiding from the Springboks, which was ominous, but Graham said he was confident that once the team had all its best players available, dramatic improvement was possible.

'I've been associated with a lot of winning rugby teams and I naturally expect that to continue in Wales,' he told the gathering.

Although Raewyn sat beside him at the press conference, there was no way she could instantly down tools and relocate to Wales. She had her own important coaching role, with the Auckland representative netball team. She would eventually join her husband early in 1999.

Graham programmed the press conference so that after the inevitable one-on-one interviews, he could exit the hotel, drive to the airport and fly off to Wales. Just one problem there … the city council had towed his car away from outside the Centra! Perhaps the NZRU had tipped them off, he thought later.

Leaving his trusty lawyer David Jones to retrieve the car, he departed in a taxi, stopping off briefly at his home to collect his suitcase, and in the process removing the telephone, which was ringing non-stop, from the hook.

As he was checking in at Auckland International Airport, there were TV cameras focused on him from every angle. He maintained a dignified attitude as he disappeared through the check-in zone.

As he entered Air New Zealand's first-class lounge, desperately needing to flop down and unwind, he found the place packed and there, large as life on the TV screen, was Graham Henry being interviewed by Paul Holmes! *Oh, hell, give me a beer!*

Grant Dalton, an icon in the yachting world, was in the lounge and offered Graham a seat next to him. They sat together all the way to London, sharing sporting experiences. Dalton was totally supportive of what Graham was doing, which he found reassuring; in fact, it occurred to Graham as they flew out of Auckland that the only negatives had come from the NZRU and the Auckland Rugby Union, which had wanted to make some money on the side.

4

Into the valleys

Like a painter assessing a blank canvas, Graham was able to start from scratch with Wales. With Auckland and the Blues, he'd always built on the previous year — and given the sequences of success enjoyed by both those teams, that approach had been nothing less than logical.

But now Graham was dealing with a nation with a proud history but one with a national team that had been embarrassed in the previous season's Five Nations Championship; the team was also coming off a 90-point battering from the Springboks, who just happened to be Graham's first opponents.

It meant Graham was going to have to start building from the ground up, which presented him with a novel and stimulating experience. He had to bring together a management team and a selection of players if his vision for Wales was to become a reality.

The management team Graham assembled featured David Pickering as manager, Alun Lewis as back coach, Lyn Howells as forward coach, Steve Black (Blackie) as conditioning coach, and Trevor James (a full-time employee of the Welsh RU) as the team's administrative manager.

Graham had learnt about Blackie on a previous trip to England when he called in on the Newcastle Rugby Club to check on three of his former Auckland cohorts Pat Lam, Inga Tuigamala and Ross Nesdale.

'You guys are top of the heap,' he said. 'I thought I'd call in and find out what makes you better than the rest.'

The answer they gave was a Geordie called Steve Black, the individual responsible for the team's mental and physical preparation. Lam assured Graham that Black was a remarkable person with the capacity to fire up players.

A 40-year-old who looked like Friar Tuck, Blackie was into positive reinforcement in massive slices. He operated as both a conditioning coach and a feel-good motivator, and insisted players had to have a full tank going into a game, both physically and mentally.

He became the perfect foil for Graham, modifying Graham's methods of preparing a team for important games. 'You've got to love your players, Graham,' he kept reminding his new coach.

With a New Zealander and a Geordie installed, Graham knew it was essential to fill the remaining positions with Welshmen.

Pickering, who'd played 27 tests for Wales and sometimes captained the side, was a successful businessman with a major shareholding in three safety and engineering companies. Lewis was the current coach of Newport with a broad reputation as the best back coach in Wales, and Howells was the Pontypridd coach, a forward specialist who related exceptionally well to his players. Lewis and Howells carried on with their club duties and were part time with Wales.

Next came the important matter of selecting his players. Graham admits that in his early days in Wales he listened to too many people and allowed himself to be influenced away from some of the players who would eventually become key components of his squad. He soon came to realize that much of what had been uttered was based purely on local bias.

He soon put out of his head everything that had been spoken about contenders for the Welsh team. Having no club allegiances, Graham reasoned that he would make up his own mind based on what he observed in front of him. He'd been coaching for 25 years, pretty successfully, and felt he knew the sort of player he was looking for.

He learnt that divisions had formed within the Welsh team because half the players were on contracts and half weren't. He was given an example of the match against England at Twickenham where seven of the players were on salaries of £30,000 to £40,000 while the other eight were on nothing. There was a win-bonus system operating, which had little merit since the team was losing more matches than it was winning. Friction existed within the squad.

So the first thing Graham did was to restructure the whole system, putting every squad member on the same basic contract with increases directly proportional to the number of caps.

Having formed a squad for the one-off Springbok game, Graham's first training session was an eye-opener: the players were walking from phase to phase — Graham had to tell them to run. They were in what he quickly identified as the 'Plod Syndrome', which has a lot to do with over-involvement in trainings and matches to the extent that no-one is ever giving more than 80 per cent effort.

It had been the practice for the Welsh squad to assemble in Cardiff every Wednesday throughout the rugby season. While this may have developed camaraderie, what was happening was that the players were hammering hell out of each other and then going home. Graham quickly deduced, because of the heavy commitments burdening the Welsh players, that less was better than more.

For the Springbok game, the players assembled at midday on the Monday and went through a gym session in the afternoon. On the Tuesday, they staged a long training session in the morning and a lighter workout in the afternoon. Then Graham sent them home.

The players had Tuesday and Wednesday evenings in their homes, allowing them to relax while maintaining their intensity. After reassembling on the Thursday, they went through the team plan before travelling across to the Wembley Stadium in London, where the game was to be played. Friday was about fine-tuning ahead of the game on the Saturday.

The game was won by South Africa by 28 points to 20, after it had been 20–all with less than five minutes left to play. While it meant Graham's reign as coach had started with a loss, the result was a hell of an improvement on the 13–96 result in South Africa.

From the moment he arrived in Wales, Graham was totally energized. If he'd taken over the All Blacks he would have been expected to achieve instant success and win every international, but becoming coach of Wales was an entirely different challenge. Here was a team that had not achieved any consistent success for more than two decades: as well as the embarrassingly large totals conceded to France, England and South Africa in recent times, the team had failed to qualify for the World Cup quarter-finals in 1991 and 1995 and was ranked only eighth in the world (behind New Zealand, Australia, South Africa, France, England, Samoa and Argentina).

Graham journeyed throughout Wales, calling on every club, and also checked out Welsh contenders playing their rugby across in Ireland and England. He was pleasantly surprised with the quality of talent on display, which, he now realized, emphasized that Wales's problems lay in the developmental and competitive structures. The current set-up was counterproductive to producing a successful international team.

Graham's groundwork was winning support. Stephen Jones wrote in the London *Sunday Times*:

> The Welsh can see that he is doing more for their rugby than any previous coach. He's taken coaching sessions at some of the tiniest clubs in Wales. They're so tiny that not even many Welsh people have heard of them. And he's certainly infected the players with his own excellent form early on. He's been incredibly thorough, re-motivated them and made them want to play again. Henry's uncomplicated methods have restored organization and confidence to Welsh rugby. There's not been a single word of criticism of him.

To launch Graham's career as coach, the Welsh Rugby Union indulged in some innovative marketing, producing a poster that received worldwide publicity. The striking poster had Graham standing in front of the full Welsh squad, kitted out in scarlet jerseys and white shorts, with a message proclaiming, 'Guide Me, O Thou Great Redeemer' with a secondary line reading, 'Wales: Bread of Heaven.'

The poster provoked an amazing variety of reactions. While most rugby people seemed to think it was appropriate, a number of church people didn't, some branding it blasphemous.

The Welsh Rugby Union received a letter from the Rev. Phylip Henry Rees, representing the Pisgah, Ebenezer and Martletoy Baptist churches. 'Like yourselves, we wish to see Welsh rugby successful again,' he wrote, 'but ultimately our God will not be mocked by such language. There is only one redeemer and that is JC our Lord, not GH.'

While most pundits were predicting a Springbok victory by 20 or 30 points to launch Graham's Welsh career, Graham genuinely believed his team could win. They were opponents with which he was familiar, and understanding the intensity of the Tri-Nations Championship and the Currie Cup competition, he knew Nick Mallett's men would be wearied.

A dodgy penalty try awarded to South Africa in the first half and a rush of blood from a Welsh player at 20–all, causing a kickable penalty to be reversed, proved costly, although Graham knew, in the finish, that his team had lost because his players didn't know how to win. It was a shortcoming he would work on.

Paul Ackford wrote in the *Sunday Telegraph*:

So how did he do it? How did Graham William Henry, Wales's New Zealand-born coach, transform a side who were on the wrong end of a 15-try, 96–13 thrashing into a team four months later who were leading the Boks with three minutes of the match remaining? Any fool can work with quality but only a genius can transform mediocrity. The greatest tribute you could pay to Henry was that he gave Wales back their rugby nous.

Disappointed his team didn't finish the job against the Boks, Graham balanced the budget a week later when his team defeated Argentina 43–30. Although under often severe pressure from the Pumas' scrum, the Welsh brilliantly utilized what possession they did have to score four spectacular tries.

Next up was the Five Nations Championship, a competition that would determine just how much progress the Welsh had made under their new coach.

The answer seemed to be not a lot because after two matches

the Welsh sat forlornly at the bottom of the ladder with no points. The Scots, who were regarded as the competition's easy-beats, upended Wales 33–20 at Murrayfield and the Irish prevailed 29–23 at Wembley, ostensibly a home game for Graham's team.

Graham's entry into Five Nations rugby was catastrophic. He had spoken to his Kiwi fullback Shane Howarth in the changing room before the game and told him he thought Scotland might switch the kick-off and pressure Matt Robinson who was playing his first test. Graham didn't tell Matt this because he didn't want to make him anxious. As it turned out, that's exactly what the Scots did. John Leslie claimed the kick-off and Scots were seven points up in less than a minute! The Welsh players were accustomed to playing in a particular manner and when the pressure went on, they resorted to kind, abandoning the pattern Graham was wanting to introduce.

If the Scottish international was an exercise in frustration, the Irish game a fortnight later became a nightmare. Graham anticipated the Irish would try to intimidate his team through aggression and so instructed his players to get into them physically, a command that was completely misinterpreted.

Graham's players got into them all right, but with a total lack of discipline. The Welsh players lost their cool and in the process annoyed the referee who turned against them. At one stage Wales was down 6–26 before clawing back to 23–26.

So after two Five Nations outings, things were looking bleak for new coach Henry — played two, lost two, with the giants of the competition, France and England, looming ominously ahead. The Welsh were on target for the wooden spoon.

Not everyone was convinced Graham was the man to turn Wales's fortunes around. He received a letter from the chairman of the Ebbw Vale club offering him a one-way air ticket back to New Zealand!

Graham would concede now that the Welsh players had to go through the agony of the Scottish and Irish defeats to find themselves as a team. Only then did the Welsh players collectively buy into Graham's game plan, the high-intensity, wide-ranging approach he'd wanted them to execute from the start.

With a new front row and another Kiwi (Brett Sinkinson) introduced as an openside flanker, the Welsh headed for Paris where they hadn't won since 1975. Their opponents, Grand Slammers in the previous two seasons, hadn't lost a Five Nations match in three years.

Analysis of the first two internationals revealed opponents were running off fly-half Neil Jenkins, satisfied he posed no threat as an attacker. So the policy in Paris was for Jenkins to operate as a runner. Legendary French fullback Pierre Villepreux would say later he never thought it possible that Jenkins could run so incisively. The French were completely unprepared for his daring raids.

The French were stunned by Wales's relentless attacks and found themselves 28–18 down at half-time. Although Graham's team yielded the initiative in the second half, they held on to win 34–33, thanks to Thomas Castaignede missing a last-minute wide-angle penalty.

Huge emotion unfolded after the final whistle, even from the coach who usually maintained a reserved stance regardless of the situation. Wales's first win in Paris in 24 years ranks among the very special moments in Graham's career.

Graham had told his players to be bold and keep being bold, because being bold wins rugby matches. The Quinnell boys, Scott and Craig, would tearfully remind Graham later that their famous father, Derek, who played a huge number of games for Wales, never once sampled victory in Paris.

The Stade de France, a magnificent new stadium, housed 70,000 spectators and it was said they could have sold it five times over. Graham was thrilled Wales had turned on a performance worthy of such an occasion.

Tim Glover would write in the *Independent*:

Anyone who witnessed one of the biggest upsets in France since the revolution would have been privileged to say 'I was there'. It had to be seen to be believed, and even then seemed unreal. Wales not only won in France for the first time since 1975, they did so with panache, élan and chic, not to mention cheek. It was a tour de force, exhilarating and breathtaking in its approach and, in terms of entertainment, utterly compelling.

Stuart Barnes wrote in the *Daily Telegraph* that:

> Wales's epic victory (on a Homeric scale of 0–10, it reads 11) against a fatally over-confident France deserves a few video replays for no reason other than gratuitous pleasure. This was a classic game of rugby. Graham Henry has re-established his redeemer credentials on the streets of every town in Wales ... for in Paris we saw the unstinting self-belief of the 1995 All Blacks, one of the greatest of all teams but one that lost the World Cup final. Earlier in the week, Henry considered victory in Paris as his coaching Everest, the biggest challenge of his career. On Saturday he was resetting his sights. 'There are many more mountains to climb. This is hopefully the start.'

Sue Mott, writing in the *Daily Telegraph*, said that in eight months Graham had transformed a team and a nation:

> With that blazing 34–33 victory over France, the Welsh dragon is firing again after at least a decade of being a depressive newt. 'It was breathtaking, one of the greatest games I have ever seen,' said Gareth Edwards, one of the greatest names of Welsh rugby, so he would know. And everyone gives credit to Henry, the coach who has imposed southern hemisphere professionalism on a British basket case.

Wales now faced a three-week wait for the climax to the campaign: the clash with Five Nations front-runner England at Wembley. After beating France comprehensively at Twickenham, England, guided by Clive Woodward, was on target for a Grand Slam. The previous season it had whipped the Welsh 60–23.

Ten days before the England international, Graham and Raewyn visited St David's, a delightful little town on the Irish Sea coast, famous for its cathedral, a place that houses the tomb of St David, the patron saint of Wales.

There to attend a prize-giving at the local school, Graham was taken on a conducted tour of the cathedral. Unnoticed by anyone, he slipped quietly into the chapel and dropped to his knees. Not being a regular worshipper, he was self-conscious, but being the only person in the chapel at the time he asked St David for assistance. He said the Welsh people had experienced difficult times and there was a lot of unemployment in the Valleys and the only thing that could alleviate the negativity was a win over the 'old enemy' England. The Welsh players needed his help.

With 10 minutes remaining in the Five Nations decider at Wembley and Wales six points in arrears, Graham looked skyward and said, 'Well, St David, if you're going to come through, now's the time!'

Not 30 seconds later, Mark Taylor was the victim of a controversial late charge which presented Wales with the penalty from which it set up an attacking lineout. This led to a Scott Gibbs try which, with Neil Jenkins's conversion, brought Wales an amazing 32–31 victory.

The result, which allowed Scotland to slip through and claim the Five Nations title, brought ecstasy to an entire nation. Winning the Five Nations would have been special but nowhere near as satisfying as defeating England.

Neither religion nor superstition had played any part in Graham's life before he moved to Wales but he found happenings could influence a person. The editor of the *Wales on Sunday* newspaper had sent him a pair of red underpants, featuring the Welsh crest, as a promotional gimmick.

Graham happened to be wearing them when Wales defeated France in Paris. He wore them again in Treviso when Wales downed Italy in a non-competition match a week later. Deciding they were now definitely lucky, he wore them again at Wembley for the England game.

Graham had quickly come to appreciate that for the Welsh, England was the game of the year. The attitude throughout Wales seemed to be that it didn't matter what else happened as long as England was defeated. It was not just a rugby mentality that shaped this attitude: over the centuries the English were the landowners and factory owners while the Welsh were the labourers, so it wasn't hard to see where the motivation stemmed from.

Graham's match strategy was to maintain discipline throughout, no matter what the provocation, and to keep England away from the Welsh 22 for as long as possible. Video analysis revealed Woodward's awesome pack was lethal inside or close to the opposition 22. One of England's favourite ploys was to drive through to the goal line from lineouts.

Graham's team came of age in this game. England probably played its best game of the championship and effectively won the contest but finished behind on the scoreboard, thanks to Neil Jenkins's goal-kicking and Gibbs's stunning late try.

Graham said at the press conference that England hadn't respected Wales as a team. 'Oh, they respected certain individuals,' he said, 'but not Wales as an opponent. If you've smashed a team by 60 points the year before, it's hard to cleanse the sensation of superiority from your subconscious.'

David Hands wrote in *The Times*:

> They were calling Graham Henry the Great Redeemer before this international season began. Maybe the age of miracles is still here after Wales, against all but their own expectations, concluded their temporary tenancy of Wembley with a victory so dramatic that few could have believed it, even though they were among the 79,000 to witness it. Henry, not quite walking on water as he fought his way through the hordes, has turned Wales into a superbly competitive team with a furious belief in themselves.

The *South Wales Argus* declared on its front page, 'Wales is talking about nothing else this morning. Yesterday's last-gasp rugby victory over England has restored pride in our national game. It was quite simply an unbelievable day. Can there have been a better day in recent Welsh sporting history?'

The *South Wales Echo* said, 'Forget the usual Monday morning blues — there was joy in the Welsh air today. As the nation went back to work, commuters seemed to have more of a spring in their step than usual. Even those with hangovers were feeling unusually lightheaded — who needs aspirin when you have just beaten the English at rugby?'

And Andy Howell wrote in the *Western Mail*, 'Wales was the laughing stock of world rugby stuck in the last-chance saloon when

Graham Henry took over on 28 August. Eight months on, he is being hailed as a saviour, the man who saved Welsh rugby from the depths of despair.'

Raewyn was at Wembley to witness Wales's epic win, having flown across to join her husband early in 1999. Graham had mentioned in an interview that his wife coached the Auckland netball team and this was pounced on by locals. Almost before Raewyn had discovered where the local supermarket was, she'd been invited to coach the Cardiff team — and she finished up coaching the rep team, the B team and the under-21 team.

Netball, in fact women's sport in general, had a low priority in Wales and Raewyn found she had to start pressuring the journalists who came to the house to talk rugby with Graham to garner any publicity for the sport at all.

Netball was essentially social and she caused a stir when she suggested to her Cardiff players, as they headed to North Wales for a tournament, that they should sacrifice drinking for the weekend.

'Bloody hell,' said one girl, 'you mean I've got to pay to come on this trip and I'm not allowed to drink!'

Following Leigh Gibbs's appointment as CEO of Welsh Netball, Raewyn was instantly promoted to the post of Welsh coach, which was pretty special having husband and wife coaching two of Wales's national sports teams.

She rated it the most enjoyable coaching experience of her life because all the players were as keen as mustard and without egos. Her training schedules changed many of their lives. Raewyn made them all go to the gym, some for the first time in their lives.

She developed a strong friendship with the team's sports psychologist, Lynne Evans, who would spend many hours with Graham and Raewyn discussing aspects of team preparation and behaviour.

Two months after the epic victory over England, Graham took his Red Dragons off to Argentina, a notoriously difficult country to tour; indeed, the Welsh had never claimed a series there. But this time they returned triumphant, winning both tests in Buenos Aires, 36–26 and 23–16. With this success, Wales had become the first northern hemisphere nation to win a series in that country.

Graham was chuffed. His forwards had stood up to the Pumas' powerful scrum, the backs had constructed quality tries and Neil Jenkins had continued on his winning way as a goal-kicker.

Then it was back to Cardiff for a special occasion: the opening of the Millennium Stadium. The opponent? The mighty Springboks!

Seven months earlier, Graham's debut as an international coach had been against the Springboks at Wembley. His team had lost 20–26, and while most of the Welsh players regarded this as a minor triumph given the 90-point humiliation from their previous meeting with the Boks, Graham was annoyed. He knew his team could have won.

Rob Howley, the Welsh captain, would nominate Graham's reaction to the loss as a defining moment. 'I think most people in Wales were happy with the performance, considering what had gone before,' said Howley, 'but Graham was obviously disappointed we had lost. He stressed to us that we'd been in a position to beat South Africa, and hadn't. Most other coaches would have been satisfied, I'm sure. Graham wasn't.'

This time there would be no gnashing of teeth. South Africa and Wales had been doing battle since 1906 and never before (and not since) had the Red Dragons come out on top. But all that changed on 26 June 1999 when Graham's men won 29–19.

The occasion merited a full house — but only 27,500 souls were there to see Wales's historic victory. No, it wasn't through poor marketing or any unprecedented apathy on behalf of the Welsh rugby fans; the simple fact was that, for safety reasons, only one-third of the new stadium had been approved for use for this opening encounter. Although it has to be said the 27,500 fans present made enough noise for the 81,000 who would have flocked in had they been given licence!

Wales had won its previous five internationals, which included defeats of France, England and Argentina, in Buenos Aires. When the team staged its final training session at Sophia Gardens in Cardiff, Graham stood on the sidelines feeling totally redundant. The players, he considered, were so totally in control he had no need to interfere. He knew his team would defeat South Africa.

And defeating the Springboks was pretty special for Graham. Call him old-fashioned, but he'd grown up in an era when South Africa was the ultimate foe. When the nation had been ostracized because of its apartheid system, and with the emergence in the 1980s of Australia as a rugby force, modern-day players had begun to regard the Wallabies as the team to beat. But for Graham, the ultimate victory is still against South Africa.

So it would not be exaggerating to say he encountered pure ecstasy after his team's win in the magnificent Millennium Stadium. Each team scored two tries, but with Neil Jenkins, at the peak of his form as a goal-kicker, adding 19 points with his boot, Wales had 10 points to spare. Not only had history been created, it had come about in style.

After the game, Graham walked around the stadium positively purring. This was a very special occasion, one of the magical moments of his coaching career, not just because of the victory but because his players had performed to the peak of their powers.

What a way to celebrate the opening of the new stadium!

This was the team's sixth consecutive victory. Wales was on a roll, and there was more to follow: Canada and France, too, were swept aside at the Millennium Stadium, leaving Wales in good shape for the fourth Rugby World Cup, which it was hosting. This was a remarkable turnaround given that the nation had been in despair when Graham arrived 12 months earlier.

Wales was allocated the most intriguing of the five pools for the World Cup — some dubbed it 'The Pool of Death'. Though they might also have branded it 'The Kiwi Connection Pool' because three of the four nations involved claimed New Zealand coaches: Argentina was prepared by Alex 'Grizz' Wyllie, Samoa by Bryan Williams and Wales by Graham; Japan was the odd nation out, but its squad was awash with former All Blacks and New Zealand representative players.

Remarkably, the three Kiwi-coached teams finished level with seven points each, the result of Wales beating Argentina, Argentina beating Samoa, and finally Samoa upsetting Wales.

This was the first occasion a World Cup had featured five pools, necessitating repechages to cull the number of qualifiers down to eight for the quarter-finals.

Had Argentina lost to Japan in the final pool match, Wales would have been plunged into the repechage section. Graham admitted to being in 'a nervous state' until the Pumas' victory was assured and a quarter-final contest, against Australia, confirmed.

The drama didn't halt there. Cagey 'Grizz' Wyllie, reasoning his team was better off playing Ireland at the neutral venue of Lens in France in its repechage game than Scotland at Murrayfield, advised his players not to win by more than 48 points against Japan. The final score of 33–12 gave the Pumas an appointment at Lens where they pulled off a massive upset, eliminating the hapless Irish.

News of how divine intervention had helped Wales defeat England at Wembley had so wowed the Welsh players that they insisted Graham visit St David's and enlist their patron saint's support for the quarter-final clash with Australia.

'Good thought,' said Graham, 'but it's a long drive to St David's, a six-hour turnaround, and I'm afraid I don't have the time.'

'We'll get you there,' replied one of the players, who obviously had great influence because the next thing Graham knew a helicopter had been arranged to fly him to St David's. In the circumstances, he could hardly refuse!

The Welsh had made massive strides in a remarkably short time under Graham but they were outgunned by the 'streetwise' Wallabies in their quarter-final at the Centennial Stadium.

Australia led 10–9 at half-time and although it was still 10–9 with 11 minutes left to play, a touch of genius from fly-half Stephen Larkham created the match-winning try. The Wallabies went on to win 23–9.

'I was hoping for a miracle, which didn't eventuate,' Graham said at the press conference. 'The Wallabies were too quick and streetwise for us.

'We've come an incredibly long way and now we've got to go on. Ideally, we need a northern hemisphere Super 12 that will provide high-quality, high-intensity rugby for the leading players, week in and week out.'

Heavy rain before and after the kick-off meant the contest wasn't the spectacular event most people were anticipating. Closing the retractable roof would have helped, but the IRB wouldn't give permission for that: the game had to be open to the elements. Which, as Wallaby Tim Horan quipped, 'Having a retractable roof and not using it when it's raining is a bit like having a Ferrari in the garage and taking the bus!'

When one of the Welsh players observed that St David hadn't come through for them on this occasion, Graham drolly replied that St David had told him not to be so greedy.

If New Zealanders were disappointed for Graham, they were devastated a week later when the All Blacks capitulated in unbelievable fashion against France, conceding 33 points in the second half of their semi-final against a team they had defeated 54–7 in Wellington four months earlier.

When the All Blacks then also dropped their third-place play-off contest to the Springboks, procuring enough possession to score a dozen tries but in the event managing none, it prompted John Hart to announce his resignation as coach.

Graham didn't quite know how he felt about that. Shocked at how the All Blacks had unravelled during the World Cup, he knew that had he remained in New Zealand he would now be a leading contender, perhaps *the* leading contender, to take over the team. But once he'd committed himself to Wales, the NZRU had said it wouldn't deal with him ever again, and as long as the so-called 'Henry Clause' remained in place, there was no future for him back in New Zealand.

But nothing is forever and by year's end, David Moffett would be replaced as CEO by David Rutherford, while several of the existing board members would, at the next AGM, be dumped after the NZRU disastrously (for their country) conceded co-hosting rights to the 2003 Rugby World Cup. One of the most significant changes the revamped board would make would be to throw out the Henry Clause.

That was in the future, though. In the immediate wake of the 1999 World Cup, Graham's challenge was to shape Wales into a team that could win the Six Nations.

Unfortunately, that didn't eventuate. Three excellent victories in the 2000 championship, against Italy and Scotland at the Millennium Stadium and Ireland in Dublin, were overshadowed by heavy losses to France, at home, and England at Twickenham.

England, denied the title so dramatically at Wembley 12 months earlier, emerged triumphant on this occasion, with France, Ireland and Wales finishing equal second (although Wales with the poorest differential was officially only fourth).

It didn't help that Wales had lost some of its Kiwi connection for the championship after a *Sunday Telegraph* 'Grannygate' investigation disclosed that neither fullback Shane Howarth nor flanker Brett Sinkinson qualified to represent the country. Both had ostensibly qualified through their Welsh grandfathers, but they didn't have any! Sinkinson's grandfather was born in Oldham, England, and Howarth's in New Zealand.

Howarth had by then appeared 19 times at fullback for Wales. He was devastated by the revelations, having genuinely believed he qualified to represent Wales, which is why he relocated his family to Newport. 'I'd hate people to think I was some kind of mercenary,' he told the author at the time, 'but having had a taste of international rugby, I was keen for more. And when Graham said he wanted me, I was dead keen. I'd already turned down Roger Uttley who wanted me to play for England.'

Howarth couldn't believe what was going on when the story made worldwide headlines. 'I didn't have the foggiest where my grandparents were born. How many people do? But when I made inquiries back home, I was informed one was born in England, the other in Wales. Thomas Williams, my mother's father, I was assured had been born in Cardiff.'

Graham had first become aware of Howarth's supposed eligibility when Howarth's agent back in Auckland, Roger Mortimer, whispered in his ear before he left to take up the Welsh coaching appointment. Bearing that in mind, he watched Howarth play several matches for Sale before declaring him his best fullback option.

Graham was confident Howarth's ancestry was in order but he

had some suspicions about Sinkinson's, so he requested the Welsh Rugby Union check them out. When the union cleared them to play, Graham naturally presumed the appropriate groundwork had been completed. But obviously it hadn't.

Eventually, Graham had to front to the International Rugby Board, along with chairman Glanmor Griffiths; their case heard by a three-man panel. Although the Welsh union was found guilty of fielding unqualified players, the matches won when Howarth and Sinkinson played were allowed to stand, which was a huge relief for the administration. Fortunately, Wales wasn't the only country caught up in the Grannygate scandal.

As a result of Grannygate, the IRB changed the eligibility rules so that a player could represent only one country.

Having had his team twice finish among the also-rans, Graham considered his options going forward. Perhaps a genuine New Zealand forward coach might make a difference, but who was the best New Zealand forward coach?

Rex Davy was going about his business as a hugely successful real estate company manager in West Auckland when the phone rang late one afternoon. It was Graham Henry.

'Great to hear from you, Graham,' said Davy. 'What can I do for you?'

'Well,' said Graham, after a modicum of small chat, 'I would appreciate it if you can find out who the best forward coach in the country is.'

'OK, I'll make a few inquiries. I presume this person would have to be prepared to move offshore?'

'Very possibly.'

'OK, leave it with me.'

Graham knew his friend would diligently follow through on his request. He had enormous regard for Davy, who'd been a stunningly successful manager of Graham's Auckland and Blues teams and a great student of the game.

Not many days had passed before Davy phoned Graham with the answer. 'The man you want is Steve Hansen, the assistant coach to

Wayne Smith at the Crusaders. Oddly, he played all his rugby as a centre, but everyone assures me he's the best forward coach in the land.'

'Thanks, Rex. Let's see what eventuates.'

Because Hansen was contracted to the New Zealand Rugby Union, Graham could not legitimately approach him about an off-shore appointment, so he approached a 'secret agent' to undertake some inquiries on his behalf. The secret agent was no less than Christopher Doig, whom Graham considered the most talented individual he had ever met. They had taught together at Auckland Grammar School, Graham being an expert in physical education with Doig tutoring in English.

Graham remembers when Doig announced he was heading to Austria to train as an opera singer. Aware of his talents as an English teacher and a sportsman, Graham said, 'What the hell are you doing that for?' Years later, when Doig became an internationally renowned tenor, Graham acknowledged his thinking had been rather narrow at the time!

He continued to marvel at Chris Doig's boundless energy and abilities. His operatic talents aside, Doig served on the Arts Council, was CEO of New Zealand Cricket and, at the time of his sad death in 2011, was a member of the New Zealand Rugby Union.

Anyway, Doig wasn't destined to be a detective because after a short time on the Hansen case he fielded a phone call from the man he was 'tracking'!

Hansen had first become curious when Todd Blackadder and Matt Sexton, the captain and the hooker of his champion Canterbury NPC team, each asked him when he was off to Wales. Once was amusing; twice was decidedly fishy …

'What do you guys know, I don't?' Hansen asked Blackadder.

'Well, there's someone been asking questions about you, and it seems like Wales might need a forward coach.'

Under pressure, Blackadder conceded that the 'secret squirrel' just might be a fellow by name of Christopher Doig.

With his curiosity well and truly aroused, Hansen tracked down Doig.

'What the hell are you asking questions about me for?' he demanded.

'Well, I confess I am operating on behalf of someone else,' replied Doig. 'That someone is Graham Henry, who is looking for a forward coach to assist him with the Welsh national team. Do I take it you might be interested?

'Yeah, I might be.'

Hansen had been assistant coach to Robbie Deans with the Crusaders and had succeeded Deans as coach of Canterbury. His team would go on to win the championship in 2001, smashing Auckland 53–25 in the semi-final and beating Otago 30–19 in the final. Interestingly, given what had gone on with Graham back in 1998, Hansen was also experiencing contractual problems with the NZRU.

His positive response to Doig led to a phone call from Graham, who explained that he needed a specialist forward coach to help transform Wales from good losers into champions.

'Are you genuinely interested?' asked Graham.

'Yeah, I'm in if you want me. But I wouldn't be available until after the NPC finishes in October.'

Unbeknown to his bosses, Hansen was flown across to Cardiff for an interview with David Pickering, Alun Phillips and Graham. There were two or three other candidates.

When he was called back in, it was to offer him the job. He accepted and the following day he flew back to New Zealand and broke the news to Canterbury chairman Mike Eagle and CEO Steve Tew, two individuals soon to make their mark at national level.

Hansen arrived in Cardiff in November 2001. The next several months would not unfold in the manner he anticipated: he was in for one hell of a roller-coaster ride.

5

Taking on too much

High summer in Wales does not exactly equate to high summer in New Zealand, where Graham spent the first 50-odd years of his life. In 'Godzone', his preferred attire was shorts and a cotton T-shirt, a quick dip at the nearest beach was a way of life, and the household chef enjoyed heaps of down time because meals were more often than not being prepared outside on the barbecue.

Notwithstanding that, Graham was enjoying his second summer in Wales. He was winding down after another full-on season in charge of the national team, one in which Wales had performed adequately although not as spectacularly as in the previous year when, under Graham's guidance for the first time, the men in scarlet had notched up those 10 consecutive test victories.

He would be required to fly out to Canada to offer some guidance to and observe the performances of the Welsh Development team, but that wouldn't be too demanding. Even if a pullover was often an essential piece of summer clothing in Marshfield Village, Castleton, between Newport and Cardiff, where the Henrys had established themselves at a residence suitably named the Coach House, Graham was in relaxed mode, his life right at that moment uncomplicated.

That was until he fielded a phone call from Donal Lenihan in Cork, the same Donal Lenihan, bank official and former Irish and British and Irish Lions test lock, who had recently been named manager of the British and Irish Lions rugby team for the 2001 tour of Australia. He knew Donal wasn't ringing to wish him a happy birthday (the date being 8 June and Graham having that very day clicked over 54 years on the clock).

'Graham,' said Lenihan, 'congratulations on your achievements with the Welsh team.'

'Thank you,' said Graham, wondering where this was leading.

'I wonder if you could get yourself across to Dublin next week. We're sorting out the coaching arrangements for the Lions tour and I have a proposal you may be interested in.'

'Sounds exciting. See you in Dublin.'

As he prepared to board the Aer Lingus plane for the short flight across the Irish Sea, Graham wondered which role Lenihan might have in mind for him. It surely wouldn't be as head coach because this was, after all, the iconic Lions team we were talking about, a team with an illustrious history dating back more than a century. Many famous Scotsmen, Englishmen, Welshmen and Irishmen had guided the team's fortunes down the years on tours of South Africa, New Zealand and Australia. Graham vividly recalled the deeds of the 1959 and 1971 teams in New Zealand, the '71 team especially because, under Carwyn James's astute guidance, they'd created history by winning the series against the All Blacks. Graham had bought a copy of James's book *The Lions Speak*, in which a number of the leading players wrote chapters about their specialist positions. It had been Graham's virtual bible when he first broke into coaching.

The Lions lit up the rugby fields in the major southern hemisphere nations every four years. The prospect of a Kiwi being given charge of them seemed as preposterous as a Brit or a South African being appointed coach of the All Blacks. Nah, it just wouldn't happen.

'Graham, we'd like you to be the head coach of the British and Irish Lions,' said Lenihan, soon after Graham had been ushered into his hotel suite in Dublin.

Graham was flabbergasted.

Graham could have said no, probably should have said no. He will tell you now that right at that moment his ego seriously obscured his decision making.

He was already fully committed as the national coach of Wales.

He didn't need to overload himself with the massive responsibility of coaching the British and Irish Lions in a three-test series against the world champion Wallabies on Australian soil. It was hard to recall any individual who had taken on the Lions coaching role while still in charge of their national team.

But Graham Henry being Graham Henry didn't hesitate to accept. Not only did he regard it as a huge honour and privilege to be offered the position, he also saw it as another opportunity to demonstrate to those blinkered individuals administering the game back in New Zealand who had invoked what became known as the Henry Clause, David Moffett pre-eminent among them, that he could do the business as a coach at the highest level.

It was a serious mistake because the decision was ego-based: he would concede when he reflected on the tour years later that when he accepted Lenihan's invitation it was about him, not about the team. But Graham learnt from that mistake and became more 'ego-less'; he came to recognize that it was the team performance that mattered, their achievements that brought pleasure and satisfaction.

Before Graham could be confirmed as Lions coach he required the blessing of the committee of the Welsh Rugby Union, to whom he was contracted, and that was no shoo-in, for Graham had maintained a fiery relationship with his employers. He'd had many challenging meetings with them, finding many of their attitudes violently at odds with how he believed the game in Wales needed to develop.

He understood precisely why many of the Welsh committee members acted the way they did: they had existed in the Welsh rugby environment for the last 50 or 60 years and were totally answerable to the clubs that controlled them by the voting process. Being a member of 'the committee' gave them an important status in their community — but to survive they had to placate those clubs.

A couple of weeks before Lenihan made public his committee's preference for the Lions coach, Graham had to excuse himself from the Welsh Development team tour in Canada and return to Cardiff to confront the WRU and convince a majority of the committee they should release him for the tour. Graham argued that the long-term benefits of him coaching the Lions and the experience he would gain would comprehensively outweigh any short-term inconveniences.

As manager, Lenihan had made an impassioned plea to the WRU not to stand in the way of Graham becoming the Lions coach. The Lions committee's brief to Lenihan as manager had been basic: To recommend the best available coach, irrespective of nationality. Which is what he had done.

A number of the Welsh committee voted against releasing their man, their main argument being that the joint coaching roles of Wales and the British Lions were too great for one person. Graham would now concur with that logic but at that June 2000 meeting he managed to convince a majority of the committee that he could adequately handle both jobs.

It's fair to say Graham's appointment did not meet with unanimous acclaim. Not only was he an outsider but he had headed off some well-qualified rivals, most notably Clive Woodward, who had impressively turned England's fortunes around.

The contest for the appointment only developed because the genial Scotsman Ian McGeechan had declared himself unavailable for a fourth consecutive term in office. McGeechan was the Director of Coaching for the Scottish Rugby Union and patently the Lions' No. 1 choice. He ticked all the boxes and, having guided the 1989 tour to Australia (series won 2–1), the 1993 tour to New Zealand (series lost 1–2), and the 1997 tour to South Africa (series won 2–1), he had become a virtual Lions institution. The Lions management had made strenuous attempts to get him on board again, but on this occasion he declined.

The announcement a Kiwi was to take charge of the British Lions caused a storm of controversy and divided the media and rugby personalities. Clive Woodward said, 'I can't believe he has got the job. It's a joke. It doesn't make any sense. Why, oh why, are we not taking a British coach?' And Roger Uttley, an England stalwart who'd been part of the coaching team when the Lions last toured Australia in 1989, described Graham's appointment as a huge slap in the face for all rugby coaches in the British Isles. 'All we've done is to say to our senior coaches, "Sorry, guys, you're doing a good job domestically but internationally you can't hack it." If I was them, I'd be hacked off.'

Gavin Hastings, the fullback whose contribution to the Scottish and British Isles causes had been massive, also fired a salvo at Graham's selection. 'The Lions team is a special institution,' he said, 'something with its own ethos and ethics. These days with New Zealand, South Africa and Australia fed their high-protein diet of Tri-Nations rugby, it's only a traditional Lions party and the Barbarians that are left to continue the legacy. That is why the appointment of a New Zealander hurts.'

Zinzan Brooke, a massive contributor to Graham's Auckland and Blues teams in the nineties, leapt to Graham's defence, branding as 'pathetic' the criticism his selection was causing. 'It doesn't matter a jot that the task of leading the British Lions has gone to an outsider,' he said. 'Graham is a winner — he cannot be any less committed than a British or Irish coach. He knows the players better than any British coach and can successfully combine his Welsh and Lions coaching roles. If you want to criticize Graham, you will have to join the back of a very big queue. If you actually want the job, you will be at the front of a very short queue! The simple truth is the Lions were crying out for a coach and they couldn't find one. I find it pathetic the way some current coaches and past players are reacting.'

Graham was aware of the criticisms. He knew that the criticisms were not of him personally but of the decision to appoint as coach a person who was neither British nor Irish, and to an extent, he understood and accepted them. It wasn't the first time in his career he had come under fire but his results on the paddock had always silenced those critics. Right through his coaching career, now extending over two decades, with the Auckland Grammar School First XV, Auckland Colts, Auckland and Blues, he had maintained a success rate in excess of 85 per cent. That placed him among the top echelon of coaches in the world.

There were some parallels with the appointment of Carwyn James, whose team had revolutionized the rugby game in 1971. Graham wrote after his appointment:

There are some strong similarities between our situations. Neither of us had coached the national side of our homeland before we were appointed to coach the Lions. Both of us were outsiders 'in exile'. I had given up my place in the All Black succession to come to Wales while Carwyn never got to coach the national team in Wales, and many of his ideas took a while to be accepted by the establishment. We were both invited to breathe new life into an ailing patient and swapped hemispheres to do so. Allowing for the evolution of the game in the last 30 years, I believe we're preaching the same 15-man rugby gospel.

The Lions expedition plunged Graham into a new coaching mechanism where he was surrounded by a cluster of specialist coaches — Andy Robinson (assistant coach), Dave Alred (kicking coach) and Phil Larder (defensive coach), all from England, plus Steve Black, the Welsh fitness coach, as conditioner. Graham's coaching experiences until then, with Auckland, the Blues and Wales, had involved him as the head coach with one assistant coach, a manager and a fitness person. And that was it. He was used to coaching independently, usually with one assistant, and having responsibility for the entire package. He found the new challenge of operating with three quality specialist coaches around him demanding and challenging.

He knew that to be successful in Australia, he needed to 'get outside himself'. He was accustomed to taking responsibility for virtually every aspect of team preparation himself; now he was required to operate rather like the conductor of an orchestra where he had to create an environment that inspired every individual to perform to his absolute potential. It represented an exciting challenge.

Graham was thrilled that Steve Black, or Blackie as everyone knew him, had come on board. They had worked in tandem at Wales, with Graham mightily impressed with his extraordinary ability to extract the best from players. To Graham, Blackie was the most positive man he'd ever met. An example was when he phoned him just prior to the team announcement. 'How are you, Blackie?' And the man replied, 'Magnificent ... no, better than magnificent!'

Graham owed Pat Lam, for it was Lam who had made Graham aware of the remarkable individual that was Blackie. 'You've got to get this fellow on your team,' said Lam, Newcastle's captain who had worked with Blackie, when Graham was beginning to construct his Welsh coaching team soon after his arrival from New Zealand in 1998.

It was Blackie who told Graham in his early days with Wales that 'It's not enough to know your players, Graham, you have to love them.'

Blackie's philosophy was encapsulated in a chapter he wrote for Nick Bishop's book on that 2001 Lions tour, *Henry's Pride*.

There's no doubt in my mind that 80 per cent of sport is played in the mind, the other 20 per cent is physical condition. The mind influences the body and tells it what it can achieve. It's a wonderful instrument I told the players once, after a defeat. Don't worry about it, we'll put it right. Now from 4.15pm to 6.15pm we're going to feel like shit, really bad. Let's really get into it! After half an hour or so, they'd had enough of that feeling, and were raring to go, to feel happy and enthusiastic again. They'd accepted what had happened; they knew both ends of the psychological spectrum and they'd decided where they wanted to be. In coaching, a lot of people stress advancement through the technological aspects, but you'll never grow that way. You can go into football clubs and see coaches employing the same methods, and it's got no personal innovation at all, no personal commitment. With good coaching, the second-best team can beat the best team. You never win anything by copying because by the time you've copied it, the original has already moved on. You're always playing catch-up. So I made a decision with coaching to do it differently. At least to try doing it differently. Be different, and you'll make a difference.

The Lions team was announced at a press conference at the Crown Plaza Hotel, Heathrow Airport, having been selected (with some assistance from Graham) by a five-man panel comprising Derek Quinnell (Wales), Simon Halliday (England), John O'Driscoll (Ireland), and John Rutherford and Ian Lawrie (Scotland).

England's inspirational leader Martin Johnson was predictably named captain of the 35-strong touring party, which was announced after a most thorough selection process. The selectors settled on 18 players from England, 10 from Wales, six from Ireland and three from Scotland

In analysing the squad, Graham had to admit that the only players he really knew were the 10 Welshmen. One of the selectors asked if he was prepared to take the English utility back Austin Healey on tour because of his reputation for being disruptive. 'Yes,' said Graham, 'We'll get him right.' It was a call that would come back to haunt him.

Writing in the *Observer*, Eddie Butler graphically described the press conference: 'It was a whopper. It might even have set a world record for the number of microphones and biros at the ready for a rugby story. This was bigger than the Rugby World Cup, and quite an ordeal for the coach in the middle of it all. All the holders of the instruments of communication wanted a piece of Graham Henry.'

A couple of weeks before the announcement of the touring party Graham had spent a few days in Ireland, at the home of Donal Lenihan. Upon his return, and in the absence of his good wife Raewyn, who was away with the Welsh netball team, he had thrown his shirt into the washing machine, failing to notice that the shirt pocket contained his New Zealand passport. When he discovered his awful mistake, it was to the realization that his name, address and photograph had been expunged from the document. No longer did it confirm his identity — everything had been washed away!

There was just enough time to secure a new passport, except that the photos Graham sent away with the application to the New Zealand Consulate were returned because he'd trimmed the top few inches off his head in the photo booth! Fortunately, Graham was now reunited with Raewyn and she took charge. Thanks to her efficient efforts, a special courier service and an understanding consulate, Graham received his new passport less than 48 hours before the team departed Heathrow Airport for Australia.

The Lions spent a week in camp at Tylney Hall in Hampshire in the last week of May prior to their departure for Perth. Their objective was to build the finest players of four nations into one close-knit team. Lawrence Dallaglio, a survivor of the 1997 Lions tour of South Africa, recalled the words of Graham's predecessor, Ian McGeechan: 'You will be walking down a street in 15 or 20 years' time and you will see a guy who is now alongside you in this room. There will be a look between you — you won't need any more than that.'

The camp, organized by the same Impact Group who had prepared the 1997 team, was not exclusively about scrums and lineouts or defensive or attacking ploys. It was about implementing the Lions culture that the team comes first — hugely important when you have players drawn from four different countries, a unique situation in world rugby — and binding 35 players together into a powerful unit capable of outgunning rugby's world champions, physically and mentally.

The players were stretched beyond their comfort zone but in a supportive environment. One exercise involved climbing a pole to a platform 20 metres above the ground before diving backwards 'into the unknown'. Graham found this high challenge particularly demanding, as did several of the players.

The week at Tylney Hall was especially valuable for Graham, who urgently needed to get to know his players and support staff. He recognized that, notwithstanding his outstanding achievements previously, he needed to coach to a higher level than ever before and use to ultimate effect the coaching talents of Robinson, Larder and Alred.

A senior players group that comprised Martin Johnson, Lawrence Dallaglio, Keith Wood, David Young, Rob Howley and Jonny Wilkinson was established, their function being to provide a link between players and management and to keep the lines of communication open.

One of Graham's early challenges was in trying to comprehend baggageman Pat 'Crash' O'Keefe's Cork accent and impish sense of humour.

'Am I speaking too quickly or are you thinking too slowly?' O'Keefe inquired after Graham had asked him to repeat a question for a third time.

'One of those,' replied Graham. 'Listen, Pat, I've had a call from an irate Irish journalist who's unhappy with the ratio of Welsh and Irish players in the team.'

'Aah, don't worry about him, Graham … that fella can't even cross his legs!'

One aspect of the Lions squad that gave Graham cause for optimism was the special strength among the loose forwards. In openside specialists Richard Hill and Neil Back, blindsider Lawrence Dallaglio and No. 8 Scott Quinnell, he believed he possessed the best loose forward combination in the world, one that would truly torment the Australians.

But alarm bells had rung when Dallaglio suffered a major injury playing in an English premiership match a few weeks before the team assembled, tearing part of the soft tissue around the cruciate ligament in his knee.

After initially appearing in danger of withdrawing altogether, he made exceptional progress and when the team arrived in Perth, there was optimism he would be ready for the third match against the Queensland Reds. Graham certainly hoped so, for he was counting on Dallaglio being a major part of his weaponry in the test series.

Sitting in the grandstand at Perth, Dallaglio obviously survived the tour opener, which is more than could be said for two other hapless members of the team: Scottish No. 8 Simon Taylor, who was being groomed as Dallaglio's understudy, and England hooker Phil Greening, both highly talented players

Greening broke his leg making a tackle in defence training while Taylor lasted 27 minutes of the Western Australia game before damaging his knee ligaments. Both were invalided out of the tour. It was the start of an unbelievable injury toll list that would reach catastrophic proportions and seriously diminish the strength of the team by the end of the tour.

Graham and his fellow coaches, Andy Robinson and Phil Larder, drove the team hard in Perth, unquestionably; too hard. The coaches were hyped, probably over-keen in wanting to impart their knowledge and make a difference. The objectives were admirable: to have the players at peak, in terms of technical and tactical awareness, for the three internationals. But Graham would also tell you now that in his desperation to be successful, he didn't manage the other coaches well enough. He drove the players too hard, his personal ego to be successful getting in the road of good common sense. He was more conscious of the end result than of individual player welfare and he concedes in hindsight he burdened many of the players with tactics and game plans that were too complicated, too complex and therefore too demanding. And in that first week in Western Australia, when the team was based at Fremantle, with scant regard for the jet lag that was affecting many of the players, he drove them ruthlessly. It was the catalyst for English scrum-half Matt Dawson's untimely outburst at the time of the first test.

In his defence, coaching an international team on an overseas tour was a new experience. Graham's solitary 'tour' experience was on Wales's brief (and successful) two-test visit to Buenos Aires. All his previous coaching with Auckland and the Blues involved only brief journeys out of New Zealand to South Africa and Australia.

However, while many of the players, and Graham himself, would tell you that first week was excessively brutal, it meant the 2001 British Lions hit the ground running.

They obliterated Western Australia 116–10 in Perth and four days later, some 3000 miles east-nor'-east in Townsville, overwhelmed a Queensland President's XV 83–6, scoring a staggering 31 tries in the two games.

In the context of the test series against the Wallabies, the results held scant significance because the opposition was so weak, but they did reveal attacking patterns that made the Australians aware Henry's men were going to be a major threat.

Those concerns were magnified tenfold when the Lions then swept aside the Queensland Reds 42–8 in the first serious contest of the tour at Ballymore, prompting one Sunday newspaper subeditor to write: 'Australia on Red Alert as Lions Roar On'.

The performance against the Reds plainly rattled a few Australian cages and prompted Eddie Jones, heir apparent to Rod Macqueen as Wallabies coach and coach of the next opponent Australia A, to declare he was disappointed with the amount of foul play in the Queensland game. He urged match officials to 'keep an eye on it' when the Lions took on his side at Gosford, with the obvious implication that the Lions, not their Australian opponents, were mainly responsible. It was the start of a propaganda war plainly designed to focus referees' attention on the Lions' tactics in a bid to destabilize the team.

It had an instant effect. In the Australia A game at Gosford, three days later, controlled by New Zealand's Paul Honiss, the penalty count was 9–24 against the Lions, a huge proportion of those penalties being given away in and around the tackle area. Graham concluded the ref was looking at only one team. However, his greater concern was the inept performance turned on by his midweek players for four-fifths of the game. They allowed Australia A's locks Justin Harrison and Tom Bowman to control the lineout and not until they were 6–22 down did they finally secure sufficient ball to alter the momentum. Three tries in the final 12 minutes left the Lions coaches ruing what might have been. They eventually lost 25–28; the result providing a valuable reality check for the tourists.

If the Lions thought the loss to Australia A would bring a halt to the orchestrated litany of criticism of their tactics, it only encouraged it. Rod Macqueen, the Wallaby coach, declared the Lions guilty of twisting the scrum before the ball came in and of attacking jumpers in midair at the lineout. Bob Dwyer, the New South Wales coach, focused on the Lions' 'illegal' play at the breakdown, claiming the Lions should have received more yellow cards than they had.

Graham could see what the key men in Australian rugby were trying to achieve. They had recognized from the Lions' performances, particularly in the demolition of the Queensland Reds, that the tourists could hurt them in the scrums, lineouts and breakdown, and so they were using their publicity machine to try to build a refereeing shield, to protect themselves in those areas.

So at a press conference at Manly, two days before the New South Wales game, Andy Robinson set about redressing the account. He dealt with the scrum and the driving maul. 'Scrummaging is very much part of rugby,' he said. 'Now it seems as if we are going to have league-type scrums, where they are not contestable. It is affecting the nature of the game. In the northern hemisphere, you are allowed to scrummage, and looking at Tuesday night's game you weren't allowed to scrummage at any stage. Also, Australia A stifled our driving maul by coming round the sides and dragging us down. Part of that was very, very dangerous because the guy would actually just roll on the floor of the maul and pull it down, which is highly illegal.'

It didn't end there. The Lions resolved to have exhaustive interviews with referees before each match, to establish beyond doubt what the requirements were in every aspect of the game. The tourists wanted an equal perception, so that refereeing wouldn't be a deciding factor in the test series. They resolved to fight the phoney war so the test series was played on level terms, rather than how Australia wanted it to be played.

Whatever the Lions hoped to achieve with their counter-propaganda counted for absolutely nothing in the next game against the New South Wales Waratahs, a game which ranks as one of the ugliest, bloodiest, most unfortunate international rugby contests ever staged. The Lions won convincingly 41–24 but the occasion is remembered more for the on-field warfare.

Graham is convinced the Waratahs, prepared by former Wallabies coach Bob Dwyer, set out to injure as many touring players as possible. In the opening seconds of the game Tom Bowman flattened his opposite lock Danny Grewcock with an elbow to the head and was yellow-carded, spending the next 10 minutes in the sin bin. In the second half, Duncan McRae, the Waratahs fullback, landed 11 unanswered punches on fly-half Ronan O'Gara, who was lying prostrate on the ground at the time. That incurred a red card and a seven-week suspension. Before the finish, referee Scott Young despatched two forwards from each side to the sin bin so that for 10 minutes the game was contested between one team of 12 players and one of 13.

Graham, who says he has never coached any of his teams to use violence to achieve their ends on the playing field, was angry that Dwyer attempted to rationalize the Waratahs' actions afterwards, and took a crack at him in the press conference. 'At some point you've got to have the will simply to accept the facts as they are,' he said.

Graham said he believed the attitude of the New South Wales players in the second half and the behaviour of coach Dwyer afterwards revealed a great deal about the character of Australian sportsmen under pressure. They were, he believed, fulfilling a role that, by whatever means possible, would deny the Lions the chance to develop confidence and momentum.

Graham quickly learnt that this was the brutal reality, part of the total package at the very top level of international sport; that you form your own set of values you coach by, and that obviously not all coaches will be the same. Suck it up and move on!

Graham could have become despondent as he viewed his bruised and bloodied warriors in the dressing room afterwards but he sensed his team was coming together, its determination hardening a week out from the first test.

'What doesn't kill you makes you stronger,' he quipped to Blackie.

The *News of the World* correspondent wrote, under a heading 'Bloody Disgrace':

> The bomb that has been ticking under the Lions tour of Australia finally exploded with full ferocity as the name of rugby was dragged through the gutter at the Sydney Football Stadium. Australian test referee Scott Young sent five players to the sin bin and dismissed another for a frenzied attack on Ronan O'Gara. Tom Bowman charged into Danny Grewcock from the kick-off, catching him in midair. He was first off to the sin bin. Neil Back had his head stamped on and Duncan McRae landed 11 punches on O'Gara and was given a red card.

One terribly costly injury the Waratahs weren't responsible for involved Lawrence Dallaglio, who Graham anticipated would have a major influence on the outcome of the test series. It wasn't to be. Even after demonstrating superb patience and professionalism throughout the rehabilitation of his knee and after being held back by the medical team until they were convinced he was ready for combat, he reinjured the same joint against the Waratahs. He could run in a straight line but the injury impacted painfully on his mobility and flexibility. His tour was over.

Also injured against New South Wales was centre Will Greenwood, while earlier in the week both Mike Catt and Dan Luger had dropped out of the tour. Hooker Rob McBryde was about to be invalided out of the tour as well. The injury list was expanding at an alarming rate. Apart from being disruptive, the swarm of injuries was affecting the bonhomie and confidence of the touring team because many of the casualties were first-choice test players.

The shocks didn't end there. On the Monday following the Waratahs game, while the team was quartered at Coffs Harbour, the New Zealand-born liaison officer Anton Toia died of a suspected heart attack in the presence of several players at the local beach after attempting to swim ashore from a boat. Graham had known Toia for more than a decade, for he had been the liaison officer when the Auckland Blues teams visited Queensland. He was a top man, always considerate and positive, and had become a close companion, respected by both players and management.

His death produced an eerie echo of the original Lions tour of Australia back in 1888. Early in that tour, the Lions' popular captain Bob Seddon drowned while sculling down the Hunter River.

With a game against New South Wales Country Districts to be played on the Tuesday prior to the first test in Brisbane, Graham chose to pit his test squad against the Tuesday squad at the Monday training session.

It seemed an entirely logical way, to Graham's Kiwi mind, to go about things. That is, until David Young approached him after training.

'Can I have a word, Graham?'

'Certainly,' replied the coach, wondering what the Welsh captain had on his mind.

'A lot of the boys are upset that they're been written off and relegated to the status of also-rans without being given a chance to stake a claim for a test place.'

Graham was shocked. He'd indicated earlier in the tour that the team that played against the Waratahs would be a shadow test XV and that the NSW Country Districts game at Coffs Harbour wouldn't present much of an opportunity for players to press for test selection.

'Well, I'm sorry if I've upset players doing it this way but it seemed the most logical way of doing things.'

'I'll tell the boys,' said Young, 'but a lot of them feel they've been cut adrift.'

In hindsight, Graham realized he had misread the situation and should have been more sensitive because individual agendas counted for more in British and Irish culture than they perhaps did in New Zealand. Graham acknowledged that he could have communicated the selections more tactfully.

Tensions eased as the first international drew near, with the mid-weekers branding themselves Dai's Driftwood (after their captain Dai Young) and adopting the song by Travis as their theme tune: 'We're driftwood, floating on the water!'

Given the Waratahs bloodbath, the death of Anton Toia, the growing injury toll, the negative reaction of those not selected in the test XV and the imminent clash with the world champion Wallabies, it had been a particularly challenging week for Graham. But his humour stayed with him. At the Friday press conference a journalist asked about the 'Grumpy Lions' tag the media had applied to the tourists.

'I think it's a load of rubbish,' said Graham. 'How's that for grumpiness?'

Two of the backs selected by Graham for the first test, English winger Jason Robinson and Irish centre Rob Henderson, had remarkable stories to tell.

Robinson, a freakish talent thrust into the limelight with league club Leeds at 17, had by the mid 1990s become an incorrigible party-goer with a taste for alcohol and gambling, someone only too willing to yield to temptation. Fortunately, by the mid 1990s the Wigan team also featured former All Black Inga Tuigamala, a committed Christian, who was concerned at the way Robinson was wasting his life. He approached him one day and told him that, in a dream, he had seen him standing on top of the world, which suddenly crumbled beneath his feet. It was the warning Robinson needed to hear, because at the time two women were expecting his children! Tuigamala's concerns had a profound effect on Robinson, who pledged to change his life. He became a born-again Christian, gave up drinking, married the girl he wanted and committed himself to a family which now includes four children. After a distinguished league career, he finally made the switch to rugby, joining Sale, in 2000.

Henderson resurrected his playing career after being left out

Zinzan Brooke, Grant Fox and Shane Howarth in a lap of honour after Auckland's win in the 1993 NPC final against Otago at Eden Park. *PHOTOSPORT*

Graham, as coach, and Zinzan Brooke, as captain, would lose the Ranfurly Shield in 1993 but win it back in sensational fashion two years later. *PHOTOSPORT*

Wales's new coach prepares for the 1999 Five Nations Championship. By the end of that campaign he would be hailed as the Redeemer. *TRANZ / ACTION IMAGES*

Graham oversees a British Lions training run in Brisbane in 2001 alongside his conditioner (and motivator) Steve 'Blackie' Black. *TRANZ / ACTION IMAGES*

The 2001 British Lions demonstrate togetherness at training at Manly, Sydney, before the New South Wales game. *Tranz / Action Images*

Winger Dafydd James across for one of the Lions' four tries in the 29–13 defeat of Australia in the first test at Brisbane in 2001. *PHOTOSPORT*

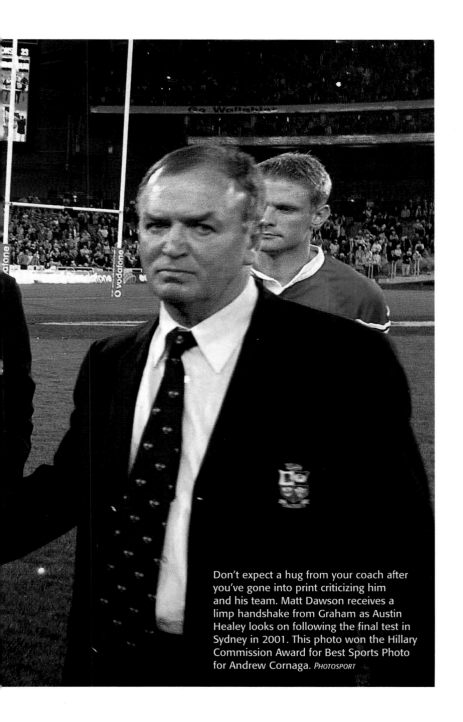

Don't expect a hug from your coach after you've gone into print criticizing him and his team. Matt Dawson receives a limp handshake from Graham as Austin Healey looks on following the final test in Sydney in 2001. This photo won the Hillary Commission Award for Best Sports Photo for Andrew Cornaga. *PHOTOSPORT*

Graham, surprised and delighted at being reappointed All Black coach in 2007, fronts the media as NZRU chairman Jock Hobbs looks on. *Photosport*

Two trophies nicely in the bag in 2007 — the Bledisloe Cup and the Tri-Nations Cup — giving joy to Steve Hansen, Brian Lochore, Graham and Wayne Smith. The trophy they most wanted that year, the Webb Ellis Cup, would sadly elude them. *RugbyImages*

of the Irish World Cup squad in 1999, a happening that jolted him into action. Before that, he'd had a fondness for curries, cigarettes and fizzy drinks. He was a premiership journeyman who played overweight and got by on talent with a minimum of application. One British journalist even recalled an occasion when a packet of cigarettes dropped out of his shorts as he took the field as a replacement in a club game! A rigorous diet and a fitness regime had converted him from a beer barrel shape into a serious athlete.

It was a typically beautiful afternoon in Brisbane for the series opener and when the teams ran onto the field, the vocal support emanating from vast blocks of red-jerseyed fans was overwhelmingly in favour of the Lions.

The Lions coaches had studied Australian fullback Chris Latham's play extensively in the run-up to the test and had identified chinks in his defensive armour they felt they could exploit. They observed a vulnerability to a good kicking game. Doubts could be created by putting up high balls in front of him, and being a natural left-footer, he could be pinned down in the right-hand corner. Recognizing what a potent force Latham could be as a counter-attacker, Graham wanted his team to drastically reduce his options.

The first high ball after seven minutes paid an immediate dividend. Latham, rushing forward, failed to secure the ball, leading to the Wallaby forward who picked it up being ruled offside. Unfortunately, Jonny Wilkinson missed the goal. However, it showed the Lions' homework was paying off.

The Lions were in dynamic form and so taunted Latham that he was replaced at half-time by Matt Burke, by which time the Lions were ahead 12–3. The Lions fans roared and the locals fell silent as the advantage was extended to 29–3, four tries against none, an almost unbelievable score line.

Where would it end? Well, unfortunately, it ended there and then for the Lions, pretty much. Not only did they not score any more points, they yielded the initiative to Rod Macqueen's men. The final 25 minutes would become a watershed for the team's fortunes over the whole series.

In that final phase, the Wallabies scored two tries to none (woeful goal-kicking restricting them to 10 points) while the Lions conceded eight penalties, had Martin Corry and Phil Vickery sin-binned and (subsequently) Colin Charvis cited, kicked quality possession away and generally came apart under pressure. But the tourists held on for a resounding 29–13 victory. One up, two to play!

For Graham, who had been under immense pressure, the result brought sheer relief. He positively beamed when Donal Lenihan described it as 'one of the great Lions performances'. The exhaustive analysis of the Australians, dating back into the previous year, had come to fruition on the pitch. The team had scored sparkling tries, utilizing the thrust of Brian O'Driscoll at centre and the pace and elusiveness of Jason Robinson on the wing.

Former great David Campese, writing in the *Australian*, lauded O'Driscoll's performance. 'It was so refreshing to see a backline player at this level who backs his skill and speed. He ran to gaps and then he went through them. The more I think about it, the more I think this was a stunning result.'

Paul Ackford, writing in the *Sunday Telegraph*, described the result as a 'full-blown slaughter'. 'The Lions have had a hard time of it in Australia with a posse of Australian players and coaches continually popping up to criticize the so-called illegalities at the tackle, scrum and lineout areas and underpin their game. Well, the Lions were in control, scoring four great tries. Brian O'Driscoll was the star as the Wallabies were humbled.'

Several of the British Lions had been offered large amounts of money to write newspaper columns during the tour. Keith Wood, for one, turned down a five-figure sum from one of the dailies, because rugby was his total focus.

But many of the players did commit themselves to tour diaries (Graham understood as many as 24 of the 37 originally selected were putting their names to tour diaries), which is not an issue when the All Blacks tour because, interestingly, the players themselves have voted against it. But it is surprisingly permissible under the British Lions structure. The Lions management wanted all player columns to be put on hold for the duration of the tour but that became impossible to enforce because the contracts the players had in place pre-dated their Lions tour contracts.

One who chose to pen his thoughts, for the *Daily Telegraph*, was England scrum-half Matt Dawson, who'd been a major contributor to the Lions' series win in South Africa four years earlier. On this particular tour he was relegated to a backup role behind Wales's Rob Howley, which may have been a factor in the blistering column he wrote for UK consumption to coincide with the first international. The Lions management became aware of it on the Saturday evening after the test.

Dawson accused the tour management of running a harsh regime rife with internal splits and treating the players like children. He also claimed that coach Henry had failed to inspire trust among the squad and that some players had even threatened to quit the tour.

He talked of 'mindless training', of the players 'not enjoying themselves', and the coaching staff taking things too far. 'We are not being trusted,' he wrote. 'If it all goes wrong, then players will get the blame because coaches have done all they can.'

Dawson claimed that Graham's team talk before the Australia A game didn't inspire him at all: 'too much shouting and screaming. Picked out individuals to wind them up, but all very childish.'

He also accused manager Donal Lenihan of treating the players like kids. 'As if we wanted to lose. They have flogged us for three weeks. Defeat [against Australia A] was waiting to happen.'

He also wrote that in the wake of the Australia A game at Gosford, lost 25–28, some of the players had decided to leave the tour. 'We said if this should happen, we would implement peer pressure but, to be frank, with so many young players, it is hard to avoid.'

Once the Lions' victory celebrations subsided, the management team had to deal with Dawson. This was not an inconsequential matter, for his inflammatory statements had sprouted wings — selective extracts were being reproduced throughout the sporting world. Despatching him from the tour was one option, but in the event the Lions management settled on a significant fine.

Chris Hewett wrote in the *Independent* that Dawson had put together 2000 words of 'condemnatory bile', accusing Graham

Henry and the rest of the Lions hierarchy of presiding over the biggest managerial disaster since Brian Clough embarked on his ill-fated sojourn at Leeds United. Hewett wrote:

> Unfortunately for Dawson, the Lions instantly produced one of the finest performances in post-war rugby history to beat the world champions at the Gabba. The score line: Henry 1, Dawson 0. Yesterday, Dawson was suitably contrite. He sought out Donal Lenihan and apologized for his rank-breaking behaviour in lambasting the coaching team in a newspaper Tour Diary. He then contacted the coaches concerned and apologized all over again. Dawson's agent David Williams conceded he had overstepped the mark. 'Matt feels he has let the tour down. He also feels he should keep quiet for a day or two!' Dawson wrote that the training regime was too ferocious, that Henry's man-management style was unsympathetic and that many players had not been given a fair shot at test selection. He broke the first rule of rugby touring that tales are never told out of school and he contravened the spirit and letter of his contractual agreement with the Lions. Graham Henry gave an assurance that Dawson would not be sent home.

Dawson, besides apologizing personally to the team's managers and coaches, then stood up and repeated his apology to a forum of players. He was obliged to consume a massive portion of humble pie in his next column in the *Daily Telegraph*:

> I have had to contend with the great low of seeing the reaction to the article I had written and cope with the realization of what I had done. I was disappointed in myself for taking the gloss off what had been a fantastic evening for all concerned [and] putting in jeopardy that trust and confidence that had built up within the whole group. That means a lot to me. What makes me really tick is the sense of being part of a group. I like to be liked and I like to give my all for those around me. That has been put under strain and I'm disappointed it came to that.

The game against the ACT Brumbies in Canberra three days after the first test brought an ironic conclusion to the whole affair.

Dawson handled the kicking duties, even after Ronan O'Gara came on as a substitute in the second half. The game strongly resembled the Australia A contest which the Lions lost but on this occasion, thanks to a mix of desperate tries and Dawson's goal-kicking, they managed to stay in touch.

But they were still 23–28 in arrears deep into injury time, so deep that the hooter sounded for full time. 'Oh hell,' said Graham to Phil Larder, 'one mistake and we're gone.'

Henry's Lions weren't intending to make any mistakes though. They just kept recycling the ball and advancing on the Brumbies' goal line. More than a dozen phases had been executed when the tourists worked the ball left where giant prop Darren Morris daringly flipped it behind him ... blind ... and somehow found Austin Healey, who jinked past the last two defenders to score.

It was 28–all as Dawson stepped forward for the conversion close to the touchline and sensationally nailed it! He looked more shocked than elated as he walked slowly away clutching the Lions badge above his heart.

Ian McGeechan, Dawson's coach at Northampton (and on the 1997 Lions tour) later lauded Dawson's focus and concentration after all that had gone on. 'To put over what wasn't an easy kick shows just how much winning, and winning in a Lions jersey, means to those players. When you saw him turn away, his first reaction wasn't to anybody else, it was straight to the badge on his chest.'

And so it was off to Melbourne for the critical second test that would either see the Lions gain an unassailable advantage or the Wallabies level up the series. Graham felt there had been an important psychological shift and on the evidence of performances at the Gabba, he now believed the Lions were the better team. But he also knew that Australian sportsmen are at their most dangerous when their backs are to the wall, a belief he made sure he conveyed to his players.

What was obvious, and understandable, as a consequence of the first test outcome, was that the Australians had closed ranks and decided to make the tourists' chances of winning the series as difficult as possible. Rugby retains a lower profile in Australia than rugby league and Australian Rules and has to fight for survival, meaning a series loss to the Lions would severely impact on the sport. Graham understood this, and even had some respect for the lengths to which the Aussies were going to get their team across the line first.

This manifested itself in several ways. In the lead-up to both the second test (in Melbourne) and the third test (in Sydney), the tourists were given local club grounds to train on with scant privacy, the sessions blatantly being videoed.

Sydney was experiencing an extremely wet winter which resulted in one of the Lions' training sessions being cancelled because the club venue they'd been allocated was under water. But no alternative arrangements were made, so Graham was obliged to put his players through their paces at a local park. Hard to imagine a British Lions team ever being forced to make its own training arrangements in South Africa or New Zealand, but it happened in Australia in 2001.

Graham has no doubts that if Anton Toia had still been with them, an adequate alternative training plan would have been implemented, but it didn't happen in Sydney, another example of the hard-bitten Aussies ruthlessly lengthening the Lions' odds on winning the series.

For the Melbourne test, staged at the (indoor) Rules venue of Colonial Stadium, the Lions were allocated a long, narrow changing room which Graham and his fellow coaches found totally unsatisfactory for the final preparation for an international game, and at half-time.

To diminish the influence of the Lions supporters — who by the time of the Melbourne international had swollen in numbers to more than 20,000 — the ARU demanded that anyone purchasing tickets for the game by telephone or through the Internet had to have a valid Australian address and then, at the not inconsiderable cost of $40,000, supplied gold scarves and hats to their supporters as they entered the ground.

The Ockers resorted to even more devious tactics for the final test in Sydney — they turned out the stadium lights in the sections where the red-clad Lions supporters were grouped!

But as Graham now knows, these are realities that need to be handled. Coaches need to be on task, totally focused and not distracted by events they cannot control. Adjust and stay on track!

However, the Australian administrators' attempts to win at all costs didn't prevent the Lions from controlling the opening 40 minutes of the second test. They took the game to Australia from the kick-off and through a glut of possession, a steady stream of penalties — courtesy of South African referee Jonathan Kaplan — and through consistently breaching Australia's first line of defence, played most of the spell in Australian territory. But a lack of poise and accuracy meant the Lions went to the break only 11–6 ahead, having scored just one try when with better finishing the tourists could have been 15 or 18 points in front. The winning of the series dissipated because the Lions failed to secure those opportunities, which was hugely frustrating for Graham.

To Graham's dismay, the second test and the entire series underwent a complete metamorphosis in the third quarter. Jonny Wilkinson, of all people, started it. Believing there was an attacking opportunity out right on Dafydd James's wing, as the Lions sought to attack from their own half, he threw a long, high pass. But the pair of hands it found were not James's but Joe Roff's, one of rugby's champion interceptors. The defence had no chance of stopping him and suddenly it was 11–all.

Less than five minutes later, Roff was in again, benefiting from a stampeding run off stolen ball by his captain, John Eales. Burke's conversion and penalty goal soon after had Australia 21–11 ahead.

The Lions never recovered against the resurgent Wallabies, eventually going down 14–35 to level the series. The Lions had lost the second half 3–29, the very score, trainspotters noted, the Lions had led the first test by in Brisbane after an hour!

The long, narrow dressing room hadn't helped Graham at half-time address problems he'd identified. He couldn't see everyone's face and he knew he wasn't getting his message across to some of the players, but he carried on regardless. It contrasted vastly with Brisbane where Graham had spoken with clarity and direction during the break after which the Lions had gone out and inside 10 minutes put the game beyond Australia's reach.

Adding injury to insult at Melbourne, the Lions lost their outstanding loose forward Richard Hill to concussion, after Nathan Grey blatantly elbowed him in the face, and their halfback Rob Howley to a cracked rib. They also had Wilkinson carried off on a stretcher. At the time it was presumed his leg was fractured but it turned out to be only deep bruising and he recovered in time to participate in the test series decider.

The casualties in Melbourne brought the total number of serious injuries on tour to an unbelievable 12, eight involving players who were test candidates. Lions team doctor James Robson estimated that he had been interrupted by injury emergencies on no fewer than 22 of the 29 nights he'd spent in Australia up until the end of June.

Such was the extent of the casualty list that Graham found he had only 12 fit players for the Tuesday training session before the final test. That improved as the week rolled on, with several of the test squad being held together by sticking tape and plaster, but on the Thursday Austin Healey, chosen to play on the right wing and operate as backup halfback to Matt Dawson, developed back spasms. When these didn't clear and with no other fit halfback in the squad, Graham recruited Andy Nicol, the former Scottish captain who was in Australia on a supporters tour. On the eve of the game, Nicol was unwrapping his tour gear and trying to memorize moves written on bits of paper!

Healey's injury ruled him out of the deciding international, which should have made him a non-event, but, shockingly, he would command more headlines worldwide that weekend than any other member of the touring party.

Graham, having worked painstakingly to bond 15 reasonably fit players together for the decider, entered the lobby of the team's Manly hotel on the Saturday morning where he was confronted by a couple of British journalists. 'Have you read Austin Healey's comments in the *Guardian*?' one of them asked.

'No,' said Graham. 'I have no knowledge of what he has written.'

'Well, he's provided the Wallabies with ample ammunition for today's game.'

Graham's heart sank. First Matt Dawson, now Austin Healey. What the hell was going on? Were these guys on our side or not?

He was handed the offending article, which had appeared in Friday's *Guardian*, timed to cause most damage when it was reproduced back in Australia.

Healey's article, in part, read:

They call me one of the troublemakers. Matt Dawson and me, the lip machines. Matt says this, I say that; what's going on? Anything we say comes back to this back-end of the world with a whole lot of spin. Well, spin this, you Aussies: up yours. Is that enough to get into the *Sydney Morning Sun Telegraph* load of shite? I went out among the big waves and got thrown all over the shop. Thank you very much, I said, and went straight back to dry land. I'll take on the ape [Justin] Harrison but not Mother Nature. Did I say the weather has been crap? Just another thing to get up your nose, what is it with this country? The females and children are fine and seem to be perfectly normal human beings, but what are we going to do with this thing called the Aussie male? Look, it got so bad I found myself agreeing with Graham Henry the other day. He said he didn't mind them being the best in the world at this or that, but why did they have to rub our faces in it the whole time? It doesn't half make you want to beat them.

Elsewhere in the diary, Healey referred to Harrison, who was in the Wallaby starting XV at Sydney for the first time in the series, as a 'plank' and a 'plod'.

Graham was shocked: Healey's other columns had been published on Saturdays, but this one appeared on the Friday, meaning it could be read in Australia before the game started. For such provocative comments to be quoted back in such circumstances smacked of sabotage. It came as no great surprise to Graham to learn subsequently that Healey's column was ghosted by former Welsh international and journalist Eddie Butler.

'Will that guy never learn?' Graham said to the journalists present, as he reeled from what he'd just read. 'I am amazed a Lion would give the opposition such perfect ammunition for a team talk. If the comments had gone through the agreed media scrutiny, as they should have, they would never have been approved.'

Healey himself was dismayed. At a disciplinary meeting held in Dublin following the team's return he claimed unequivocally that he did not write the article and nor did he agree with what it said. If it had been referred to him, Healey said, he would certainly have found it unacceptable and would have required it to be changed.

While Graham felt Healey had to accept responsibility for what appeared, because the column bore his name, he had sympathy for Healey, who was genuinely distressed by what was published. Graham's greater anger was directed at Butler, who was guilty of a most serious breach of trust. What was written represented Butler's ramblings, not Healey's at all.

As Martin Johnson said to Graham, what possible motivation could Austin have had to make such comments when he was struggling to get himself fit for the most important match of the tour and probably of his entire career?

Butler's article was timed to cause the maximum possible damage to the Lions. As with the Dawson column, he was guilty of not passing it through the usual vetting channel, the Lions media liaison person, Alex Broun, and while all Healey's previous columns had appeared on a Saturday, this one had came out on a Friday.

Branding Justin Harrison an 'ape' was precisely the sort of ammunition Graham didn't want presented to the Wallabies. The series rested on a knife-edge and it wasn't going to take much to tip the series one way or the other.

The Australian Rugby Union was already doing its bit to secure the vital edge for Rod Macqueen's men. Another $40,000 had been outlayed to ensure every Australian fan in the stadium wore a gold scarf and hat, while empty areas of Stadium Australia, which was under construction, were draped in gold banners with an overhanging legend GO WALLABIES.

And the media were right in behind the Wallabies. Nick Bishop wrote in his tour book that the Australian media had closed ranks behind the Wallabies.

The kindest comment you can make is that their patriotism tests their objectivity as newspeople to the limit! But it's amazing to witness how sporting success is used as a rallying call to the nation. The odds are stacked against the Lions and their supporters. They are facing a country united behind its sporting icons, and they have seen first-hand the killer that lurks behind the sunny disposition of the Aussie sportsman. They are in their very own Rorke's Drift, a last outpost. But they have been here before and they know how to fight for their lives.

In the calm before the storm out in the middle of Stadium Australia, the rival coaches found themselves adjacent to each other. They shook hands and wished each other well. But Macqueen felt he couldn't miss the opportunity.

'I just want to personally thank Austin Healey for his words,' he quipped.

Graham didn't respond.

Macqueen, a decade on, insists that Healey's comments did not feature in the Wallabies' preparations. 'They may have given Justin Harrison a boost, but we were more focused on our own game plan. People possibly thought we had Austin's comments plastered on our dressing room wall, but, no, that wasn't the case.'

The contest itself, refereed by New Zealand's Paddy O'Brien, was a battle royal, the tightest and most desperate of the three internationals. What had gone before mattered little as the two teams, with the Lions calling on their last reserves of energy, gave it everything.

The Lions led 10–9 after the first quarter, the Wallabies were ahead 16–13 at half-time, the Lions went ahead 20–16 early in the second half only for it to level out at 23–all with one desperate final quarter to be played. What drama! What a series!

You could have made a fortune betting on Jonny Wilkinson as a goal-kicker at Twickenham over the past several years. He almost never missed, especially when England's games hung in the balance.

Now he had the chance to put the Lions ahead at the most critical stage of the series. But twice he was astray with makeable penalty goals — some claimed he struggled with the Indian-born Summit ball used in the series — while at the other end Burke goaled two opportunities from almost identical situations.

And so, with time running out, the Wallabies led 29–23, only for the Lions to surge on to attack and set up a lineout seven metres from the Australian goal line. It presented a golden opportunity for the Lions to execute a driving maul, which had been one of their aces throughout the series, and claim a series victory.

The throw would go to skipper Johnson, on whom you could risk your house in such circumstances, and the Wallabies would be stretched to the maximum in trying to keep their line intact.

The Wallaby forwards wanted to take the safe option and drive into the opposition the instant the Lions claimed the lineout throw but Harrison — the man Healey, in his column, had branded an 'ape' and a 'plank' — wanted to contest the ball.

Harrison explained later that he gambled because he was certain the ball would be thrown to Johnson. 'I took a punt and it came off. The other guys were into me to defend it, but I wanted to have a crack at it. In the finish, they backed me. Those sorts of things are not supposed to happen. Maybe the moons were aligned for me.'

Harrison's fingertips got in the way of Johnson's safe take, enough to disrupt the Lions' golden plan. At that instant, although there were still a couple of minutes remaining, the series was lost. Australia 2, British Lions 1 — game, set and match to Rod Macqueen and his plucky Wallabies, who'd rebounded resolutely after being comprehensively outplayed in the first three halves of the series.

Regardless of how the players or he as coach would be assessed — and history is invariably cruel to touring sides that lose test series, no matter how narrow the margin or the circumstances — Graham was full of admiration and pride for his players. Given the number of walking wounded — Graham had barely managed to round up 15 players to start the final game — their effort in taking the Wallabies to the wire represented a monumental achievement. They were perhaps one clean lineout take from an amazing series victory.

The Lions had scored the same number of tries in the series as the Wallabies, seven, but where the Lions had succeeded with only seven penalty goals, the Wallabies had landed 12. Ironically, the previous Lions team to South Africa in 1997 had scored only three tries against the Springboks' nine but the 13 penalty goals kicked by Neil Jenkins (compared with five by South Africa) had allowed the tourists to claim a series victory.

Graham didn't return to the UK with the team; instead, he and Raewyn headed north to Burleigh Heads on the Gold Coast, where his parents were holidaying, for some much-needed rest.

As a coach, Graham hated losing. With a career success rate of around 85 per cent, losing was not something he had to endure too often. Given the massive significance of a series involving the British Lions, this loss left him gutted.

The previous year, when he had asked the Welsh Rugby Union committee to release him for the tour, some delegates said they considered he was taking on too great a workload. At the time, he interpreted their observations negatively. Right now, he acknowledged they had been right.

Lions tours in this modern, professional era are unique; indeed, they are the only rugby tours still in existence. They bring together the finest players from four very different nations and the coach's challenge is to mould them together into a winning combination.

They are completely different from All Black and Springbok squads because every player chosen for a Lions tour, with rare exceptions, is a front-line test player. They regard selection for the British Isles as the pinnacle of their careers and, once involved, each player is grimly determined to win test selection.

But whereas the New Zealand, South African and Australian squads number 28 players, meaning only half a dozen players are on the outer when the test squad is named, a 37-strong Lions touring squad presented major challenges for the coach. While every individual, as an established international, considers himself to be in the reckoning for the test XV, the fact is that with every test announcement, 15 players are left disappointed. That's a lot of disappointed players on the sideline.

Many of the younger players, who were touring as established internationals and naturally fancied their chances of winning test selection, were aggrieved at missing out. The single-minded attitude of the coach towards winning the series failed to impress them. It was something Graham had emphasized back in the UK before the team departed for Australia, that winning the test series was significantly more important than the aspirations of any individual, but in the heat of battle on tour, most of the players forgot that.

The situation was exacerbated because in the final three weeks of the tour, the Lions played three internationals and only one other fixture (a Tuesday outing against the Brumbies in Canberra). It meant about 40 per cent of the touring party were largely surplus to requirements throughout that time. That would be challenging enough for one nation to deal with; for four, it caused a huge degree of frustration.

Ever since he'd stepped up to the élite level as a coach, Graham had prepared for crunch provincial matches by pitting his reserve players against the selected 15. The reserves' job was to simulate the tactics the opposition were expected to adopt in the upcoming game.

The Auckland and Blues teams and, to a lesser degree, the Welsh players who'd come under Graham's guidance were familiar with these tactics and prepared accordingly. But the Henry Method offended many of the Lions who'd missed test team selection. They felt Graham was demeaning them by using them as cannon fodder in training.

Graham, with only two and a half years of international coaching behind him, was unfamiliar with probably 70 per cent of the Lions players before they assembled. He concedes that he probably could have expressed himself better to those players who missed test selection and spent more time with them as individuals. At the time, though, he considered his greater priority was to win the test series.

Graham will tell you that in 2012, as a coach with a decade of international experience, he would now handle the Lions situation quite differently. Back in 2001, though, he was still finding his way as an international coach and there were many times when he was struggling to get his head in the right space.

If the Lions had won the series, probably there would have been no recriminations. But that hadn't happened. And as a consequence, Graham's immediate future as a rugby coach was about to seriously unwind.

He had, he realized, over-emphasized results at the expense of the process, and had placed excessive pressure on the players at training. Given their demanding schedules back in the UK, he should have eased them more gently into the tour. Had he done so, the group harmony would have been better and the results might have been different.

Graham knew he wouldn't be Mr Popularity back in Wales because desperately few of the 10 Welsh players who had toured had featured in the internationals. While this was circumstantial, he knew it would be interpreted differently back in the Valleys. Only winger Dafydd James, halfback Rob Howley (until he was injured) and No. 8 Scott Quinnell claimed regular positions in the test starting XV, while Colin Charvis was involved exclusively as a reserve.

Graham much admired his Welsh skipper David (Dai) Young as a prop but the selectors opted for Phil Vickery and Tom Smith in the front row, not because they were better scrummagers but because they offered more around the park; and Mark Taylor, a highly promising centre, was never going to displace the team's outstanding midfielder Brian O'Driscoll, who rivalled captain Martin Johnson as the player of the tour.

Others consigned to the status of midweekers were fly-half Neil Jenkins, a hero of the 1997 campaign but who had major injury concerns, hooker Robin McBryde, prop Darren Morris and flanker Martyn Williams.

Paul Rees captured the mood back home when he wrote in the *Guardian* that when Graham returned to Wales he would face more jeers than cheers. 'Leading the charge will be some of the Welsh Lions who have admitted privately rather than publicly they are angry not just at the way they were treated as training fodder on the trip but because their national coach failed to tell them they were not in the frame for the tests. "Graham has some fences to mend," said one.'

Graham would have loved to have spent several more weeks relaxing on the Gold Coast, but it was time to don his cap as Welsh rugby coach again. A new season beckoned, one with an unusual twist. Because the Irish international had been postponed the previous season following an outbreak of foot and mouth disease, it had been slotted in at the beginning of the new season.

6

Gloomy times

Graham was in a reflective mood as he flew back to the UK in August 2001, the Lions assignment completed. His competitive nature meant he was grossly wounded through having dropped the series to the Wallabies. He wasn't accustomed to coming second, and it hurt.

The series was now behind him, and his employers, who had generously released him for the Lions tour, would be wanting him to refocus on matters Welsh. There were autumn internationals looming plus the make-up Six Nations fixture against Ireland.

It was three years since Graham had so ambitiously relocated from New Zealand to Wales. In that time, he'd converted the Welsh national team from an embarrassing easy-beat into a side that was now competitive with the best teams in the world, and he'd had a major influence in restructuring the sport in Wales.

Back in 1998 when he'd first arrived, the Welsh squad had no indoor training venue at which they could practise defence, scrums and lineouts, the contest at the breakdown, or tackling. Training outdoors was counterproductive because it was so cold — often down to −10°C — making it impossible for coaches and players to seriously focus. Also, Graham had had quite enough of chatting to the media after training and being so cold he could scarcely enunciate his words!

Graham located an equestrian centre at Bridgend. Although it was spacious, the horse droppings were an additional challenge and Graham remembers one player finishing up in hospital with a poisoned leg.

But it enhanced the Welsh players' attention. The temperature was a manageable zero degrees and the team performance lifted accordingly.

The Copthorne Hotel outside Cardiff was the team's base, but it wasn't conducive to preparing an international rugby team. It had developed into one of the social hubs of the city, with every man and his dog there to be close to the Welsh players. There was huge demand for photographs and autographs and a quick personal chat about the next game, which was very distracting for the coach.

So David Pickering, the team manager, and Graham journeyed around Wales in search of the ideal venue. At the Vale of Glamorgan Hotel, they fell into conversation with the owner, Gerald Leek, who was one of Wales's most successful businessmen.

'So what exactly are you guys looking for?' asked Leek.

'We need a barn, Gerald.'

'How big?'

'About half the size of a rugby field.'

'What for, precisely?'

'So a rugby team can train indoors, regardless of the weather.'

'And what else?'

'Just the barn, Gerald — we are desperate.'

'What would you want on the floor?'

'Mud.'

'Mud? What about the dust?'

'Spray a bit of water on it before we train.'

'You can't do that.'

'Why not, we've been training at an equestrian centre on sawdust and horse shit.'

'OK.'

'Seriously, we would need to think carefully about what goes on the floor of the training area. And it would be helpful if the building also incorporated toilets, changing facilities and offices.'

'Sounds like you want a bloody palace,' said Leek, 'but leave it with me.'

Messrs Henry and Pickering had planted a seed that would lead to the creation of the WRU indoor stadium, 30 kilometres west of

Cardiff towards Bridgend. It is now an outstanding facility, featuring two football-sized pitches with surfaces of rubberized astro-turf as well as two grass pitches with the exact dimensions of the Millennium Stadium's. In addition to a number of general offices and a platform from which individuals can look out over the practice facilities, there are weightlifting rooms, team rooms, a physio and masseur centre, an analysis room, and more. It is unquestionably the No. 1 training centre for any national sports team in the world.

Since the establishment of the indoor stadium, Gerald Leek and his Vale of Glamorgan Hotel team have also created separate ultra-modern facilities for both the Cardiff rugby team and the Cardiff City football team. They train alongside each other.

Back to the story. Graham felt uneasy as he returned to his home at Castleton. He couldn't put his finger on it, but he sensed that his time in Wales could be running out.

Graham and Raewyn had rolled up their sleeves and got stuck in from the moment they'd arrived in Wales. They'd given everything a go. Lord knows how many rugby clubs there are in Wales, literally hundreds, and Graham had visited a large percentage of them, from the mightiest to the most humble. And Raewyn, after starting out coaching the Cardiff netball team, was now in charge of the Welsh national side, preparing it for upcoming international fixtures and ultimately the world championships in Jamaica.

While Graham admired the Welsh people's absolute devotion to the game of rugby, as the national coach he found it suffocating because they made him a national celebrity. He didn't dare go to the local supermarket because everyone from schoolchildren to grandmothers wanted to talk to him and everyone wanted a photo and an autograph. Long queues would form! If he went out for dinner at a restaurant, he was obliged to sit between two friends, or someone would immediately plant themselves down beside him and engage him in a rugby conversation. He felt he was owned by every Welshman. That was a major reason why he'd chosen to live at Castleton, midway between Cardiff and Newport, rather than close to or in any of the cities.

Back in New Zealand, notwithstanding his success as a rugby coach at NPC and Super 12 level, Graham had maintained a comparatively low profile. A visit to the supermarket never produced more than an occasional 'Hi, Graham'. It was all so different in Wales where the nation's mood seemed to rise and fall on the performance of the Welsh rugby team. They were either on Cloud 9 and totally carried away — or in total depression. There was no middle ground, and this impacted on Graham as the national coach.

Wales warmed up for the 2001/02 season with an 80-point romp against Romania but then had to tackle Ireland in the Six Nations fixture that had been postponed seven months because of the outbreak of foot and mouth disease.

Whether it was perceived or real, as a consequence of events on the Lions tour, when a number of the Welsh boys missed out on the test team, Graham felt he no longer had the total support of his players as he prepared them for the clash at the Millennium Stadium, where a win would elevate Wales to runner-up in the championship. For the only time in his coaching career, he felt he had lost the dressing room. And when that happens, Graham knew, it was time to move on. When you're coaching top sporting teams, your body language needs to be 100 per cent and you expect every player to be right on the money. But when you're struggling with self-esteem because of your own situation, and you can't get your message over, you know you're in trouble.

In the event, Graham's team was smashed by Ireland by 35 points to 6. In Dublin the previous season, Wales had won 23–19.

Further disappointments were to follow that autumn. Although the Welsh disposed of Tonga comfortably enough, cracking the half-century, they crashed to defeat at their fortress of Millennium Stadium to both Argentina and Australia.

If Welsh rugby was off the boil as Christmas approached, Graham was in a state of near depression. The Lions tour was the root cause of his troubled state of mind. He realized now that with so little experience at international level, even of touring, he should never have taken on a job of that magnitude. Hindsight is a great thing.

With the experience he has gained coaching the All Blacks on countless overseas missions and at Rugby World Cups since, Graham believes he is now adequately equipped to handle a challenge as monumental as the Lions tour of 2001 had been. But he wasn't then. The tour had knocked him about mentally. It had taken a serious toll.

He had 18 months remaining on his Welsh contract. How would his bosses react if he tendered his resignation? He had the feeling that unless he got out, he would die! It was about surviving as a person, not a rugby coach.

Of course, if the Lions had won ... well, none of those issues, such as the Welsh players being disgruntled about missing test selection and upstarts like Matt Dawson and Austin Healey or their ghost writers sounding off in their tour diaries, would have mattered. Success engenders an entirely different mental state.

Being the lone Kiwi in the Lions' den hadn't helped. Because he knew few of the management team well personally, it became a very lonely tour for him. While Blackie and Alun Carter, the team analyst, were good mates, their first responsibility was to the players. Graham pined for people like John Graham and Rex Davy, his Auckland buddies, with whom he used to talk through his concerns and worries. Ironically, they'd made the journey to Australia to attend some of the Lions' matches and support their old colleague, but believing they would be interfering and that Graham was too heavily committed, they had left him alone.

John Graham and Rex Davy would have helped ease the pressure, provided much-needed balance, and got him exercising more. He had sacrificed workouts in the interest of the team's needs, several times going more than 24 hours without a break. When you're constantly on edge, it's important to exercise. As the tour of Australia rolled on, Graham worked out less and less.

He had been lonely on the Lions tour. Now he was lonely at home because Raewyn was away in Singapore with a couple of Welsh netball teams at an Asian tournament.

David Pickering became so concerned at Graham's low mental state that he phoned Raewyn in Singapore and suggested it might be a tonic if he joined her and got away from Wales for a while.

'If he's that low then, yes, 10 days in Singapore could help,' said

Raewyn. 'But I've got two teams here to look after; I won't be able to spare him much time.'

Then she had a thought. John Wood, who had been a groomsman at their wedding, lived in Singapore, and they had remained in touch.

'Leave it with me,' she said, whereupon she looked up Wood's number. To her delight, he was home and, even more marvellously, he indicated he would love to host his old mate Graham Henry.

So while Raewyn went diligently about her netball duties, Graham flew in from Cardiff to be met at the airport and hosted by Wood. His old friend even organized a week's holiday for the Henrys at the world-famous holiday retreat of Phuket after the netball commitments were completed.

Blue skies, sweltering temperatures, crystal-clear waters … where better to relieve yourself of life's pressures? If you couldn't unwind there, you weren't going to unwind at all.

But to Raewyn's dismay, Graham didn't unwind in Phuket. Nor did he sleep particularly well. He was wound up like a clock. He'd taken along some rugby planning but couldn't bring himself to concentrate on it. His world just seemed to be going round in never-ending circles.

It was crisis time. By the end of the so-called holiday, during which he had several meaningful discussions with his wife, Graham's mind was made up: he would resign as the coach of Wales. It was a no-brainer. His greatest concern was that he would be abandoning Wales 18 months out from the 2003 World Cup, although he was positive Steve Hansen would prove a more-than-adequate replacement.

Back in Cardiff, he set up a meeting with chairman Glanmor Griffiths and fellow board member and good mate David Pickering and broke the news. Pickering wasn't surprised, but he and Griffiths immediately set about trying to convince Graham that it was a passing phase and that things would work out.

'You've achieved wonderful things here. You'll be starting afresh when the Six Nations kicks off next month,' said Griffiths. 'And you'll have your new forward coach, Steve Hansen, here. Things will come right; you wait and see.'

Having explained to them that, in the good Kiwi vernacular, he was 'buggered', Graham was so encouraged by their loyalty and support he agreed to stay on for the Six Nations Championship, subject to things working out.

Steven Hansen could see that Graham wasn't right. He knew his mate wasn't the same positive individual who'd guided Auckland and the Blues to just about every title going back in New Zealand. 'It was obvious he was struggling,' he would reveal later. 'The Lions tour was probably the first time in his coaching career he had not achieved his goal and it had knocked his confidence. He was really down.'

To a sideline observer, in the weeks leading up to Wales's opening encounter in the 2002 Six Nations Championship, against Ireland at Lansdowne Road, life appeared to be operating normally. But Graham knew it wasn't. Players for whom he had the greatest respect undoubtedly weren't happy.

Behind the scenes, Graham was in turmoil. He explained this to David Pickering and his wife, Justine, over a meal at his kitchen table in the week leading up to the Irish game. 'It's not a case of not wanting to go on,' he said. 'The fact is the fire in the belly has gone. The deep-down desire isn't there any longer. I know I've lost the dressing room. I believe it's time to go. I have nothing more to offer. I'm buggered mentally and physically; the boys deserve a lot more than I can give them.'

It was always going to be a challenge for Graham's team in Dublin. Even if the coach had been right on his game and the players had been supporting him 100 per cent, victory would have been a gigantic challenge. But much worse than that, the occasion became a nightmare for all concerned.

Ireland won 54–10, a record score by the men in green at Wales's expense.

This was one of the few games Raewyn didn't attend because she was in camp with the Welsh netball squad. But she was aware of the hiding Graham's team was taking.

When the final whistle sounded, she said to her mate Lynne Evans, 'I think that result means he'll be going home.'

'But he can't just abandon you here in Wales,' said Evans.

'He's really down. I've never known him to be so low. He just wants to get back to New Zealand.'

Naturally, the reviews of Wales's 50-point battering were not kind. One read:

> Wales was reduced to a shambling mess and their coach Graham Henry will do extraordinarily well to retain his job beyond the end of the month. At a cringing post-match press conference, the magnitude of the loss and the poverty of performance scarcely seemed to have sunk in. It was the second worst defeat in Wales' history. They were awful and seemingly without hope. 'All we can do as coaches is work to the best of our abilities,' said Henry. Eddie O'Sullivan, Ireland's new coach, was delighted with the result.'

Another said:

> The Welsh supporters unable to cross the Irish Sea or land at Dublin Airport because of gales were the lucky ones. For at Lansdowne Road the Welsh team was caught in a hurricane that swept Ireland to a record win. If there is still a monastic retreat in the Emerald Isles, the visiting coach Graham Henry was probably searching for it last night. The storm that awaits the New Zealander in his adopted home will be even more ferocious and it is difficult to see him surviving in his well-paid job.

The moment he arrived back home in Cardiff the following day, Graham set up another meeting with Glanmor Griffiths and David Pickering.

'I hope you will please accept my resignation now. I'm absolutely buggered,' he said. 'I'm sorry we performed so poorly in Dublin.'

Griffiths and Pickering still tried to convince Graham to stay, emphasizing he had the support of the Welsh Rugby Union committee and that things would turn around.

But Graham knew in his heart it was all over. He had hit the wall and he had to leave. He knew the players deserved better.

First, though, he had to ensure that Steve Hansen was prepared to take over the reins. So he called him and asked him to come round. 'There's a major problem,' he said, 'and I'm hoping you can resolve it.'

When Hansen, or Shag as Graham had come to know him, arrived, the desperate nature of the situation was explained to him.

'If that's what you want to do, go for it,' said Hansen, who knew Graham was dropping him, as a coach, in the deep end. Hansen could see Graham was no longer any use to Wales.

Three days after the 54–10 walloping, which was greeted with alarm and despair throughout Wales, Graham's resignation was announced. The official statement read:

After a meeting between Graham and senior officers of the [WRU] union, it has been agreed by both parties that Graham Henry will leave his post this week. Both sides have thought deeply about this decision and believe it has been taken with the best interests of Welsh rugby in mind. Kiwi Steve Hansen has taken charge for the remainder of the Six Nations.

Graham, in an interview with *BBC Sport*, identified burnout as the reason for resigning.

He said the all-consuming demands of the job had left him jaded. Henry, whose record with Wales is 20 wins, one draw and 13 losses, admits he's not the coach he was when he arrived in 1998. 'When I arrived we had a great run of victories and both the Welsh team and myself were carried along on a wave of adrenalin as we won ten games in a row. There's so much passion and commitment in Welsh rugby and Wales as a whole and it really has been a pleasure to be the national coach.' However, the last two results against Ireland produced a 16–90 score line. 'In light of recent results I've had to take a look at myself in the mirror and ask some harsh questions. I still think I'm a good coach but I don't think I am coaching as well as I can. The intensity of the rugby that Wales and the Lions have played since I arrived, as well as the all-consuming nature of the job I came into, I believe has led to a burn-out factor in my coaching. It is no knee-jerk reaction to the result in Ireland, but being brutally honest, I feel the time has come for the team to hear a new voice.'

Graham owes a huge debt of gratitude to Glanmor Griffiths and David Pickering, who gave him a path out of Wales when they could have made things massively difficult for him. There was speculation in the media that Graham had been sacked, but that wasn't the case. He departed with his dignity, if not his mind, intact, thanks to Griffiths, Pickering and Graham's trusty lawyer back in Auckland, David Jones, who together hastily sorted out a redundancy package. (Although, right at that depressing stage of his career, money wasn't important to him; he just wanted to get himself right.)

Following Graham's departure, the Welsh Rugby Union promoted Hansen to the position of interim coach. He would eventually be upgraded to national coach and would go on to coach the team at the Rugby World Cup in Australia in 2003 and through to 2004.

When he announced his resignation, Graham added that he wouldn't be going anywhere in the immediate future because his wife, Raewyn, was coaching the Welsh netball team and his son Andrew was playing for Cardiff.

That was a smart thing to say because it put the media off the scent. Almost before any of them realized, Graham was on a plane bound for New Zealand.

He didn't want to abandon his wife, who was committed to the Welsh netball team through until the World Cup, but he knew if he remained in Cardiff he would suffocate. He was at the lowest ebb in his life and desperately needed to get back to his roots. As he settled into his seat on the Air New Zealand flight out of Heathrow and took a deep breath, he wondered if he would ever coach a rugby team again.

His journey deposited him not in Auckland but in Christchurch, where he linked up with his mother and father, who immediately expressed concerns about his state of health. They had never seen him so down. They were genuinely concerned about his mental state.

After a couple of weeks unwinding in Christchurch, Graham and his parents took a break in Akaroa, the delightful French settlement at Banks Peninsula, southeast of Christchurch. Graham had holidayed at this seaside fishing resort a number of times in his youth. With the media pretty much unaware he was back in the country, he was able to relax. Running every day around the Akaroa hills became a tonic.

The fresh air, the relaxed atmosphere of Akaroa, his mother's cooking, and the complete absence of rugby commitments was the essential panacea for Graham, who gradually began to thaw. Finally he had reached the point where he was able to re-establish himself in Auckland and reacquaint himself with his old mates. He acknowledged the wisdom in the adage that there's no place like home.

Meanwhile, back in Cardiff, Raewyn was also making a serious reassessment of her life. She could chuck everything in and return to Auckland, too, but she was reluctant to abandon the Welsh netballers, who were bringing her enormous pleasure.

They'd beaten Scotland and Ireland to qualify for the World Cup in Jamaica in mid 2003 and she'd pledged her commitment to the team until then. But, hell, that was 17 months away!

There was also the matter of their house. She didn't require a property of that size for herself. Hmmm, it was time to share a couple of wines with her good mate Lynne Evans, after which everything became clearer.

She would sell their property, board at Evans's house, and have month-about in Wales and New Zealand through until the completion of the Netball World Cup in 2003. Amazing what can be achieved with some positive thinking!

The house sold in double-quick time — for almost double what the Henrys had paid for it — and Welsh Netball accepted Raewyn's month-on, month-off schedule. (Well, they could hardly complain since they weren't paying her anything!) And over the next year and a half, Raewyn accumulated a staggering number of air points.

One day Graham fielded a call from Tokyo. The caller was a Mr Yamamoto, who was calling on behalf of the coach of the Waseda University rugby team. It represented something of a blast from the past. Back in the late 1980s, when Graham was headmaster at Kelston Boys' High and John Graham was headmaster of Auckland Grammar, Hiroshi Ito, who had taught at Auckland Grammar and subsequently worked as interpreter for Japanese rugby teams touring New Zealand, had invited Messrs Henry and Graham to Tokyo to assist with coaching of the Waseda University team. There they had met Yamamoto, their liaison person, who was fluent in English and a 'top bloke'.

Located at Shinjuku in Tokyo, Waseda dates from 1882 and is one of the most prestigious universities in Japan, indeed in all of Asia. Graham and John Graham did their bit and were delighted when Waseda subsequently won the Japanese universities title.

'Graham,' said Yamamoto, 'how lovely to talk to you again. Would you be interested in returning to Tokyo to help prepare our Waseda University team for the championship fixtures coming up?'

Graham couldn't believe his luck. What a breath of fresh air. How better to complete his convalescence than to work with totally enthusiastic young Japanese rugby players. No responsibility, no preparing match schedules, no after-match interviews, no claustrophobic fans.

'There's nothing in the world I would rather do right now,' replied Graham. And he meant it.

'Just one thing, Mr Yamamoto — I need to bring a forward coach with me. OK?'

'Of course; you just let me know who that will be.'

Whereupon Graham made a phone call to Wales, to a certain David Young, prop for Wales and the British Lions. This delightfully funny man, besides being a quality rugby player, possesses excellent leadership qualities and, most importantly as far as Graham was concerned, is a natural coach.

Young, concerned at how Graham was faring after his hasty departure from Wales, was delighted to receive the call and didn't require a second invitation to commit himself to the role of forward coach of Waseda University.

While working with David Young in Japan wasn't exactly a case of getting back on the horse, it represented a significant phase in Graham's recovery. It also provided an important opportunity to save some face.

At Waseda, for the first time in many years, Graham wasn't required to prepare match schedules or painstakingly analyse videos of opposition teams. So Graham had time to work out with Young in the gym virtually every day and, when he wasn't involved in coaching sessions, he read a lot.

Waseda University went through to win the championship — after the imported coaches returned home — which was a source of immense satisfaction for both Graham and David Young.

Importantly, the Japanese sojourn got Graham's coaching juices flowing again. Not in a I-want-to-take-charge-of-a-Super 14-team-right-now sense, more simply in a I-believe-I-still-do-have-something-to-offer-as-a-coach way.

First things first, though: Graham had to re-establish himself in Auckland. This was a challenge because his dear wife, Raewyn, had remained in Wales, still heroically coaching the Welsh netball team. Furthermore, many of the belongings he was attached to were still in the house at Newport, which was now on the market.

Graham began catching up with old mates like John Graham, Rex Davy and George Duncan, who were all relieved to find that the fellow whose coaching talents they'd so admired before he took off to the other side of the globe appeared to be pretty much back to his old self.

He startled them, though, when he told them what he had in mind: he was going to ask David White, the CEO of Auckland Rugby, whether the Auckland coaches would like the assistance of a technical adviser for the NPC campaign that was coming up.

Graham's mates were almost unanimous in their reaction. They asked him why the hell he wanted to become involved again with an Auckland union that had treated him so ungraciously when he was departing for Wales. 'You've been there, done that, coached the Colts, the Bs, Auckland and the Blues,' John Graham said to him. 'Why do you need to start again?'

Because, Graham told him, he needed an avenue back into rugby coaching.

And so it came to pass that he knocked on the door of the CEO of the Auckland Rugby Union, David White, offering his services. He and David White went back to Auckland Grammar School days.

When Graham was running the hostel, White was a junior house master, who developed into an excellent sportsman, going on to play cricket for New Zealand and rugby for Grammar Old Boys at senior level. He is currently the CEO of New Zealand Cricket.

White said he would sound out his coaches, Wayne Pivac and Grant Fox, but it would be their call. Their team had been crushed by Canterbury in the semi-finals the previous season and so they might be looking to bolster their coaching structure.

Despite making the initial approach himself, Graham wasn't optimistic; he feared Pivac would perceive him as more of a hindrance than a help. But it wasn't long before Graham received a phone call from White. Yes, he could offer him the position of technical adviser/defence coach for the 2002 NPC campaign at a fee of $20,000.

'Will you take it?'

'Yes, thanks, and I'm grateful to Wayne and Foxy for giving me the opportunity.'

And with that, Graham headed to his fridge for a beer. He was almost back on the horse.

Mind you, $20,000 was a drastic drop in salary from the £250,000 he had been receiving from the Welsh Rugby Union. But he felt good again. The depression had lifted. You couldn't put a price on that. He would have taken on the defence coach/technical adviser's role for nothing. The money wasn't important. He'd been given a lifeline back into rugby coaching, which, he recognized, remained his great passion.

Also, because he didn't now have the responsibilities of the head coach, it meant he could ease himself back into coaching.

Being a defence coach instead of the head coach was an entirely new experience for Graham. He realized it would be entirely inappropriate to usurp the established coaches' power, or to be confrontational. While senior in age, he was junior in rank among Auckland's three coaches.

Subtlety, he reasoned, represented his best method of making an impact. As an early riser, he quickly identified a way of getting messages across without offending the official coaches.

If the early bird gets the worm, the early coach gets to write first on the whiteboard. Graham, a seriously early person — wide awake at 4.30 most mornings — would regularly arrive at Eden Park around 6 a.m., two to three hours ahead of his colleagues. On the whiteboard mostly used for planning purposes, he would itemize lessons from the previous weekend's game, how the team had generally performed, and what needed to be done going forward.

Wayne and Foxy would eventually get around to reading Graham's comments. It was a subtle, non-confrontational way of identifying issues that required attention.

'What do you mean by that?' one of them might ask. 'Why would you pinpoint that?' the other would say.

It was the first time Graham had ever had to use such tactics to try to get his message across, because he had always previously been the coach, the man in charge. Now he was third in line, but he didn't consider that should necessarily stop him having his five bob's worth! Still, he wasn't the coach and the last thing he wanted to do was upset his colleagues. It was an enlightening time. The man who would guide the All Blacks to World Cup glory, ultimately, was required to learn new skills. It was an experience he would treasure and one he considers helped shape him into a better coach, giving him a greater insight into how assistant coaches operate in their roles.

Fox, his old mate, didn't identify any drastic change in the personality or attitude of the man who'd coached him a decade earlier. As far as Foxy could see, Graham was still a charming, dedicated rugby person with an incredible passion for coaching.

But that didn't mean they saw eye to eye on every aspect of how the Auckland backs should prepare for a match in 2002. One particularly tetchy session unfolded as Auckland prepared for an important early-season game.

'Listen, Graham, you might have played it that way back in 1993, but this is 2002, and this is how we're playing it on Saturday,' Fox snapped at him.

'I think you're wrong,' said Henry.

'Well, I'm sorry, mate, but you're overruled on this one.'

Whereupon a ruffled Foxy exited the board room before he said anything else he might later regret.

That was around 4 p.m. Two hours later, they were sharing a beer. It was nothing more than robust discussion, two passionate individuals striving to achieve the same end in different ways. And there were several similar animated discussions early that rugby season before it was obvious they were all on the same page.

But it all worked out for the best. Pivac, Fox and Henry combined to perfection, collectively guiding Auckland to victory in the 2002 NPC. The team bounced back from an opening loss to Taranaki to claim third spot in round-robin play before achieving what many would have considered impossible: upsetting Canterbury in a gripping semi-final in Christchurch, scoring five tries to two. Canterbury, blessed with such outstanding achievers as Ben Blair, Aaron Mauger, Andrew Mehrtens, Justin Marshall, Scott Robertson, Richie McCaw, Chris Jack, Norm Maxwell, Greg Somerville and Mark Hammett, was a raging hot favourite to retain the NPC title — but found Auckland too hot to handle. As did Waikato in the grand final in Hamilton when the Blue and Whites won 40–28.

Ali Williams, one of Auckland's high-profile players, confessed in a light-hearted book he wrote in 2009 that in those early days he was guilty of often mischievous behaviour, including the night of that NPC final win over Waikato.

The players decided it would be appropriate to fill the NPC trophy with beer and pass it around for everyone to have a celebratory drink. Nothing wrong with that, and Williams was delegated to top up the trophy with brown ale, which he did. But he didn't stop there. On a whim, he tossed a handful of Viagra tablets into the brew. And as the trophy passed from player to player, to coach Henry, to player, some commented on the pleasant malty flavour of the brew!

Williams reports that towards midnight an agitated Auckland coach sought him out. 'You're responsible, I believe. How the hell am I going to get rid of this!'

It's a hilarious story, although Graham claims it is a figment of Williams's imagination, and believes he may have planted the seed for its appearance in Ali's book by having related a similar story about how a certain Welsh official was 'got at' in that manner.

Graham's input into Auckland's success led to him being invited by coaches Peter Sloane and Bruce Robertson to become technical adviser to the Blues Super 12 team for the 2003 campaign, an offer he gladly accepted.

It also became a vintage year for the Blues, who lost only one match (to the Highlanders in Dunedin) in taking out the title for the first time since Graham's team had triumphed in 1997. The Brumbies were accounted for 42–21 in the semi-finals before the Crusaders — fielding 11 All Blacks with another three internationals on the reserves bench — were edged out 21–17 in a tense, tight final.

Rugby News branded the Blues' performance a superb team effort. 'It achieved something few other teams have managed in the past six years during which the Crusaders have appeared in five Super 12 finals — they created disorder in the Crusaders ranks.'

In the middle of the year the Welsh netball team headed for Jamaica and the World Cup, hoping to boost their international ranking, which influenced government funding.

Things didn't work out quite the way Raewyn had hoped, though. Their first opponent was St Vincent and Grenadines, one of the Caribbean teams, who edged Wales out in a controversial contest in which one of Raewyn's players, a Jamaican no less, was guilty of pushing an opponent over. She was stood down for the next match, which somehow turned out to be against St Vincent and Grenadines again, with the same result. The final, grading, game was against … you guessed it! … St Vincent and Grenadines — who won again.

Raewyn still doesn't know how it came about that her team engaged the same opponent three times. And the grading game, so critical for Wales, became a farcical affair when she discovered, after her Welsh team had warmed up, that the opposition were still back at their hotel. All to do with a disputed contest earlier. 'Oh, didn't anyone tell you?' an official asked Raewyn. 'Sorry, you'll have to warm up again later.' Great!

But Raewyn had more to worry about than just the failure to defeat St Vincent and Grenadines: her own health was suddenly a concern. Something was amiss internally — she wasn't sure what, but it was causing a degree of pain.

Wales didn't have its own medical person but the New Zealand team did and, after giving Raewyn a thorough check-over, the Kiwi doctor immediately ordered her into hospital, where she remained for a week. This was an experience because, being the only white patient in the hospital, she was the source of much fascination — groups of children used to line up to look at her!

The entire Welsh netball squad visited their coach before flying back to Cardiff, but even after their departure, Raewyn wasn't abandoned. Lynne Evans stayed on, as did Mary McCahill, sister of former All Black Bernie, and Suzie Fewtrell, a couple of Kiwi girls who just happened to be in Jamaica at the time of the netball championships. All three remained to comfort Raewyn, refusing to leave till she was released from her hospital bed.

When that happened, Raewyn was finally free to fly back to New Zealand and re-establish herself with Graham. The circuitous route, via Miami and Los Angeles, was exhausting but finally brought a conclusion to her Great Welsh Experience.

Naturally, after the joys of 2002, Wayne Pivac and Grant Fox invited Graham back into their camp for the 2003 NPC campaign, and he was delighted to accept. And why not? He was doing what he most loved: coaching rugby. And he was hoping for an opening that would allow him to re-establish himself as a coach at a higher level, perhaps even back at international level.

The Aucklanders took out the championship again in 2003, qualifying for the play-offs in dramatic fashion. After some mixed performances, they were lying fifth going into the final game, which just happened to be against Canterbury in Christchurch, with the Ranfurly Shield also at stake! What could be more challenging than playing Canterbury on its own turf, although in Auckland's favour was the fact the World Cup had kicked off and the Red and Blacks were without all their international stars. The Aucklanders swept the Cantabs aside 40–31, unsettling them with the quality of their counter-attacking, in which Brent Ward and Orene Ai'i were outstanding, claimed the shield and bounded into the play-offs.

As in 2002, Auckland missed out on the home play-offs, but it mattered not, although their progress to the final wasn't without drama. On the eve of the semi-final against Otago at Carisbrook, Ben Atiga received a 'We need you now' call from the World Cup All Blacks in Sydney, necessitating a backline reshuffle.

Iliesa Tanivula took Atiga's place at centre from where he emerged a hero. With time almost up and the scores locked at 32–all, Messrs Pivac, Fox and Henry advanced to the sideline ready to brief their team on the tactics required for the extra-time session.

In the final play of the game, first-five Tasesa Lavea shaped to take a drop-kick, provoking a fifth of the Otago defenders to charge frantically towards him. But instead of drop-kicking, he propped, eluded the first wave of Otago players, bolted into a gap and put Tanivula across for a sensational try beside the posts, giving Auckland the game 39–32!

In the final, played in the capital, Auckland dissected Wellington 41–29, in a match that marked Christian Cullen's final appearance in New Zealand before he headed off to Ireland to join Munster.

Graham would treasure his three campaigns as a deputy with Auckland and the Blues because when he graduated to All Black coach he understood his assistants' situations. He'd been there, done that. He'd learnt new skills, like how to get his message across without upsetting people. He was a much-better-prepared head coach, he considered, for the experience of being the third in line.

Coinciding with Auckland's impressive surge towards NPC glory, the All Blacks were swatting opponents aside with effortless ease at the World Cup in Australia. John Mitchell's team had disposed of Italy, Canada and Tonga with an average winning score of 76 points. Next up, they would tangle with dear old Wales, now in the hands of Steve Hansen, who'd certainly had his moments since being pitched in at the deep end courtesy of Graham.

Hansen's Welsh team had rather ignominiously finished up with the wooden spoon after losing every match in the Six Nations Championship in 2003. His team's losing sequence actually extended to 11 but the Welsh union remained loyal to him and his best as a coach was to be seen at the World Cup.

Graham wasn't at Telstra Stadium in Sydney for the Welsh game because he had accepted an invitation for himself and Raewyn to lead a supporters group to the play-offs, in addition to which he was providing comment for Welsh Television. The Henrys' itinerary had them in Brisbane that weekend. Observing the action from afar, he was enthralled with what unfolded.

The Red Dragons gave the All Blacks one hell of a fright. They led 34–28 approaching the three-quarter mark, setting themselves up for a massive upset, before the All Blacks finally engaged top gear and pulled away to win 53–37.

In the quarter-finals the following weekend, the All Blacks rebounded from the Wales onslaught to crush the Springboks 29–9, leading their fans to believe they were on target to finally secure that elusive Webb Ellis Cup. Australia, England and France also played themselves through to the semi-finals.

Back in New Zealand, the nation was hugely upbeat leading into the semi-final clash with the Wallabies, especially as the All Blacks had whipped them 50–21 in a Tri-Nations game in Sydney four months earlier.

But previous results count for nothing in sudden-death World Cup fixtures, as astute coaches are all too aware. And New Zealand's World Cup dream came crashing down, yet again, at Telstra Stadium. A shock early intercept try to Stirling Mortlock gave the Wallabies an advantage they never relinquished. The All Blacks scored only one try, going down 10–22 in a meek performance.

It relegated them to that scenario rugby players consider the equivalent of kissing your sister: having to play off for third. Whether you win or lose that contest, no-one really cares. The dreadful fact is: YOU'RE NOT IN THE FINAL!

In the months ahead, when Graham had the opportunity to quiz the players on why the All Blacks unravelled in the semi-final, one valid reason promoted was that being based in Melbourne — where they had played two pool matches and their quarter-final — militated against them.

Melbourne, fabulous city that it might be, is not a rugby venue — Australian Rules controls the whole city's thinking. If a Rules star as much as sneezes, it's news. The sport draws 80,000 to a club fixture. League does tolerably well, especially when the Storm is leading the

NRL, and soccer benefits from the huge multicultural population based in the city and attracts consistently good crowds. But rugby just doesn't cut the mustard. It remains the odd sport out in this vast city.

Being stuck away in the silo of Melbourne meant the All Blacks missed all the World Cup hype that was being generated in Sydney. The Wallabies, quartered in Sydney, were fortunate to be right in the mix. You could see which team had absorbed that World Cup hype when they clashed on 15 November — and it wasn't New Zealand. The All Blacks were hot favourites, especially after the Wallabies had only just sneaked past Ireland by one point (in Melbourne, interestingly enough; the Wallabies' only game there) but it was the hugely focused Aussies who won, and they did so emphatically.

The loss cast a pall of gloom across New Zealand. As Graham would come to appreciate four years later, New Zealanders, and the media in particular, are fearfully intolerant of All Black coaches when their teams lose, particularly at World Cups.

Graham was in the grandstand at Telstra Stadium when the All Blacks came crashing down and in the week that followed leading up to the final, in which Martin Johnson led England to a famous victory — secured in injury time through a Jonny Wilkinson dropped goal — Graham undertook some serious planning regarding his coaching future.

It had long been his ambition to coach the All Blacks. He'd respected John Mitchell as a coach and admired what his team had achieved since his appointment in 2001, which included two decisive Tri-Nations wins. But Graham was also aware there was an element of dissatisfaction at NZRU level that Mitchell hadn't embraced the major stakeholders in the game, or the media.

If the All Blacks had triumphed at the 2003 World Cup, Mitchell would undoubtedly have been reappointed, regardless of his off-field shortcomings. And Graham would have returned to Auckland and found something to occupy his time. He certainly wouldn't have challenged Mitchell for his job.

But the comprehensive defeat in Sydney had changed all that. Graham would give it a go.

7

Come in, Smithy and Shag

When Graham decided to challenge John Mitchell for the All Blacks' coaching role, the New Zealand Rugby Union required him to nominate his assistant or assistants.

In his mind, this was pretty straightforward. He wanted Steve Hansen as his forward coach and he wanted Wayne Smith to organize the backs.

Nothing complicated there — except Wayne Smith didn't want a bar of it. And that wasn't too hard to understand. He'd been John Hart's technical adviser when the French blew the All Blacks off Twickenham at the 1999 World Cup, and then, less than two years later, after he'd succeeded Hart as the All Black coach, he'd been unceremoniously sacked by the New Zealand Rugby Union.

His results through 2000 and 2001, when his assistant was Tony Gilbert, were mixed — 12 wins, six losses and a draw. But several of the losses were by the narrowest of margins in desperately exciting contests, such as the 2000 Bledisloe Cup test in Wellington when John Eales heroically landed a last-second, wide-angle penalty goal for a 24–23 victory. A week later, Smith's All Blacks went down to the Springboks in Johannesburg 40–46.

The pivotal moment in Smith's reign as All Black coach came in a radio interview with Murray Deaker after the All Blacks had sustained yet another narrow, agonizing loss to the Wallabies — this time 26–29 in Sydney — which meant the much-prized Bledisloe Cup remained in the hands of the Australians. At this time, New Zealand's foes over The Ditch were enjoying the most successful era in their entire history, including winning the 1999 Rugby World Cup.

The interview took place the morning after the game. Deaker's broadcast position was a hotel room in Sydney and Smith, who had just finished a press conference, was in the lobby of a different hotel.

The questions were straightforward until Deaker said, 'Wayne, given the failure to win the Bledisloe Cup, do you think you're the right person to coach the All Blacks at the next World Cup?'

Smith's fatal mistake was to hesitate. Not a brief moment of reflection but a protracted silence. Finally, he said, 'I don't know.'

A TV3 crew from New Zealand were waiting to record an interview with Smith and were startled when the usually mild-mannered Smith declared, after signing off from Deaker, 'That guy's nothing but an arsehole.'

'Oh, who was that?' asked the TV3 interviewer.

'Bloody Deaker.'

Smith's hesitancy under questioning would ultimately cost him his job. The print media picked up on the interview and speculation became rife. Although he reapplied for the position, his hesitancy was interpreted as indecisiveness, a trait the rugby fans of New Zealand considered was entirely inappropriate for an All Black coach.

The New Zealand Rugby Union obviously agreed. They replaced Smith mid year, an unprecedented happening, replacing him with Mitchell, who with Robbie Deans as his assistant, had charge of the All Blacks when they toured Ireland, Scotland and Argentina in November and December.

One individual who didn't concur with the multitude was Graham, who was following developments from afar. He knew Smith as a passionate rugby person, totally committed to the game, with black blood running through his veins. With Smithy, the players always came first. Graham knew that's why he would have hesitated when Deaker started grilling him. Whether his reappointment would be the best thing for New Zealand rugby is what Smith would have been weighing up when the question was put to him.

Graham knew Smith's hesitancy during the interview represented nothing more than his total honesty. But Deaker and his listeners plainly interpreted this honesty as a weakness.

Smith was devastated by the whole episode, especially in the weeks that followed when it began to impact negatively on his wife, Trish, and his sons, Josh and Nick.

He had no sooner digested his rejection by the NZRU than he received a phone call from Lloyd Jones, brother of prominent and outspoken New Zealander Bob Jones, these days a board member of the Northampton Rugby Club in England. He said if New Zealand didn't want him as coach, Northampton most certainly did. The Northampton Saints had a proud history and had even hosted the 1905 All Black Originals. They were currently in the relegation zone in England's premier competition and needed a coach of Wayne Smith's calibre to put them back on the path to prosperity.

Smith accepted the offer, and the family relocated to Northampton where he committed to a long-term future with the club. In the two seasons following his arrival, he turned the club's fortunes around and converted them from easy-beats to a much-respected opponent. Smith and his family had settled in wonderfully well in Northampton and loved the place.

Which is where he was when Graham's phone call came through in December 2003.

Smith was sitting in bed taking some notes when his wife, Trish, brought the phone through to him. 'It's Graham Henry calling from New Zealand,' she said.

As Smith entered into a conversation with Graham, Trish was standing in the doorway mouthing the word 'NO!'

'Hi, Graham; what's new in your world?'

Graham didn't waste words. He was going to challenge John Mitchell for the All Black coach's berth and he wanted Steve Hansen and Wayne as his associates.

Trish advanced towards the bed. Silently, she shouted to her husband, 'WE ARE NOT GOING BACK TO NEW ZEALAND!'

Wayne nodded to her.

'Listen, Graham, I'm happy with my lot at Northampton where I've made a long-term commitment. The family is pretty settled here.

My immediate answer to you is no, but let me think about it for a couple of weeks.'

The next day he adjourned to the local pub with his assistant coach, Brendon Ratcliffe, and told him about Graham's offer.

'So are you interested?' asked Ratcliffe.

'Absolutely not. I am loving my time here, and I told Graham that. It's a million to one against me having another go with the All Blacks.'

He repeated those sentiments to Trish when he got home. 'I'm definitely not getting involved with the All Blacks again.'

'It's a relief to hear you say that,' replied Trish.

If Smith thought his answer would discourage Graham and force him to go locate another attack coach, it didn't.

In the succeeding days, he fielded calls from Steve Hansen in Cardiff and good friend Gilbert Enoka, who would become Graham's mental skills facilitator (and one of the key people in the management team over the next eight years), in New Zealand. Unlike Smith, Hansen had been absolutely delighted to receive a call from Graham. The Welsh Rugby Union had intimated it would be appointing a new coach of the national team, meaning at the conclusion of the Six Nations Championship Steve would be unemployed.

Graham felt he owed Hansen one after abandoning him in 2002, although that wasn't why he offered him the position of forward coach. Simply, he regarded Hansen as the best forward coach around and he wanted him on his team. For the same reason, he wanted Smith to complete what would come to be acknowledged, given their international experience, as the Dream Team.

By the time Hansen and Enoka had done their hard sells on Graham's behalf, Smith was wavering. He engaged in some deep thinking. He had always been keen to work with Graham and he had a high regard for Hansen, who had captained the Canterbury B team when he was running the NPC side. He decided to approach the Northampton club's owner, Keith Barwell, a delightful, fatherly figure with whom he had become very close, about the dilemma he now found himself in.

Smith had a contractual obligation to Northampton and felt morally obliged to honour that. If Barwell wanted him to stay, he would dismiss the All Black offer and get on with coaching the Saints.

'If you were my son, I would advise you not to go, after the pain you endured previously,' said Barwell. 'But you're not my son and I'm not going to prevent you going, if that's what you want.'

Graham was over the moon when Smith phoned him back to say yes, count him in. Smith said he was looking forward to working with Messrs Henry and Hansen. He said he believed they could achieve something special with the All Blacks.

Smith had first encountered Graham back in 1997. As the newly appointed coach of the Crusaders, who'd finished a dismal last in the inaugural competition, he had attended a coaching seminar presented by Graham — and he couldn't believe what he was hearing. Here was the coach of the champion Auckland Blues revealing all their secrets, even down to the minute detail of how far back from the scrum the halfback should stand. Smith took copious notes, most of which he implemented into his Crusaders schedule that season.

As he exited the meeting, he was still pondering why Graham would give all his trade secrets away, when the penny dropped. Of course, that was it! What Graham was revealing was the 1996 model, and in the meantime, he'd moved on. He was so innovative he could afford to reveal the previous year's plan that he'd now dispensed with.

John Mitchell and Graham were the only applicants for the All Blacks' coaching position. Each travelled to Wellington to appear before an NZRU sub-committee comprising CEO Chris Moller and board members Mike Eagle and John Graham, with deputy CEO Steve Tew assisting; chairman Jock Hobbs did not involve himself in the process because of his relationship to Robbie Deans, Mitchell's assistant (Hobbs and Deans are brothers-in-law).

Graham had respect for what Mitchell had achieved on the field as All Black coach. The team had played some great rugby and had a highly successful win/loss record. But Graham knew there would be enormous pressure on Mitchell because he'd been smashed mentally with the World Cup defeat by Australia. Also, he'd been copping it from the media, who had become progressively disenchanted with him because of his indifferent attitude towards them as well as to the major stakeholders in the game during his tenure as coach. Graham knew it would represent a huge challenge for Mitchell to get himself up to reapply for the position, particularly with his negative undertone.

Graham fronted up to the sub-committee with eight pages of handwritten notes. He knew his credentials stacked up handsomely: four NPC titles with Auckland, two Super 12 crowns with the Blues, a sequence of 10 straight wins with Wales, including historic victories over South Africa, France in Paris and England at Wembley, plus his experience of coaching the British Lions in Australia. Also, since his return from the UK, he had been involved in two NPCs with Auckland and one Super 12 with the Blues, all of which were won.

From his notes, here's what Graham pitched to the sub-committee:

Why All Black coach? Best person in world rugby to coach All Blacks with the coaching staff available (Hansen and Smith). The objectives: the All Blacks are consistently No. 1/goal to bring home World Cup in 2007/build a team of proud young men.

Respect the position: Proud to be a New Zealander/aware of the importance of rugby in the country/acutely aware of the responsibility of All Black coach/role model and ambassador/following people like Neil McPhail, Jack Gleeson, Brian Lochore, Laurie Mains.

Love the game: Thirty years a coach at all levels, 23 of them amateur/ tenacity and perseverance/Why I went to Wales/involvement with Auckland upon my return.

Huge passion for coaching: It's my profession/every session to be better, more stimulating, more thought provoking/increase knowledge and skills/want the guys to be totally prepared and totally motivated/ the harder and smarter you work, the better you play.

Selection: Have a proven record as a selector for identifying talent/ spent time agonizing over selections/critical to get it right/accountable for fielding the best team/process must be methodical and disciplined.

Experience and maturity: Maturity moulded from highs & lows, victories & defeats/better coach for four NPC and two Super 12 wins/experience with Wales and British Lions, in particular — many lessons learnt/ Wales fanatical/total involvement in Wales/total disarray there/Lions and working with three other coaches, a new experience/the Matt Dawson & Austin Healey sagas/injuries/handling press conferences/ losing some Welsh relationships/coach burnout/negotiating release of Welsh contract.

I'm a team person: When I have struggled, have always turned to my managers (Rex Davy, David Pickering)/NZRU board plus staff and All Black management and All Blacks need to be one/NZ rugby high performance unit/acutely aware that All Blacks need to build relations and communicate as a rugby family/involve commercial partners, media, broadcasters, fans/NZers get to know their players/ players to communicate with their fans through the media/part of leadership development and team culture/part of our preparation and team balance.

Extension of school-teaching: Ability to see the big picture on and off the field/see what we are trying to create and achieve/ability to sell and communicate that vision/through guided democracy develop attitudes, knowledge, skills, physical requirements and, most importantly, mental requirements/that is the game we play, the culture we live by/important area — management helping players take responsibility and ownership by developing leadership and decision-making skills.

Stable, supportive, enjoyable private life: Raewyn/children/friends.

Above all, leadership: Who are we?/ Who do we represent?/traditions and history of NZ/traditions and history of NZ rugby/playing for the people/pride in and respect the country.

Graham was told to report back to NZRU headquarters the next morning when he would learn of the board's decision. When he arrived, Chris Moller and Jock Hobbs were there to meet him. They escorted him into the boardroom.

'Congratulations,' said Moller, 'you have been appointed coach of the All Blacks.'

Graham has no recall of what he said in reply but he knows that for the rest of that day, after fronting the media, he couldn't get the smile off his face!

It is, after all, a monumental occasion when you're asked to coach the national team of a country as passionate about its rugby as New Zealand. It had always been Graham's ambition and now, after a 30-year journey preparing teams, he had won the ultimate appointment as a rugby coach: to coach the All Blacks — to coach New Zealand.

His induction as All Black coach was all the more remarkable given that just over five years previously he had been thoroughly abused by the CEO of New Zealand Rugby and warned if he took up the coaching appointment in Wales he would never hold a coaching position at national level in New Zealand, ever again.

But nothing is forever. After the NZRU had the 2003 World Cup hosting rights stripped from it, the board was overthrown, and Moffett resigned as CEO, to take up a position, ironically enough, as chief executive of the Welsh Rugby Union. With the changeover, the so-called Henry Clause was drop-kicked out the window.

As Graham shared a toast with Raewyn and family and his great mates John Graham and Rex Davy following his return to Auckland, he reflected on the irony of appointments lost that had led to him becoming the All Black coach.

Coming to Auckland from Christchurch in 1973 to take up a teaching position at Auckland Grammar School under John Graham's leadership had provided a wonderful opportunity for Graham. Challenging, yes, but he had learnt and developed both as a teacher and a sports coach; he'd also come to appreciate the necessity for hard work and perseverance.

While deputy headmaster at Kelston Boys' High School in 1986 he had applied for the rector's position at Palmerston North Boys' High School and was miffed when he missed out, the posting going to another good rugby man and good mate David Syms. Palmerston North being such a traditional school, Graham doubts he would have been allowed to coach rugby had he won the appointment. Ironically, he was appointed headmaster of Kelston a few weeks later ... a school that thankfully valued his interest in rugby.

If he'd been made coach of Auckland in 1987 when Maurice Trapp won the job, he wonders whether he would have been successful. He was much better prepared and better qualified when he was voted into the position five years later.

Then, of course, had he not quit Wales when he did in 2002, relocating to New Zealand, he most certainly would not have come into consideration for the All Black coach's role when Mitchell faltered at the 2003 World Cup.

And if Wayne Pivac and Grant Fox had not offered him a lifeline by accepting his offer to be assistant coaches with Auckland in 2002 ... well, you could go on and on!

So fate had been kind to him. It seemed he had been directed to where he was meant to be.

Having won the appointment, Graham's next job was to convince the NZRU board that Steve Hansen and Wayne Smith should be appointed as fellow coaches, with Sir Brian Lochore joining them as a fourth selector. This opportunity came at a meeting in Wellington in early February.

It would have been a major shock if the NZRU board had rejected either of the coaching candidates, but Graham still needed to present a convincing argument on behalf of them. Graham described Smith as 'a highly competent successful coach who commands enormous respect from players who have been coached by him'. And Hansen was wanted because 'he is one of the leading coaches of forwards in the world'. Collectively, the three men had accounted for the first five Super 12 titles after rugby went professional. Graham guided the Blues to championship success in 1996 and 1997, Smith did likewise with the Crusaders in 1998 and 1999, and Hansen was Robbie Deans's deputy when the Crusaders completed their hat trick in 2000.

In defining the coaching trio's responsibilities, Graham explained that the modern game was clearly divided into three major areas, and each of the coaches would be in charge of one particular area: Steve Hansen would be responsible for the forwards securing high-quality possession from scrums, lineouts and restarts; Wayne Smith for what the All Blacks do once they have possession, i.e. the attack game; and he, Graham, would be responsible for what happens when the opposition have possession, i.e. the defence game. As head coach, he would also take an overview, with each coach assisting the others with their individual responsibilities.

His philosophy was that the trio of coaches' major objective would be to produce a smart rugby environment. 'Talent rarely beats brains at international level,' he assured the board.

Graham explained that on the field the All Blacks would strive to take the initiative. 'That means taking the high ground in the contest and playing the game at such a tempo and skill level that the opposition finds it difficult to compete.' He said this would be based on self-belief honed by in-depth preparation and organization as well as constant positive reinforcement of the players' execution in relation to this high-tempo, highly skilled game. Add huge defence that would reflect the 'steel' the players had in both individual attitude and the pride they had in the team, and you had the total package.

The NZRU was suitably impressed with the Dream Team's qualifications and duly appointed Messrs Hansen and Smith to join Graham as All Black coaches for a two-year term. And Sir Brian was appointed a selector.

Ted and Shag and Smithy represented the new face of New Zealand rugby coaching.

They first got together in London in March 2004, a logical venue given that Hansen and Smith were still rounding out their contracts with Wales and Northampton, respectively. Their meeting coincided with the Wales-England Six Nations match at Twickenham, Hansen's penultimate game as Graham's successor in charge of Wales. Unfortunately, he wasn't able to celebrate the occasion with a win, England taking out a spirited encounter 31–21, although he would bow out with a handsome win against Italy in Cardiff a week later.

Among the major discussion topics at their inaugural meeting was the captaincy. Reuben Thorne had been Mitchell's man and was the incumbent but the feeling was that Thorne's time had come.

The individual the 'Three Wise Men' settled upon was Tana Umaga, a veteran of 53 tests dating back to 1997. Mitchell and Deans had surprisingly left him out of their World Cup squad, but coming up 31, Umaga still had an enormous amount to offer as an inspirational player and leader.

Ted and Shag and Smithy talked a lot about leadership and were unanimous Umaga was their man. No Polynesian had ever captained the All Blacks before, although Buck Shelford, a Maori, had been a sensationally effective leader back in the 1980s.

Umaga himself got 'a hell of a shock' when Graham phoned him to break the news. 'Heck,' replied Umaga. 'After missing out on the World Cup, I thought my days as an international were over, and now you're asking me to be captain. I'd be honoured to accept.'

Graham deemed Umaga's appointment an obvious decision. He was excited about working with 'T', who was a world-class player, gave his all and had tremendous respect from his fellow players.

The England-Wales game they attended was entertaining, but neither side would go on to win the Six Nations Championship that year. That honour went to France. However, the occasion was valuable for Ted and Shag and Smithy because England was to be their first opponent in three months' time.

Before then, it was necessary to put a fresh management team in place.

Darren Shand was selected as manager from a large number of applicants, among them a couple of imposing All Blacks: Andy Haden, who'd had a stint operating as marketing manager for NZRU in the 1980s, and Andy Dalton, who had been the NZRU president in 1999/2000 and who would later become CEO of Auckland Rugby.

What won it for Shand — Shandy as he would become known — was that he was already proven as a professional rugby manager, of the hugely successful Crusaders.

He came to the position by an unorthodox route, having launched his working career in the tourism industry in Queenstown. He'd dabbled in rafting and skiing, until AJ Hackett, the bungy-jump king, offered him a job. Shand became part of the management team eventually helping run the world-famous bungy-jump operation on the Kawarau River. He became a Jump Master!

After five years of that, though, Shand was ready for a fresh challenge, and in 1998 he applied for the position of sponsorship manager with the Canterbury Rugby Union. He impressed Steve Tew, the Canterbury CEO who was one of the interviewers, and was appointed, little thinking that the pair of them would go on to make their marks on rugby's highest stage.

The Canterbury coaches at that time were Robbie Deans and Steve Hansen. Deans, soon aware of Shand's exceptional organizational talents, invited him to become manager of the Canterbury team. Previously, the position had always gone to an amateur board member, so Shand broke that tradition when he became the first paid employee to manage the Red and Blacks.

When Deans stepped up to the Crusaders coaching role in 2000 — succeeding Smithy who'd taken charge of the All Blacks — Shand went with him. They guided the team to Super 12 success, repeating the feat in 2002.

Shand was encouraged to stand for the All Black manager's role in 2003 after the incumbent Andrew Martin fell out with coach John Mitchell, but because he had a young family, Shand declined. However, when Mitchell's men crashed out of the Rugby World Cup in Sydney and it became apparent a fresh management team was going to be created, he decided to put his name forward. The rest, as they say, is history.

Another good Crusaders person who came on board was baggage-man Errol Collins, nicknamed Possum, a man with an engaging personality and a great sense of humour.

They were joined by three of the Blues medical team: Graham Paterson, who became team doctor, muscle therapist George Duncan, who'd had a 20-year association with Graham, and Paul Wilson, physiotherapist with both Auckland and the Blues.

Graham Lowe came on board as the strength and conditioning coach. He would play a major role in helping build the All Blacks into the best-conditioned and most-feared team in the world. His talents would eventually see him lured away by the BMW Oracle America's Cup racing team and in 2009 he would become High Performance Director with Scotland Rugby.

To these were added scrum coach Mike Cron, then working for the High Performance unit of the NZRU — and who Graham considers to be without peer in the world — and sports psychologist Gilbert Enoka, who would become an extremely important member of the All Black team over the next eight years, working with both players and management.

Enoka prefers to be described as a mental skills coach rather than a sports psychologist because he knows such a title doesn't sit easily with most rugby fanatics in New Zealand.

His association with Canterbury, and ultimately New Zealand, rugby began when he was teaching at Hillmorton High School in Christchurch — along with netball coach Leigh Gibbs — and Wayne Smith, then with the Canterbury Sports Depot, used to call in selling sporting equipment.

The three of them used to have animated discussions on sport in general and eventually Smithy and Bert, as Enoka would become known, became the best of friends. When Smith took over as coach of the Canterbury rugby team, he involved Bert as a mental skills coach.

Now Enoka had made it to All Black level.

Graham was hugely stimulated by the All Black challenge. He was aware of the legacy he was inheriting: a remarkable team that over a century had contributed massively to New Zealand's identity while maintaining a winning record in excess of 70 per cent. No other sporting team in the world in any code came close to equalling that. The challenge was to enhance the All Blacks' legacy, to try to elevate them to new levels.

But if Ted and Shag and Smithy were excited to be preparing the men in black for Tri-Nations and Bledisloe Cup challenges and an end-of-year European tour, they were soon to become disillusioned. To their amazement, they found they had inherited a group of rather dissatisfied individuals. Here was the most successful professional team in the world, with an incredible 100-year legacy, but the current players, although proud, were not enjoying the environment.

The culture was not what the new coaching trio had expected it to be, with many of the players preferring to play for their franchises more than for the All Blacks. This was a culture Graham could not live with.

It was something the three of them, with help from Sir Brian Lochore, were going to have to sort out if the All Blacks were to aspire to No. 1 status in the world again.

Another matter that had Graham bemused from the start was the influence Justin Marshall was exerting on the team. Graham found that Marshall was the most influential individual in the team. He talked the most and had become the team's unofficial leader. In fact, he talked so much, not many others got the opportunity to say anything at all. He was the captain, Graham perceived, in all senses bar the title.

The JM show, through no fault of Marshall's, had obviously been permitted to develop to the point where he virtually ran the team, on the field and off.

Graham could see that Marshall was possessed of a huge motor and great pride in his ability to play well game after game. Single-handedly, he had swung the course of more than a few All Black matches since his debut in 1995. At 30, like Umaga, he still had plenty to offer, but Graham didn't see how they could develop other leaders as part of the collective leadership philosophy with Justin in the team.

Because they were brand new as selectors/coaches and because Mitchell's team, notwithstanding the calamitous World Cup semi-final performance, had been performing creditably, the selectors largely maintained the status quo in 2004. Their policy was to have a good look at the current culture before making any decisions on what changes were needed, if any.

The team that played England twice and scored two handsome 36-point victories over the reigning world champions didn't vary significantly from that which had participated at the World Cup seven months earlier.

Mils Muliaina, Doug Howlett and Joe Rokocoko were retained as the back three, Dan Carter (as a second-five), Carlos Spencer and Marshall directed operations behind the scrum, with Richie McCaw, Jerry Collins, Marty Holah, Chris Jack, Ali Williams, Greg Somerville and Keven Mealamu still in the forward mix.

A notable newcomer was Jono Gibbes at blindside flanker with centre Tana Umaga (now the captain), lock Kevin Robinson and props Carl Hayman and Kees Meeuws all recalled.

Henry's All Blacks completed their domestic programme undefeated. After the encouraging wins against England, Argentina and a Pacific Islands team, they eked out Tri-Nations victories against the Wallabies (16–7 in Wellington) and the Springboks (23–21 in Christchurch).

Apart from the fact only two tries (both to Howlett) were scored in 160 minutes of action against Australia and South Africa — a stat uncharacteristic of teams prepared by Graham Henry — the All Blacks were, to all intents and purposes, progressing satisfactorily under their new management.

But the coaches knew there were problems they couldn't immediately resolve, problems that would manifest themselves initially in Sydney and horrendously in Johannesburg.

The Sydney game was lost 23–18. Interestingly, it would be the only occasion in his 106 games as coach that the All Blacks would fail to score a try. It meant a victory at Ellis Park was essential if the Tri-Nations was to be won.

The Johannesburg game represented a special occasion within South Africa, being the 10th anniversary of Freedom Day when apartheid was abolished. On every seat at Ellis Park, organizers placed a small drum. Those drums make a lot of noise! And after the Springboks took the field, Nelson Mandela wandered out to shake each player's hand, as he had on the occasion of South Africa's famous World Cup final victory in 1995.

The All Blacks had already received a preliminary warning of the emotions rampant in Johannesburg that day because as their bus approached Ellis Park, Bok supporters pounded on the side of it, chanting 'Bokke, Bokke!' Graham and many of the players had never experienced this kind of atmosphere anywhere before.

In the coaches' box high up the grandstand at Ellis Park, Graham soberly watched as Nelson Mandela offered a word to each Springbok. He turned to Smithy and Shag and said, 'We're in for a hell of a game, boys!'

And a hell of a game unfolded. The All Blacks rebounded from a half-time deficit to lead 26–25 with 15 minutes remaining. But there was no stopping the Springboks on this auspicious occasion and with two late tries they dealt the All Blacks a 40–26 hiding.

In the Tri-Nations wash-up, South Africa came first with 11 points, Australia had 10 and New Zealand just nine. Not a flash start to Graham's All Black coaching career! More embarrassing was the fact the Springboks scored 13 tries, the Wallabies nine and the All Blacks a meagre four.

If that was cause for despair, Graham couldn't believe what unfolded that evening at the team's hotel — a mock court session run by two hardened campaigners, Justin Marshall and Carlos Spencer.

Court sessions were nothing new. They had been around for decades; they were indeed a legacy of the amateur era, something teams indulged in to promote team spirit, particularly on traditional overseas tours which back in the fifties, sixties and seventies could extend to three and four months.

At the Johannesburg session, the judges dispensed rough justice to a variety of individuals, reserving their severest penalties, which mostly involved sculling substantial amounts of alcohol, to team officials. Graham observed a couple of his colleagues being reduced to an almost comatose state. One management member, who rarely imbibed, even finished up so intoxicated he admitted later he genuinely feared for his life!

What Graham observed that night he considered totally unacceptable. The magnitude of the drinking he deemed inappropriate for a professional sporting team. What unfolded was ugly and embarrassing and went outside the parameters of what great sports team are about, particularly in the modern professional era. He presumed it reflected what All Black teams had been indulging in before he inherited the side. He didn't institute an inquiry or approach those responsible. Perhaps the Johannesburg court session was a one-off, an exception. He didn't care about that. What he knew was that he couldn't live with that culture and resolved that from that moment, as long as he was coaching the All Blacks, there would never be another court session. And there wasn't.

The binge drinking wasn't the only aspect of the All Black culture Graham was concerned about. It was obvious John Mitchell had erected a fence around the All Blacks and not allowed anyone else in. It was a throwback to the amateur days and while it may have suited Graham's predecessors, it wasn't how he ran a rugby team. Graham had always embraced the sponsors, the stakeholders, the public and, after a slow start admittedly, he had even come to work amicably with the press. That's how he wanted things to be at All Black level. Obviously, there was a lot of work to be done. And not all of it was about building a winning rugby team on the field.

The next morning, Wayne Smith slipped a note under Graham's door. Smithy preferred to confront people when he had a problem, but on this occasion he felt a handwritten letter would more poignantly convey his feelings of concern. He knew Graham was devastated with the loss at Ellis Park and unhappy with aspects of team culture, but he felt it was important Graham understood he had grave concerns, too.

'Graham,' the letter read, 'I came back to New Zealand to coach because of you. I wouldn't have come back for anyone else. I support you 100 per cent but it is important we sort out our problems. Let's go on together and fix this thing, Wayne.'

Graham, who would become universally acknowledged for his impish grin, bore no semblance of a smile as the All Blacks readied for their journey back home from Johannesburg. He wouldn't look this humourless again until the All Blacks exited the World Cup at the quarter-final stage in 2007.

Smithy's letter would never be referred to. But, by God, Graham and his team would certainly set about 'fixing things'.

On the long, monotonous flight back across the Indian Ocean, Graham did some calculations. In three months the All Blacks were scheduled to embark on a four-match tour of Italy, Wales, France and England. There were major issues to be dealt with, based on the unsettling experiences of the past couple of months. If the All Blacks' flagging fortunes were to be revived, there had to be a drastic reassessment of the team's parameters.

Across the aisle from him, Smith was being brutally honest with manager Shand: 'We have a dysfunctional team — if it's not fixed, I won't be back.'

Soon after their arrival back in New Zealand, a meeting was convened in Wellington. Present were the three coaches, Sir Brian Lochore, manager Darren Shand, team facilitator Gilbert Enoka, captain Tana Umaga and vice-captain Richie McCaw. They assembled at NZRU headquarters, selected a room and locked the door. It was three days before they completed their deliberations.

Graham considers it the most important meeting in his eight years as All Black coach. Every aspect of All Black culture was addressed. The major objective of everyone present at the meeting was to create an environment in the All Blacks that would stimulate players and make them strive to become part of it. These were the guidelines by which the All Blacks would operate in the seasons ahead and, as it turned out, right through to the triumphant 2011 World Cup campaign.

The three rules governing off-field behaviour, developed over time, became:

1 You're an All Black 24/7.
2 Every one of you will prepare for every match. If there are 30 in the touring party, all 30 will prepare, even though only 22 will be directly involved in the game.
3 No women will be in our hotel. If your partner comes on the tour, they will stay in another hotel.

After the Johannesburg debacle, a fresh policy regarding the consumption of alcohol was spelt out. It was:

• The team will have a change in attitude to drinking.
• Binge drinking will not be tolerated in the team going forward.

- We want to encourage players to have a drink, but at no time do we want any binge drinking, as has been the case in the past with court sessions, etc.
- We do not want to be policing it hard but rather want to be helping each other out and learning to control things.
- By no means do we want to stop players enjoying themselves, but we all have to front the next day.

Sir Brian came up with a catch phrase that was adopted that year and was still being quoted at the time of the 2011 Rugby World Cup: 'Better people make better All Blacks.'

The other major outcome of the meeting was the establishment of the leadership group that would become such a critical component of the team as it journeyed forward.

Starting on the end-of-year European tour, selected leaders were assigned portfolios. These senior players were now in charge of such categories as social events, interacting with sponsors, dealing with the media, buddying up with new internationals, etc.

Not everything that went amiss in Sydney and Johannesburg could be blamed on the players; Graham shouldered his share of the fault. In his report to the NZRU, he said the coaches were disappointed with the quality of performance during this series of games and that the major issue was a failure to implement the game plan.

The reasons he gave for this were a failure to ensure the players had sufficient leadership, knowledge and confidence (self-belief) to implement the game plan; a failure to ensure there was a transference of leadership, and therefore responsibility, from the coaches to the players; the players were overworked to the extent they ran out of edge in the last two internationals; it was questionable whether the group had the necessary leadership ability, game understanding and composure to achieve constantly at the sharp edge of international rugby, particularly away from home; and it was questionable whether the group understood their identity — who they are, what they stand for, and their collective and individual responsibilities as All Blacks.

Graham said the coaches were fortunate they now knew what

the challenges were. 'We have started the process of implementing actions we believe will considerably improve our weaknesses. The reality is this will take some time. It will take patience, perseverance and persistence. It won't be a quick fix. We will all need to work together in the professional game to ensure it is successful.'

If a fresh culture was to be implemented on the end-of-year tour of Europe, it meant some of the team's more powerful personalities had to be sacrificed. So when the 33-strong touring party was named, missing were the strong personalities Justin Marshall and Carlos Spencer and also Andrew Mehrtens, who at 31 was a veteran of 70 test matches dating back to 1995. It was Sir Brian who said, 'If you take him, the minute things go wrong, you'll rush him back in at the expense of the new guys.'

He was right, of course. And so Ted and Shag and Smith gambled boldly, sacrificing Marshall, Spencer and Mehrtens, who collectively boasted 172 test appearances, and introducing an assortment of rookie backs who didn't claim a test cap among them: Piri Weepu, Jimmy Cowan, Luke McAlister, Conrad Smith and Casey Laulala. Other fresh-faced backs selected were Dan Carter, who was considered by his Canterbury and Crusaders coaches at the time not to have the necessary qualities to play at No. 10, Rico Gear (one test) and Ma'a Nonu (four tests).

Graham met with Marshall at the Heritage Hotel in Christchurch and broke the news to him.

'We're not taking you on tour,' Graham explained to Marshall, 'because we're wanting to develop other leaders. We need to give them the space and the opportunity to develop.'

'I'm disappointed,' replied Marshall. 'I thought I still had something to offer.'

'And you do. Your career is not finished, but on this particular tour, we need to develop a number of young guys to lead this team in the future. If you are there, they won't get the total benefit of this opportunity.'

Marshall hadn't been dispensed with completely. He would be recalled for the 2005 series against the British Lions.

Graham was sympathetic to Spencer's cause, because he had been a spectacularly effective achiever for him with Auckland and the Blues. Some players are coach makers and others are coach killers. Without doubt, Spencer slotted into the first category: he was a player who'd definitely made his coach, Graham, look good.

Probably Spencer hadn't flourished in recent times playing alongside such an equally strong personality as Marshall. He tended to function better outside a serving halfback like Steve Devine. Spencer was still an immensely talented footballer, but with the new management wanting to develop a collective leadership structure, they knew Spencer's presence would be a negative. They also knew it would be impossible to convert him into a subordinate role, and the same went for Marshall.

Prior to the tour, Graham instigated a meeting, facilitated by Gilbert Enoka, at which about eight of the touring players, who constituted the new leadership group, were invited to speak openly about how they felt about being All Blacks and what their expectations were. The meeting was brutally honest and became charged with emotion.

To the shock of Graham and his fellow coaches, almost all of them confessed they weren't enjoying playing for the All Blacks. They identified team culture and the pressure from fans and media as major concerns. And most of them said they were closer to their Super 12 colleagues and their franchises than they were to their fellow All Blacks.

It was an eye-opener for Graham and his fellow management members, who had been striving to create an ideal environment. Here were the players saying they weren't enjoying it. It was a major issue, an attitude that had to be turned around.

The management team had plenty to muse over. It wasn't something they could fix overnight, but it was certainly something they had to remedy going forward.

The tour selection policy had the potential to spectacularly misfire, given that the coaches resolved to split their resources against Italy and Wales and not field their strongest 15 players until the French game, but in the event the team returned from its European sojourn undefeated.

After smashing Italy 59–10 in Rome, when Umaga led the side, the selectors daringly made nine changes for the Welsh contest, introducing Weepu, Laulala and No. 8 Mose Tuiali'i for their test debuts. Richie McCaw was promoted to captain, Dan Carter, who'd played almost exclusively at second-five until then, was selected at first-five, and another inexperienced individual, Tony Woodcock, was pitched into the front row.

If there was one game the two former Welsh national coaches, Henry and Hansen, didn't want to lose, it was this contest at the Millennium Stadium. So Graham felt immense relief when his boys rallied from 13–19 down early in the second half to win 26–25. It was an extremely tense game and it wasn't until Chris Jack claimed a vital lineout in the dying seconds that Graham knew the win was assured. It wasn't the most decisive of victories, but a win is a win and given the inexperience of so many of the players, the coaches took enormous confidence from the performance.

That evening Ted and Smithy and Shag encountered 'Pinetree' Meads, who is nothing if not brutally honest in his assessment of matters rugby. 'That,' he told the Three Wise Men, 'would be one of the worst All Black performances I have ever seen.'

'There's better to come,' quipped Smithy.

'There better bloody be!'

During the stay in Cardiff, an inflammatory article written in the New Zealand Herald by sports columnist Chris Rattue sparked major headlines throughout Wales. Not content with labelling the Welsh rugby team 'a disgrace', Rattue went on to brand them 'the village idiots of world rugby'.

Although the article was ostensibly written in light-hearted vein, the Welsh saw no humour in these claims whatsoever and grilled the unfortunate All Black coaches at the next press conference, which was especially awkward and highly embarrassing for Graham and Steve Hansen, who had both coached Wales. Graham wanted to talk rugby, but all the Welsh journalists wanted to ask was questions about the New Zealand Herald article. Becoming exasperated, Graham finally said, 'Look, every village has its idiot — and he is obviously ours!'

Upon his return to New Zealand, Graham wrote a letter of complaint to the editor of the New Zealand Herald, stating he thought Rattue's article lacked tact and sensitivity, and that it was an embarrassment to both the All Black touring team and their supporters touring Wales.

The editor did not reply to Graham but ran the letter in the Letters to the Editor column.

Ever since then, Rattue has hardly had a kind word to say about Graham. Graham's conclusion: You can't win with the press!

The games in Rome and Cardiff represented the first example of what cynics back home would brand the All Blacks' rotation policy. It was implemented on that tour because the coaches wanted to develop a team for the future and this meant giving raw young talented players an opportunity to perform and be assessed under pressure at test level. It seemed to Graham an eminently sensible strategy to implement at the time, one that looked to the future.

The best of the European tour, as promised, came seven days after the narrow escape in Cardiff, when the All Blacks took on the Tricolores in Paris. The All Blacks wore a Flanders poppy on their right sleeve, in remembrance of New Zealanders who had died in combat, particularly those killed on French soil during the First World War. Captain Umaga said at a press conference before the game that New Zealanders' service overseas was a big part of the country's heritage and the team's heritage. 'We want to honour their sacrifice,' he said.

At stake was the Dave Gallaher Trophy, named after the captain of the 1905 Originals, who was killed at Passchendaele in 1917.

The All Blacks ran riot against France, winning 45–6, and exceeding their coaches' wildest expectations as they ran in five tries to none. Umaga was back leading the side, teaming up in midfield with Smith, who'd made his test debut against Italy. It was the game that put Graham's All Blacks on the map. He rates it one of his greatest performances as an All Black coach and, at the time, positively purred because it reinforced what the coaching and management team were seeking to introduce.

It was the first graphic example of the new regime's hard work paying off, the coaches having inspired a group of young players to express themselves beautifully on the world stage. And what a stage: the fabulous Stade de France in Paris before 80,000 spectators. The leaders had linked arms and had played and led together.

That performance, against the team that had won the Six Nations Championship that year undefeated, was outstanding and reinforced much of the learning that had been going on since the depths of despair at the time of the Johannesburg court session a few months before.

The French captain, Fabien Pelous, was so awestruck by the All Blacks' performance, he described them as performing like 'extra-terrestrials'.

One of the more interesting selections for the French international was Norm Maxwell, who at 28 was in the twilight of his career, not because of his capabilities but because his body had taken a fearful battering through 35 test matches and more than 100 games for Northland, Canterbury and the Crusaders. He was even carrying a hole in his quadriceps as a consequence of a major injury sustained in 2003 — his body was literally beyond repair.

Maxwell was the lightest tight forward on either side, by some margin, weighing in at around 95kg. But what he lacked in bulk, he more than compensated for in fearless commitment. No rugby player ever put his body on the line more than Maxwell.

Anyway, at practice prior to the Paris match, Graham noted that Maxwell was not training.

'What the hell's going on, Shag, Smithy?' Graham asked his fellow coaches. 'He's in the team for Saturday and he's not training.'

'That's Norm; he'll be right, Ted, don't worry.'

'Are you sure? Bloody bizarre!'

'Trust us, he'll have a big one on Saturday.'

Well, Shag and Smithy were right and Graham was wrong. Maxwell turned in a blinder, for the squillionth time in his career blanking out the pain factor to secure precious lineout ball for his team and meeting the French forwards head on.

Sadly, it would be his final appearance for his country. Graham remembers him as a unique personality who never let the team down.

A 47–19 romp against the Barbarians — a team captained, interestingly enough, by Justin Marshall and including nine Wallabies — capped a wonderfully successful tour. Not only had Graham and his fellow coaches made important progress with the team culture, but they'd got the side scoring tries. After the miserable return of four tries in four Tri-Nations fixtures, the boys had run in 24 tries against Italy, Wales, France and the Baabaas. Things were definitely looking up.

This time, Graham was able to present a positive report to the NZRU.

It was a successful tour, the most positive aspect being the team management and the senior players being proactive.

It is relatively easy to improve a situation that has obvious flaws. It is a far greater challenge to maintain the standards and continue to improve. The standards achieved in the test against France [won 45–6] are the benchmark.

Contributing to the success was the implementation of a leadership group. The growth of these players' ability to lead was the key. Each of the players had a portfolio they controlled.

The players gained a great understanding and respect for each other as they developed. They grew to understand they had similar challenges as international rugby players and these challenges were better handled collectively than individually. This brought togetherness — they were 'one'. They now have a collective rather than individual responsibility and went to 'war' for each other.

What a great way to round out 2004. Graham and his team had learnt, had changed and, although not perfect, were on the way to producing quality rugby, while also enjoying the rugby and the culture in the process.

8

Bring on the Lions

Tana Umaga's appointment as captain in 2004 was proving an inspirational move. Tana is Samoan, so in choosing a Polynesian as captain, Graham and his fellow selectors had moved away from the norm. But choosing Tana hadn't been a hard decision: although now having clicked over 30, he was an experienced world-class player who related to Pakeha, Maori and Polynesians alike and led by example. Graham was always amused at how many people from Europe in particular misunderstood the circumstances that led to Polynesians representing the All Blacks. Often they were third- or fourth-generation New Zealanders.

Events had happened early in Umaga's career that identified him as a character and an individual — he'd certainly been a bit of a lad in his youth — and Graham, for one, always believed that these people could often develop into the best captains.

The two men developed an excellent working relationship throughout 2004, often discussing team and world issues over coffee, and Graham was delighted to have him as his captain for the eagerly anticipated British Lions series coming up in 2005.

He was intrigued, though, when one day Umaga, whom he referred to simply as T, asked if he could have a word with him in private.

'What's on your mind?' asked Graham.

'Ted, those team talks you give before a match, do you think they are any value?'

'I had assumed so, T.'

'Are they for us, or are they for you?'

'Well ...'

'Ted, I think they are largely a waste of time and inappropriate.'

'Thanks, T.'

Graham greatly valued Tana's honesty although on this occasion his comments left him depressed for a week.

Seriously, though, since he'd first started coaching rugby teams, more than 25 years back, Graham had always given a team talk, because that's what coaches did.

For matches of representative or international status, the talk would be delivered at the team hotel before departure to the ground for the game. Their purpose was to give direction for the contest ahead and hopefully provide some motivation.

Until Umaga asked the question, Graham rated the coach's team talk as vital a part of match day as the referee tossing a coin for the skippers. But his captain had definitely given him food for thought.

The more he thought about it, the more he appreciated where Umaga was coming from. If players needed advice and boosting a couple of hours before the match, then the coach had missed out on something during the week.

If I'm blatantly honest, Tana's right, Graham thought to himself, *the players don't need me in their ear two hours before a game*.

As a result of Umaga's questioning, Graham began toning down his team talks and eventually eliminated them altogether.

Dan Carter was a player who had been identified from a young age as being an exceptional talent. Wayne Smith remembers fielding a call one day from an official suggesting he get along to Christchurch Boys' High (which was where Carter completed his education, having started at the less fashionable Ellesmere College) to see this player who was described to him as 'just about the complete package'.

Although Smith was impressed and would see him mature into probably the best footballer in the world, not everyone was awed by his skills, certainly not as a first-five.

Brendon McCullum, these days starring for the Black Caps, was chosen ahead of Carter for the South Island schoolboys team, and for most of 2003 and for the entire 2004 Super 12 campaign Robbie Deans played him at second-five for the Crusaders, preferring to use Andrew Mehrtens and Cameron McIntyre in the No. 10 jersey. And that's how John Mitchell had gone at the 2003 Rugby World Cup, putting his faith in Carlos Spencer's experience in the vital play-maker's role. Carter, the new boy, was risked only in the pool matches, and then at second-five.

Word out of the Red and Black territory was that Carter couldn't direct a game and that his talents were better suited to the midfield. But that wasn't how the All Black coaches, particularly Smith, perceived him. Besides, the lad had excellent rugby genes in his blood: his great-uncle was Bill Dalley, a member of the 1924–25 All Black 'Invincibles'.

Smith, who had played 17 tests for New Zealand in the No. 10 jersey, not only identified Carter as a natural first-five but believed he could be developed into the All Black equivalent of Jonny Wilkinson, and with a better running game.

One of the major discussion points when the Three Wise Men were selecting their squad to tour Europe late in 2004, once they'd agreed to invest in Carter, had been whether Mehrtens should be taken along as a back-up.

Recalling Sir Brian Lochore's warning, it was Graham who said, 'If we take Mehrtens, we'll fall back on him. If we take Dan, we've got to back him.'

Graham had always invested in youth and this was another classic example, one that would reap a fantastic reward. And whenever he made calls like this, after intense debates, he was always backed by Smith and Hansen.

While Carter was naturally thrilled at being elevated to first-choice first-five, Mehrtens was massively disappointed when the touring party was named, which led to a heated argument between himself and Smith. But disputing a rugby selector's choice is a bit like a cricketer questioning an umpire's call: those decisions never get changed; it's always a fait accompli. Sadly, Mehrtens' non-selection for that tour terminated an illustrious career dating back to 1995 and featuring 70 test appearances.

The selectors copped plenty of flak at the time for dropping Mehrtens, Spencer and Marshall, but by the team coming through their northern hemisphere tour unscathed they largely placated their critics. And now their investment in Carter was about to reap rich rewards.

The Lions tour of 2005 was a precursor to the seventh Rugby World Cup. Both tours would be hosted with great distinction. New Zealanders were enormously buoyed by the tour and embraced the more than 20,000 supporters who flooded into the country hoping to witness a repeat of the 1971 series success.

Graham found the whole occasion stimulating, having coached the previous Lions team to Australia and finding himself up against Clive Woodward, who many believed should have had the job the previous time.

The Lions had a sample of what to expect in the test series when New Zealand Maori knocked them over in Hamilton. And playing an international in Christchurch slap-bang in the middle of winter, they should have known what was coming in terms of the weather. Conditions at Jade Stadium deteriorated shortly after the evening kick-off to the point they were shocking — cold southerly, rain and sleet. Not that British players don't know about those conditions, but it wasn't what coach Woodward was wanting for his team which was geared to take on the All Blacks with an open, attacking game.

The series produced the most controversial opening imaginable with the Lions skipper Brian O'Driscoll being dumped to the turf in the double tackle of Tana Umaga and Keven Mealamu in the second minute. The incident — which caused outrage from the British management and media and which was still being talked about years later — put O'Driscoll out of the match and out of the series.

The fallout from the incident would impact on Umaga for years to come. It even brought death threats from Ireland.

The All Blacks handled the conditions better than the Lions and won 21–3.

Whoever designed Jade Stadium had obviously never functioned as a coach, installing the coaches' box high up in the main grandstand. To access it after preparing their team in the dressing room on the ground floor, Ted, Smithy and Shag first had to take the elevator, which was agonisingly slow and could take two or three minutes to arrive. It conveyed them to the top floor from where they had to make their way through a crowded restaurant/bar to their box.

Aware of this challenge, the trio exited their dressing room a couple of minutes earlier than they normally would have, after delivering their half-time instructions to the players.

As they were advancing towards the elevator, which, blessedly on this occasion, was already on the ground floor with doors open, Smith suddenly spotted Clive Woodward and his fellow coaches departing their dressing room. They faced an identical challenge to access their viewing box upstairs.

'Come on,' said Smith, 'quick, get to the lift.'

Ted and Shag couldn't understand the need for such indecent haste. But once the doors closed and the elevator began ascending, Smith displayed a broad grin.

'Didn't you see who was coming up behind us?'

'No. Who?'

'Clive Woodward and his mates. Won't do them any harm to wait downstairs for a while!'

If waiting for the lift while the second half restarted in Christchurch peeved Woodward, it was nothing to the anguish he suffered in Wellington the following Saturday when, in perfect conditions this time, Carter produced one of rugby's greatest virtuoso performances.

Scoring 33 points himself, he guided the All Blacks to a crushing 48–18 victory. In the more than 100-year history of All Black test matches there can surely never have been a more complete performance by any individual.

Graham looked on in bewilderment. He had long admired Carter's talent but what blew him away in Wellington was the breadth of his skills. He not only directed operations gloriously from fly-half, he made scorching breaks, he scored tries, his tactical kicking was astute, he goal-kicked with deadly accuracy, and he tackled fearlessly.

Chris Foy, writing in the UK *Daily Mail*, beautifully captured the occasion:

On 2 July, the world realized just how good he could be the night Dan Carter elevated the artistry and ferocity of supreme fly-half play to a new dimension.

It was once said of Nick Faldo that he conquered golf; well, against the Lions in Wellington, Carter seemed to conquer rugby. The majesty of the performance was astonishing. It defied belief at times. Two years after his international debut, he touched the stars.

Gareth Thomas gave Sir Clive Woodward's team an early lead but then the All Black's Perfect 10 reduced them to rubble. He registered two tries, five penalty goals and four conversions for a 33-point personal haul which smashed the previous record of 18 by a New Zealander against the Lions.

There was an added poignancy to Carter's tour de force, as it came in the only match where he has faced Jonny Wilkinson directly, England's World Cup winning hero. What happened in Wellington suggested a changing of the guard, a sense that Wilkinson's reign as sports global icon was at an end and that the country boy from Canterbury had emerged for the next generation.

One image captured the theme perfectly — Carter thrusting aside his rival and racing clear, leaving Wilkinson flat on the turf clutching at his vapour trail.

To Woodward's relief, Carter was forced out of the final test at Eden Park through injury, but it didn't stop the All Blacks. Even with a rookie at first-five, Luke McAlister, the All Blacks still won decisively, 38–19, to complete a comprehensive series whitewash in which the All Blacks scored 12 tries to the Lions' three.

The All Black coaches were delighted to win, obviously, but, with an eye to the future — two years out from the World Cup — they took special satisfaction from the number of young players who had stamped their mark on the series. Besides Carter, there were encouraging performances from Conrad Smith, Rico Gear, McAlister, Tony Woodcock and Sione Lauaki, who collectively had claimed only a meagre 10 test caps going into 2005.

Once the Lions series was done and dusted, it's fair to say pretty much all the planning and decisions taken by Ted and Shag and Smithy throughout the remainder of 2005 and through 2006 were motivated by how they would win the World Cup in France in 2007.

Maintaining the winning sequence was an important part of that, because the three coaches all knew from painful experience that nothing caused best-laid plans to unravel quicker than losses on the field.

Which is why Graham was irritated when the All Blacks crashed to defeat at Cape Town in the opening game of the 2005 Tri-Nations campaign. The teams scored one try apiece, but penalty goals got the Springboks home 22–16.

Graham was particularly frustrated with the refereeing performance that day by the Australian Andrew Cole. Statistics reveal that the Springboks made four line and 10 tackle breaks compared with the All Blacks' 18 line and 18 tackle breaks. The Boks attempted 121 tackles, missing 35, while the All Blacks attempted 79 tackles, missing 17. Those stats confirm the All Blacks controlled all aspects of the game apart from the scoreboard.

An almost identical scenario would unfold 12 months on when the All Blacks lost to the Springboks 20–21 in Rustenburg, but this time the statistics were even more in the All Blacks' favour. At Rustenburg, the Springboks would make four line and four tackle breaks against the All Blacks' 15 line and 11 tackle breaks. The Boks attempted 169 tackles and missed 42, the All Blacks 109 and missed 14.

Statistics of that nature almost invariably result in victory to the team that does vastly more attacking, but at Rustenburg, on a challenging narrow field, English referee Chris White influenced the outcome by disallowing a classic try by Rodney So'oialo beside the posts, claiming interference to the South African defence. Graham replayed the incident many times and to this day cannot understand how the try was disallowed. He still sees it as a perfectly legitimate score.

Anyway, the Cape Town and Rustenburg experiences prompted Graham to confront IRB referees boss Paddy O'Brien the next time their paths crossed. He posed one question.

'Why do referees have trouble refereeing down the middle in South Africa more than anywhere else?' he asked him.

Paddy didn't supply an answer. Instead, he asked: 'Are you sure it's not just your perception based on disappointment when your team loses?'

Graham replied: 'You analyse the statistics of the Cape Town and Rustenburg games and explain to me how the All Blacks lost.'

Graham has several theories about referees, one of which is that most of them are 'homers', i.e. they are sympathetic to the home team. Statistics reveal that England is penalized an average of seven times when it plays at Twickenham but 14 times when it plays away. Referees seem to have a subconscious bent towards the home team.

In the UK and France, France particularly, there exists a pronounced home-and-away mentality, with teams believing it is harder to win away fixtures. In Graham's opinion, this shouldn't be the case but invariably the referee is a factor, meaning teams playing away have to lift themselves 10, 15 or 20 per cent to counteract the refereeing factor. This, Graham considers — and all serious rugby pundits would surely agree — shouldn't be so. It is a subject he is prepared to discuss with considerable passion.

The refereeing frustrations of 2005 and 2006 would be but a minor hiccup, though, compared with what would unfold at the World Cup in 2007, where the venues were nowhere near South Africa. But that's another chapter!

The Cape Town and Rustenburg games would be the only setbacks for the All Blacks throughout those two years: they played 25 games and recorded 23 victories, adding a Grand Slam and two Tri-Nations successes to the epic series win over the Lions. Their average winning score was 34–15. They were the No. 1 team in the world, by some margin.

They weren't afraid to be innovative, sometimes with amusing results.

Against the Wallabies at Eden Park in 2005, the All Blacks were awarded a penalty deep in Australian territory. With the scores reasonably close, a kick for goal was a sensible option.

But Smith had been introducing some of his Northampton concepts to the players at training, including a rather daring kick pass across field. Part of the strategy of kick passes was to force the enemy to keep their shape.

Out of nowhere, big Ali Williams initiated a quick tap before kicking the ball across field, bringing gasps from the crowd and one particular coach.

'Smithy, what the f— are you teaching these guys?' Graham bawled out, putting his hands to his head.

Next thing, winger Doug Howlett plucked the ball out of the sky and dived across in the corner, completing one of the most audacious tries ever witnessed at Eden Park.

'You bloody beaut!' shouted Graham, suddenly rising to his feet.

'Enjoyed it then, did you?' asked Smithy.

'Hmmm!'

Graham and his fellow selectors remained faithful to the same set of players throughout the 2005 Tri-Nations Championship, but when they embarked on their end-of-year tour, they went overboard on rotation. Well, Ted and Shag and Smithy didn't refer to it as rotation — they simply believed they were building their team for the future.

They took 35 players on tour and in an unprecedented display of bravado — demonstrating immense faith in their players — they fielded two completely different XVs against Wales in Cardiff and Ireland in Dublin, seven days apart.

Only the All Blacks would have the temerity to attempt this and only the All Blacks would have the depth of talent to pull it off.

While critics back home condemned Graham's 'rotation' policy, with some arguing that what he and his selectors were doing devalued the All Black jersey, Henry's men breezed through both games, winning 41–3 in Cardiff and 45–7 in Dublin, scoring five tries in each match.

Tana Umaga was captain against Wales while Richie McCaw was in charge against Ireland. Dan Carter did the goal-kicking in Cardiff and Nick Evans in Dublin. Four of the five players not selected in either starting line-up came on as reserves, with only 19-year-old Isaia Toeava missing out on any action.

Since strict guidelines concerning behaviour and drinking had been instituted following the mock court session saga in Johannesburg in late 2004, the All Blacks' behaviour had been impeccable. But a handful of players were guilty of misconduct immediately following the team's arrival in the UK in 2005.

Once they had settled into their accommodation in Cardiff, the players realized they were still eight days out from the opening match. Management conceded that a couple of beers would be a good way to help beat jet lag.

Problem was, a group of players decided the best place to have these beers was in London, in company with their old mate Andrew Mehrtens, whereupon they jumped on a fast train, determined to join him. After they'd been journeying three-quarters of an hour or so, it dawned on them London wasn't the next village. So they decided to return and have a couple more drinks in Cardiff. UK geography obviously wasn't their strong suit!

Had their socializing been conducted privately, they might have got away with it. But the UK media find All Blacks irresistible, especially when they're in the company of beautiful women, and when photos of their shenanigans appeared on the girls' social media sites, and finished up in newspapers the following day, their cover was blown.

They were dealt with in-house, management ruling they had made a bad decision. It was not a major, but their behaviour had contravened the team's strict guidelines. It certainly added spice to the training sessions leading up to the Welsh international ... and as a consequence the team played superbly. There is always a silver lining!

The All Blacks hadn't achieved a Grand Slam in the UK in a quarter of a century, not since Jack Gleeson's team captained by Graham Mourie completed the feat in farcical near pitch-black conditions against Scotland at Murrayfield in 1978. Many of those present were blissfully unaware of who had scored the All Blacks' winning try (it was actually Bruce Robertson).

Graham and his fellow managers placed no emphasis on the Grand Slam aspect of the tour whatsoever. They just concentrated on each test, the one-game-at-a-time philosophy. Once Wales and Ireland were out of the way, they had to confront England at a Twickenham that was being rebuilt (and which housed only 60,000 instead of the usual 80,000).

For the first time on tour, skipper Umaga and his heir apparent, McCaw, took the field together. It was close to the team's strongest line-up and, notwithstanding the sometimes eccentric refereeing of Irishman Alan Lewis, who in the final 24 minutes dispatched three All Blacks (Tony Woodcock, Neemiah Tialata and Chris Masoe) to the sin bin, the tourists preserved their unbeaten record, getting home 23–19.

The R word reared its ugly head again when a dozen changes were made for the Scotland test, but it didn't prevent the All Blacks comfortably rounding out their Grand Slam. As in 1978, the weather was cold and gloomy, but floodlights this time allowed everyone present to follow the second-half action and go home aware the All Blacks had indeed won 29–10.

When Graham was growing up, the Springboks were the ultimate rugby foe for New Zealanders — hell, it wasn't until 1956, after 35 years of combat, that the All Blacks finally won a series against them, while the Wallabies were never good enough to get their hands on the Bledisloe Cup — and he still regards the South Africans as the team to beat. He has enormous regard for them as a rugby nation.

A tradition has developed since Graham became the All Black coach that after internationals between the two nations in New Zealand, the South African players are invited into the All Black dressing room where they share drinks, food and conversation.

Graham found he related well to Jake White, who coached the Boks through until the World Cup in 2007, and his successor Peter de Villiers and enjoyed discussions with them immensely. He also had great admiration for John Smit, the Springboks' most-capped forward who captained his country in 64 test matches, Victor Matfield and the rest of the South African players.

The South Africans are thoroughly nice gentlemen and always call Graham 'Mr Henry'. He always reminds them his name is Graham.

What invariably happens is that the halfbacks pair off, the front rowers get together, the wingers chat with each other, and so on. The camaraderie between opponents is one of the endearing qualities of rugby, a delightful hangover from the amateur days. Fraternities enjoying each other's company is special to the game.

It was in that spirit, especially seeing what had developed with the Springboks, that the All Blacks thought it would be appropriate to invite the Wallabies into the All Black dressing room after Tri-Nations fixtures.

But to their surprise, they rejected the invitation. Thanks, but no, we're OK looking after ourselves.

It's an additional component that makes the Bledisloe Cup the trophy the All Blacks most want to win each season, more than the Tri-Nations. Graham can understand why today's rugby players rate Australia so highly and have a greater desire to beat them, even more than South Africa. Until the All Blacks evened the ledger in 2011, Australia had claimed two World Cups to New Zealand's one and, for a long period in the late 1980s and early 1990s, they'd controlled Bledisloe Cup contests; it was also the Brumbies who had ended the Blues and Crusaders' domination of Super rugby. On top of all that there's now the Robbie Deans factor. A lot of Graham's All Blacks played for Deans's Red and Black teams and don't want to bow to him now that he's crossed The Ditch.

Sadly for Graham, Tana Umaga announced his retirement from international rugby in January 2006, believing his mind and body would not survive two more seasons through to the World Cup. He wanted to spend more time with his family, especially as his wife, Rochelle, was pregnant again.

Graham dearly wanted Umaga to hang in until the World Cup, convinced he still had much to offer. He was prepared to lessen his workload or even give him 12 months' leave, but Umaga wasn't prepared to compromise. It was all or nothing. At 32, he had decided it was time to step down.

Richie McCaw was about to be invested as All Black captain.

With McCaw at the helm, the All Blacks would sweep through 2006, losing just the one contest, to the Springboks at Rustenburg.

The referee and the team's accommodation might have had a bit to do with that.

Rustenburg, prominent in Afrikaner history — it's where South African president Paul Kruger grew up — was famous for its citrus orchards, until vast platinum deposits were discovered. Now it's essentially a mining city, not a place tourists choose to stay at. So the South African Rugby Board probably thought it was doing the All Blacks a favour by accommodating them about 40 km away at the lavish resort of Sun City. The Springboks were also quartered there.

Sun City, created in 1979 as a retreat for the whites during the apartheid era and originally part of the independent state of Bophuthatswana, is to South Africa what Las Vegas is to the United States, albeit on a much smaller scale and with a lot fewer casinos.

It features four glitzy hotels, two international-quality golf courses, a cluster of spas and gyms, and endless shows. It's a fabulous place to visit if you are holidaying in South Africa, not least because the sun never seems to stop shining. But because of the distractions, it's entirely inappropriate for a rugby team preparing for an important international fixture.

Funnily enough, the game wasn't important in the context of the Tri-Nations championship, which the All Blacks had in the bag after successive victories in Christchurch, Wellington, Brisbane, Auckland and Pretoria, and perhaps this was why several players decided to let off steam at Sun City. However, the game did afford the All Blacks the opportunity to match South Africa's winning sequence of 16 tests.

Well, thanks to referee White ruling out So'oialo's try combined with the goal-kicking skills of André Pretorius, who landed the winning goal with two minutes remaining, the All Blacks went down 20–21.

Graham was grumpy, as he always was after a loss, and his humour didn't improve when a considerable number of the players hit the grog back at Sun City. It was Johannesburg 2004 revisited, and management personally found it hugely disappointing after the guidelines for acceptable behaviour had been spelt out and, Graham believed, accepted. More than a few of the touring party failed to respect the All Black jersey at Sun City.

John Smit recounts in his biography *Captain in the Cauldron* how in walking down the path from the bar to the main casino a group of Springboks came across a distinguished All Black in the bushes, much the worse for wear. The Boks helped him up and escorted him to the casino.

Obviously, there were still lessons to be learnt regarding acceptable drinking behaviour. That was something for everyone to work on.

But in terms of on-field results, 12 months out from the World Cup, there was plenty to be excited about, given the team's achievements in 2006. And there was more to come on the end-of-year tour of Europe where the All Blacks swept aside England 41–20, recording the highest score ever against England at Twickenham, France 47–3 in Lyon and 23–11 in Paris, and Wales 45–10.

In those four internationals, the team scored 18 tries while conceding only five. Dan Carter embellished his reputation and test aggregate by scoring 72 points — 26 against England, 17 against France at Lyon and 13 at Paris, and 16 against Wales.

The coaches persisted with the so-called rotation policy, with only Carter, McCaw and Carl Hayman starting in all four games. Graham considered it an eminently sensible policy because it gave all 32 players a share of the action and an opportunity to improve their standards — and it could hardly be said, given the results, the switching of combinations diminished the team's potency.

It's pertinent at this juncture to mull over the All Blacks' total domination of the French. They'd whipped them 45–6 in 2004 and this time overwhelmed them 70 points to 14 in the two contests. Seven months later, Henry's men would overrun them again, 42–11 and 61–10, in New Zealand. In these five matches the All Blacks would score 28 tries against France's three. This was obviously one opponent the All Blacks wouldn't have to worry about at the World Cup in 2007, should they engage them. Time for another Tui billboard: Yeah right!

In his report to the NZRU, Graham said the All Blacks' objective had been to play a style of game the players enjoyed and the opposition found difficult to compete with. 'Fundamentally, it is about the All Blacks controlling both the set piece and the advantage line and contact at this point. To implement this game plan effectively, the players need to be "explosive" athletes, i.e. both powerful and fast.'

Graham said 2006 saw the appointed leadership group of 2004 replaced by an elected group whose role was 'to lead by example by both exhibiting and encouraging others to live by a set of behaviours agreed by the group'. He said Gilbert Enoka's ground-breaking work in this area was pivotal to the success of the team, and Sir Brian Lochore's experience and wise counsel to individuals was invaluable.

9

Train crash at Cardiff

When a nation like New Zealand hasn't won the Webb Ellis Cup in 19 years, and its arch rival Australia has taken out the sport's supreme trophy twice, everyone from the coaches and national administrators to media and fans are prone to become more than a tad obsessive about it.

The more so when your national team, the All Blacks, have dominated the international scene for three years, winning every trophy available while comfortably swatting aside all the opponents who might be considered contenders for the title.

Since Graham had taken charge, the All Blacks had fashioned an awesome record, winning tests against England 4–0, Wales 3–0, Ireland 3–0, France 3–0, Australia 6–1 and South Africa, traditionally New Zealand's most formidable rival, 4–3 (with those three losses occurring in South Africa).

In gambling terms, the All Blacks appeared a lay-down misère to claim the sport's premier trophy in Paris in October.

But Ted and Shag and Smithy weren't taking anything for granted. They were all too aware of what had happened to Laurie Mains's team at Ellis Park in 1995, to John Hart's team at Twickenham in 1999, and to John Mitchell's team at Sydney's Telstra Stadium in 2003, and they didn't want it happening to them. They were determined to present the best-prepared All Black World Cup team ever.

Which is where that obsession thing began to intrude. To ensure the All Blacks would be in peak physical condition when they fronted at the World Cup in France in October, they introduced a conditioning window, which caused much controversy because it meant 22 of the country's finest players — including the superstars like Dan Carter, Richie McCaw, Mils Muliaina, Sitiveni Sivivatu and Doug Howlett — would not be eligible to play in the opening seven rounds of the Super 14.

The need for the conditioning window was so players could recover from the rigours of their professional code and participate in programmes to get better, faster, fitter and stronger.

The argument was promoted that if the All Blacks participated in the Super 14 competition, they would have only three weeks in January and five weeks prior to the World Cup to condition themselves.

It was calculated that without a conditioning programme, the All Blacks would be required to play 18 test matches and 13 to 15 Super 14 games, plus Super 14 warm-up fixtures, in the 12-month period from the beginning of November 2006 to the end of October 2007. This equated to between 33 and 36 games, which would have been the highest game load leading New Zealand players would ever have been exposed to.

The All Blacks hadn't completed their European tour until 25 November and if they were to peak for the World Cup in September 2007, the All Black fitness experts regarded it as imperative that the leading players did not resume competitive play until the end of March.

Ted and Shag and Smithy first had to 'sell' their concept to the NZRU board members, who were not overly enthusiastic, it has to be said, because they were committed to Rupert Murdoch's News Corporation to make available the best-quality players for his worldwide television audience.

However, the board was also committed to winning the World Cup and after digesting the All Black management's powerful arguments for resting 22 key players, they approved the conditioning window.

It was an extremely touchy issue and News Corp. conveyed the worrying message to the NZRU that if, after monitoring ratings and advertising revenues while the leading All Black stars were sidelined, it could be shown that these had decreased, then News Corp. would claim against SANZAR.

At a SANZAR meeting in Dublin, the Australian Rugby Union stated its belief that New Zealand's conditioning programme was damaging the competition while the South African representative Mpumelelo Tshume expressed his concerns about the process being followed by New Zealand.

Not only did Ted and Shag and Smithy have to convince the NZRU of the importance of the conditioning window, they also had to win over the Super 14 franchises, which led to some spirited discussions with the Super 14 coaches.

Although the All Black management ultimately received green lights from the Blues, the Chiefs, the Hurricanes, the Crusaders and the Highlanders, they recognized the backing was superficial. The franchises wanted their celebrity players, there was no doubt about that, but they were prepared to make the extreme sacrifice if it meant winning the World Cup. However, it invoked a negativity that wasn't in the greater interests of New Zealand rugby.

And their support came at a cost, with the NZRU agreeing to compensate the franchises financially if the net revenue from home matches in the first seven rounds of the Super 14 competition fell below NZRU-approved forecasts.

A survey conducted by Colmar Brunton about how the conditioning programme would impact on the willingness of fans to follow the competition revealed that 70 per cent of fans would follow it just as closely as in previous years while 21 per cent said they would not follow it as closely.

In anticipation of a drop-off in crowd numbers, the NZRU marketing department launched a number of initiatives, including third-party ticket giveaways, franchise cap promotions, and season-ticket-member breakfasts.

Graham concedes now that the decision to take the 22 best players out of Super 14 was wrong, because it was driven by the All Black management, not the players. Some of the 22, Jerry Collins foremost among them, plainly resented the fact they could not play and condition themselves at the same time. The management had created something it didn't need.

Graham admits, in hindsight, the issue should have been discussed more with the players. At the end of the day, the management needed to get the total support of the stakeholders, but that didn't eventuate, and it backfired on them.

The better way, the procedure that would apply in 2011, was a gentlemen's agreement between Super 15 coaches and All Black management as to how much rugby was appropriate for individual players.

A huge amount of time went into the fitness planning in 2007. It was done for the right reasons: with the intention of having the All Blacks at a peak of fitness when they arrived in France in September 2007. And indeed they were super fit when they set foot in Marseilles for their World Cup opener against Italy — but unfortunately it didn't produce the right results.

The meticulous planning even extended to simulating World Cup happenings while the team was touring Europe in November 2006. Ahead of the international in Lyon, the team stayed a couple of nights at the hotel in Marseilles that had been allotted to them for the World Cup. They visited Aix en Provence, where they would train during the World Cup and checked out as many match and practice venues as possible.

With the All Black stars missing for effectively half the campaign, no New Zealand team reached the final of the 2007 Super 15 competition, for the first time since 2001. The all-South African final was fought out between the Bulls and the Stormers (and won, dramatically after the final siren, by the Bulls).

The All Blacks then romped to huge victories over France and Canada in the domestic international series before claiming their third successive Tri-Nations title. This third title was not without a hiccup, though, as the team lost to the Wallabies in Melbourne on the way back home from Durban.

Jet lag and an erratic refereeing performance from Marius Jonker led to a 15–20 loss in Melbourne but the All Blacks rebounded impressively, demolishing the Springboks 33–6 in Christchurch before

Graham still regards the Springboks as the All Blacks' greatest foe. Here he chats with Peter de Villiers at a parliamentary reception in Wellington. *RUGBYIMAGES*

Dan Carter was a critical component of the backline throughout Graham's term as head coach and became one of the on-field leaders. Here he demonstrates his silky skills against France. *TRANZ / ACTION IMAGES*

The era of the computer-age coach: Wayne Smith and Graham make sure things are happening against England at Twickenham in 2005. They must have been — their team won 23–19. *Tranz / Action Images*

Despite the smiles, it was a sad moment when Tana Umaga as the All Black captain in January 2006 announced his retirement from international rugby. *Tranz / Action Images*

Cripes, no wonder the All Blacks struggled in their quarter-final against France at the 2007 World Cup. This shot of Graham and his skip was taken at a press conference *before* the game. TRANZ / ACTION IMAGES

The same pair reflect how every New Zealand supporter felt after the devastating loss to France in Cardiff. Fronting the press conference afterwards wasn't easy. PHOTOSPORT

A satisfied cluster of All Blacks after winning back the Gallaher Trophy from France at Marseilles in 2009. From left, Jerome Kaino, Anthony Boric, Conrad Smith, Tom Donnelly. *RUGBYIMAGES*

Graham enjoys the moment with Mils Muliaina, who would go on to record 100 appearances for the All Blacks. *RUGBYIMAGES*

A winning All Black team is great for the morale of the country. No wonder Prime Minister John Key is smiling. *RugbyImages*

Mental skills coach Gilbert Enoka, centre, checks procedures with Steve Hansen and Graham prior to an All Black test match. *Tranz / Action Images*

For the All Blacks, the Bledisloe Cup rates second only to the Webb Ellis Cup, so retaining it throughout Graham's reign as All Black head coach brought immense satisfaction. The players show their delight at beating the Wallabies 30–14 at Eden Park in 2011. *RugbyImages*

This may come as a surprise to some, but Graham used to operate as an accomplished first-five at senior club level. The technique survives! *TRANZ / ACTION IMAGES*

despatching a virtually unchanged Aussie team 26–12 at Eden Park, thanks to seven penalty goals from Dan Carter.

Different nations chose to protect their leading players in different ways ahead of the World Cup. While the South Africans had placed no restrictions on participation in the Super 14 — Bryan Habana, for instance, who would star at the World Cup, appeared in 14 of the Bulls' 15 matches — they despatched what was effectively a South African B team to Sydney and Christchurch for the last two Tri-Nations fixtures, losing both games to finish bottom of the competition.

And so, late in August 2007, the All Blacks flew out of Auckland bound for France and a World Cup campaign for which they were the raging hot favourites. And why wouldn't they be, having won 39 of the 44 matches they'd played since the previous World Cup in Sydney four years back?

Around the time the All Blacks were settling in at Marseilles to prepare for their 2007 World Cup opener against Italy, David Kirk, famous for captaining the All Blacks to glory in the inaugural tournament in 1987, had an article published in the London *Daily Telegraph*.

It's unlikely any of the All Blacks read it, which is a shame. Indeed, being based in France, it's unlikely they were reading any newspapers at all in the days leading up to the tournament.

Here's an abbreviated version of what Kirk wrote:

The All Blacks are once again red-hot favourites to win the World Cup. It seems that the only thing that gives other nations and bookies comfort is history.

New Zealand has indeed only won one World Cup. And that was the tournament in which the All Blacks did not start firm favourites. So, the logic goes, just because they are the best team does not mean they will win.

Look what happened in London, Johannesburg, Cardiff and Sydney. Bummed out, choked, didn't perform when it really mattered. The same will happen this time.

In 2007, the results support All Black favouritism, but what could stop them? Let's run through a few options: weather, injuries, playing away from home, referees and self-doubt.

All teams need to adapt to referee interpretations as matches unfold. A failure to read a referee and adjust could be the difference between winning and losing.

The All Blacks will be refereed more tightly than any other team, just because they are the All Blacks.

Hmmm, prophetic words!

Tradition dictates that at World Cup tournaments the host nation shall play the opening encounter. And so it was in 2007 that the French, who had won the Six Nations Championship back in March before being hammered by the All Blacks in their tour Down Under, opened rugby's greatest showcase with a match against the Argentinian Pumas.

The Pumas had been regular underachievers at World Cup events, except in 1999 when a certain gruff Kiwi named Alex Wyllie got them through to the quarter-finals courtesy of a shock win over Ireland.

They weren't expected to stay with the French, not in Paris, not against the World Cup hosts. Well, that was the theory, but the Pumas were no respecters of ceremony, scoring the only try and winning 17–12.

The result left the French fans, not to mention the French administrators, for whom the result bore serious repercussions, stunned. Financially, the result represented a horrendous blow to the host nation.

The tournament draw had been designed to have the French play their quarter-final in Paris. But after the Pumas gate-crashed the party, they were now positioned to take that slot.

There was a danger, with Ireland also in the pool, that the French could miss the play-offs altogether. Or by finishing second (which is what happened), they would have to journey to Cardiff for their quarter-final, leaving the Pumas to take on an opponent like Scotland in Paris. Those two teams weren't going to fill the Stade de France! *Quelle horreur!*

The outcome of the opening match also had huge significance for the All Blacks, because when they'd departed New Zealand, they had expected their quarter-final opponent would be Ireland, a team that in 102 years of rivalry had never beaten them. Now it seemed that if they progressed satisfactorily to the quarter-finals they would be engaging France — and this was an entirely different scenario, as the French had a nasty habit of reserving their best for contests against the All Blacks, who they had beaten on several occasions.

These unusual goings-on had no influence on events over the first month of the tournament as the All Blacks waltzed through pool play, beating Italy 76–14, Portugal 108–13, Scotland 40–nil (in a bizarre contest in which it was almost impossible to tell the two teams apart, with both wearing alternate strips), and Romania 85–8.

If scoring 46 tries while conceding four represented four pretty good days at the office for Graham's men, the All Black coaches weren't getting carried away: they knew there were much tougher opponents ahead. None of their pool opponents had extended them.

It is easy for complacency to set in when games are being won with ridiculous ease. It was something Ted and Shag and Smithy had to guard against as they headed for Millennium Stadium in Cardiff and an appointment with France.

Ted and Shag were in familiar territory. To them, a quarter-final at Millennium Stadium felt like a home game, although they knew the All Blacks wouldn't perceive it that way.

Everything seemed to be unfolding satisfactorily, apart from the fact the opponent they were preparing for was France, not Ireland.

There were several issues regarding the preparation that, in hindsight, they might have handled differently. For example, in discussion with the leadership group midweek, the question was raised whether the team needed what was known as an emotional button. These took various forms, and ahead of previous contests against France, in France, the coaches had focused on Dave Gallaher, the 1905 Originals captain who had lost his life at Passchendaele fighting for his country. Far too many young men from New Zealand had been sacrificed in the two world wars, many of them on French soil, and this point was always reinforced, with the All Blacks playing for these men. Another 'button' the management had used was film of the French beating New Zealand in the World Cup semi-finals in 1999 before demonstrating a lack of respect for the haka by performing a 'Mickey Mouse' haka in their post-match celebrations.

The feeling expressed in Cardiff was that on this occasion the team didn't need an emotional button. They were on target. *Let's just get on with the game.*

Then along came an IRB official who explained that for logistical purposes he required the All Blacks to pack their training gear on the Friday for despatch to Paris, their expected next destination. Graham was reluctant to allow this to happen because he believed you should never get ahead of yourself.

'I should have said no, we're not sending anything to Paris — wait till we win,' he lamented later, 'but they were pressuring us, for logistical reasons, and we felt obliged to go along with it.'

Another possible distraction involved some of the player agents discussing All Black futures. Several individuals who were coming off contract, Carl Hayman, Byron Kelleher, Luke McAlister, Jerry Collins, Anton Oliver, Nick Evans and Aaron Mauger (who wasn't involved in the quarter-final) were, or had been, in negotiations with European clubs and may have been thinking about life after the World Cup, an obvious distraction.

In the wash-up, the fact that these individuals were not contracted to the NZRU post-World Cup was identified as a possible reason the All Blacks might not have performed to their full potential in the quarter-final.

By the time the All Blacks ran on to the Millennium Stadium, they knew that England had sensationally upset Australia in Marseilles by 12 points to 10. It meant the team they regarded as probably their greatest threat was out of the tournament. Now all they had to do was beat France!

Ted and Shag and Smithy preferred to follow matches from the sanctity of a coaches' box, where they could converse in private if necessary and deliver instructions to their operational team downstairs without worrying about who might be within earshot.

But at the Millennium Stadium for this World Cup fixture, the three of them found themselves occupying grandstand seats, surrounded by the public. Great view, but less than ideal positioning. As the game unfolded, particularly when the All Blacks were trailing in the second half, Graham was aware people were yelling at them, but he was so focused, he had no idea what they were saying.

The result everyone considered a formality appeared to be unfolding according to plan as the All Blacks established a 13–nil advantage after 30 minutes through a cracking try by Luke McAlister and two penalty goals and a conversion by Dan Carter.

The French were playing with resolve but didn't seem capable of containing the All Blacks, although they managed to pull back a penalty goal before half-time.

The second half belonged, unquestionably, to referee Wayne Barnes. In the fifth minute he showed McAlister a yellow card, for blocking kick-chaser Yannick Jauzion, a questionable ruling. The penalty gave France another three points.

While McAlister was a spectator, Thierry Dusautoir scored a try, converted by Lionel Beauxis; that levelled the scores.

New Zealand, now desperate, especially as Carter and his replacement Nick Evans had both departed the field injured, regained the lead through a try by Rodney So'oialo but in the 68th minute when referee Barnes and his touch judges missed the most blatant of forward passes, Jauzion scored for Jean-Baptiste Élissalde to convert and give France a 20–18 lead.

Although the final 10 or 11 minutes were fought out deep in French territory, with no penalties forthcoming despite the defenders repeatedly throwing themselves into the breakdown to stifle All Black momentum, France held on for the most unlikely of victories. Host nation France was through to the semi-final.

The word had gone down from the coaches to organize a drop-kick but although a couple of fleeting opportunities presented themselves, McAlister, who'd been forced into first-five, left it until the dying moments when he was 45 metres out to attempt one. McAlister later claimed he only took the rushed kick from that near-impossible range because the referee had indicated he was playing a penalty advantage. McAlister's miss should have given the All Blacks a shot at goal; instead, Barnes promptly ruled the drop-kick represented New Zealand's advantage.

The All Blacks had dominated much of the game, enjoying an overwhelming 73 per cent territorial advantage, winning 166 rucks to France's 42 and making only 73 tackles compared with France's 331. But incredibly they had not been awarded a solitary penalty in the final 50 minutes; in fact, referee Barnes had penalized France only twice in the entire game. How was that possible?

In the near-50 test matches for which Ted and Shag and Smithy had prepared the All Blacks across four years, they had never experienced such a bizarre contest. All the key performance indicators were off the planet. They pointed to an All Black win by a substantial margin. But the boys were not winning.

The All Black coaches in the grandstand and skipper Richie McCaw and his fellow leaders in the middle knew the huge territorial advantage the All Blacks were maintaining, coupled with their dominance at rucks, would inevitably lead either to a try or a penalty within range of the goalposts. Their frame of reference had been built up over many years: maintain relentless pressure and eventually get rewarded. Except that, on this occasion, that wasn't happening.

Conversation had ceased among Ted and Shag and Smithy. In their anxiety, they had fallen quiet, trying to take in the magnitude of the situation unfolding in front of them. All their experience told them that the pressure being exerted by the All Blacks must produce points. But what had happened on dozens of other occasions wasn't happening this time. The game was going, going ... gone!

The referee's less than distinguished performance would come under close scrutiny later, but following his final whistle at the Millennium Stadium the only thing that mattered was the scoreboard: France 20, New Zealand 18.

The immediate realization was that the All Blacks had lost in the quarter-finals, their worst World Cup result ever. Two weeks out from the final in Paris, for which they were the hottest of hot favourites, they were heading home. What's the Kiwi equivalent of *quelle horreur*? Bugger, bugger, bugger!

Ted and Shag and Smithy were in a traumatized state. They were having immense difficulty digesting what had just unfolded in front of them. All that planning, all that hard work had just disappeared in a puff of smoke. It was absolute hell.

Intriguingly, because of the must-win status of the French game, the All Black management had prepared a 'What If?' chart ahead of the game. It read:

What if … the French resort to tactics of targeting people and use dirty intimidating tactics? Our response: Communicate it, as sometimes we are not aware of it on-field; make a plan; don't back down — do it together.

What if … on the way to the game, the bus breaks down and we have no police escort? Our response: Control the controllable; leaders lead; talk to the boys; refocus and readjust routines.

What if … they score a couple of tries early, hit us hard and really get up? Our response: Don't panic; don't change the way we play; composure a key; keep things simple, especially early in the game.

What if … at half-time we have not had any physical dominance and they are over us physically? Response: Ask why, find a solution and focus on tasks; identify what is not working; confidence to change once identified; talk and trust; PD in chase.

What if … we lose someone in the bin? Response: Next task; lots of communication; don't dwell on it, just make adjustments and be decisive; control what we can control.

All sensible, Boy Scout be-prepared stuff, but the one 'What If?' that wasn't anticipated was: What happens if we have a referee who gives us only two penalties in the game and none after the 30th minute?!

Deep down, Graham had a sense of outrage that his team had just been cheated of a place in the World Cup semi-finals. Something decidedly bizarre had unfolded in front of him, causing the best team in the world, his team, to be sawn off. If it had been an America's Cup yachting event, right at that moment he would have hoisted a red flag. But it was a rugby game. And in rugby, you accept the referee's decisions, you swallow your disappointment and you say nothing derogatory about anyone. Bounce of the ball, and all that… rugby's great traditions. The luck will fall your way next week. Except that, because of referee Barnes's performance, there would be no next week for the All Blacks. The French, the exemplary French who had committed only two offences serious enough for a penalty in 80 minutes, according to the referee — surely a world record for an international rugby team — were off to Paris and a place in the semi-finals while the All Blacks would be issued with flight tickets home.

The challenge right at that moment was not in comprehending what had unfolded at Millennium Stadium but in how to handle the defeat. Shattered though he was, Graham knew it was important for them all to emerge with dignity.

A deathly silence pervaded the All Black dressing room. At the Millennium Stadium, each player occupies an individual cubicle. Several All Blacks were sitting in theirs … facing the wall, stunned. They were as white as sheets, struggling to comprehend what had just unfolded. While Graham had huge respect for his players and the massive effort they had just put in without reward, he wondered how they were individually going to handle the days ahead. He knew they were going to go through hell. Graham's job was to decrease that degree of 'hell'. He would do that by encouraging the players to display dignity and pride, and walk out of that changing room with their heads up. It wouldn't be easy, but they had to make the best of a terrible situation.

Graham didn't say much at that time. What could he say that would make any difference? And if he said the wrong thing, it could make matters worse.

Every time he'd tasted defeat as All Black coach, Graham had gone to the winning team's dressing room to offer his congratulations. He hadn't had to do that too often — at Sydney and Johannesburg in 2004, at Cape Town in 2005, at Rustenburg in 2006 and at Melbourne earlier in 2007. Though sitting on a stool facing a blank wall like some of the All Blacks were doing had a certain appeal right at that moment, Graham resolved to go and congratulate the victors.

In contrast to the All Blacks, the French changing room was abuzz. They are a passionate people and, understandably, they were permitting those passions to overflow.

But as Graham entered their territory, manager Jo Maso summoned his players to be quiet. 'Thank you, Graham, for coming into our dressing room — we admire you for that.'

Graham kept his comments brief. 'I just want to congratulate you on your victory today. You played well and deserved the win. I wish you well for your semi-final next weekend.'

Graham's sporting gesture would be accorded wide publicity in France and while he appreciated that, he would much rather it had been because he was offering French coach Bernard Laporte his condolences rather than his congratulations.

One Frenchman, who appeared to be associated with the team in some capacity, shook Graham's hand and declared, 'We got away with murder today!'

'Good luck to you,' was all Graham could think to reply.

Manager Darren Shand was finding the All Black dressing room too depressing, so he decided to step outside for a little solitude. He wasn't needed in there, and the quiet of the corridor allowed him to reflect on the day's dramatic turn of events. His team's World Cup was over. There would be no journey to Paris, no semi-final, no …

His concentration was broken as he realized a group of about half a dozen serious-minded individuals were advancing towards the All Black dressing room.

Who could they be? he wondered.

Then he recognized one of them. When the All Blacks were in Toulouse for the pool match against Romania, management had arranged a sporting celebrities night and invited along some high achievers. Among them were Claudia Riegler, the Austrian-born New Zealand skier, and Antoine Dénériaz, the French alpine skier who'd won the gold medal in the downhill at the 2006 Winter Olympics at Turin.

Shandy made his way across to Dénériaz. 'Great to see you again,' he said. 'Who on earth are these people?'

'Well, that's President Nicolas Sarkozy,' replied Dénériaz, at which point the All Black manager was suddenly on full alert.

'Ah, welcome, gentlemen, I am the All Black manager — I'm delighted to welcome you to the All Black dressing room!'

The day's two preposterous results — England 12–10 over Australia, and France 20–18 over New Zealand — had turned the World Cup on its head. There were a lot of happy-looking northern hemisphere rugby individuals as Graham made his way to the press conference.

Graham had always found press conferences challenging immediately following important contests because he was always emotionally charged and often physically buggered, as he was on this occasion. For a rugby coach, it didn't get any more challenging than at the World Cup.

He always found it difficult to get in the right frame of mind and to collect his thoughts before he was being peppered with questions. Usually, he was being interviewed as the winning coach. That wasn't the situation on this occasion, and he just knew the line of questioning that would be coming his way.

Graham could blame the referee and make excuses, but he knew if he adopted a critical stance, blaming others and making excuses, it would only place further pressure on the All Blacks. And they were all going to cop enough criticism for not winning, as it was.

'We didn't play as well as we hoped we would,' he told the media, who were anticipating explosive utterances from the vanquished All Black coach. 'The French played better than we expected, the bounce of the ball didn't go our way and we failed to do the business. Good luck to France in the semi-finals.'

Graham wouldn't be drawn into anything remotely controversial. The media exited the conference hugely deflated. Graham exited it wanting to punch someone. But he kept his cool. It was the only way.

His experiences in Wales and on that difficult 2001 Lions tour had helped him through this most difficult of times. For his actions, essentially for visiting the French dressing room and for not bagging the referee, he would win the Pierre de Coubertin Trophy, awarded by the International Committee for Fair Play, an international non-government organization recognized by the United Nations and the International Olympic Committee.

When the All Blacks arrived back at their hotel, the Vale of Glamorgan, they were told to assemble in the team room. A crestfallen lot they were. Some were in tears. Most were struggling to take in the enormity of what had just happened. A team they had consistently swept aside by 40 and 50 points had just beaten them. Their World Cup dream was shattered. Graham knew he had to maintain standards and dignity and convert the worst situation imaginable into something manageable. It was an impossible situation, he knew, but the All Blacks had to demonstrate they could handle this.

'I'm helluva proud to have been associated with you,' he told them. 'You're a mighty group of young men. You've represented your country with distinction and great commitment and you've achieved some amazing results that have made you the best rugby team in the world.

'Today, we have suffered a defeat that has denied us our goal of winning the World Cup. While this is disappointing, we must not start apportioning blame. The game is over and nothing will change the result. Take it on the chin and move on. Be proud of who you are and what you have achieved. Continue to maintain the high standards of All Black rugby. There will be great days ahead for all of you, I know.'

Graham then moved through the group thanking those who were retiring from international rugby for what they had contributed to the All Blacks over the past several years and wishing them well in their future endeavours.

Besides his own shattered dream, Graham's sympathy went out to the thousands of All Black supporters, many of whom had just lobbed into Europe full of expectation. He related to them because his sons, Matthew and Andrew, were among them. God, what was he going to say to them?

That Saturday evening was one of the hardest Graham has ever had to bear. He sustained himself by extending condolences and encouragement to others. As a rugby coach, he had always hated losing. But this was more than a loss, he realized; it was, for New Zealand, a national calamity.

It seemed he hadn't slept more than a handful of minutes when his phone rang on the Sunday morning. It was Raewyn.

'How are you?' she asked.

'On a scale of ten, about one.'

'I would like you to know I still love you.'

'I'm pleased someone does.'

Raewyn was staying at the home of their Welsh netball colleague Lynne Evans, along with Matthew and Andrew.

'You can't do anything more at the hotel,' she said. 'Come and spend the day with Lynne and your family.'

'OK, I've got some media commitments this morning — I'll be there early afternoon. And I'll stay with you tonight.'

In normal circumstances, teams eliminated at the quarter-final stage of a World Cup would be checking out of their hotels the following day and heading home. But because the Rugby World Cup organizing committee officials had never, in their wildest dreams, contemplated the possibility of the All Blacks exiting before, at least, the semi-finals, they had not protected any flights from London through to New Zealand.

The earliest the travel agent could get any of them out, manager Darren Shand had been advised, was the Monday, and then only about three-quarters of them could go, on a flight that would put them into Christchurch. First priority would be given to those with families. The remainder were stuck in the UK for a further three days!

Lynne Evans had become almost part of the Henry family when Graham and Raewyn were in charge of the Welsh national rugby and netball teams. Social occasions at her place had always been special — plenty of wine and good food, plenty of laughter, plenty of good-natured ribbing.

But trying to crack hearty the day after you've lost a World Cup quarter-final was proving hugely challenging for Graham, for everyone really.

'Sorry, guys, I've let you down,' was his opening comment to his sons, Matthew and Andrew, who had a three-week World Cup package arranged that should have culminated in riotous celebrations at the Stade de France in Paris on the occasion of the grand final.

'There are no guarantees in World Cup knockout matches — we know that,' replied Matthew. 'Don't worry about us.'

Graham tried not to worry about them, but he wasn't doing a very good job of it. The atmosphere at Lynne's house was on a par with that in the All Black dressing room the evening before.

Evans recalls it as the worst day of her life, likening it to a funeral for multiple deaths. 'There was a lot of hugging going on, and tears — it was a terrible experience. What can you do at a time like that?'

What could possibly bring Graham out of his stupor? Even make him laugh? How about a likely lad by the name of Hamish Read? Hamish, Wellington-reared and Christchurch-educated — at Christ's College, like his father — happened to be the partner of Graham's daughter, Catherine.

Unlike Matthew and Andrew, who'd just lobbed into town, Hamish and Catherine had been holidaying in Europe for a couple of weeks and had co-ordinated their plans, not unnaturally, to be where the All Blacks were for the crunch knockout matches of the World Cup.

They weren't quite as traumatized as everyone else, therefore, because their travel plans weren't set in concrete and all they were going to miss out on was seeing Graham's men in black participating from here on in.

They made the best of an agonisingly difficult day. When Graham, at an indecently early hour, declared he was heading upstairs to bed because he was absolutely shattered, Hamish, without anyone else noticing, followed him up the stairs.

Graham was surprised to find him at the bedroom door.

'Can I have a talk with you, Graham?' asked Hamish.

Hamish had seemed a bit on edge, Graham had thought, which seemed entirely understandable given the events of the past 24 hours.

'Certainly,' said Graham, now curious.

'Well, I'm in love with your daughter, Catherine, and I want to marry her. I'm asking for your blessing.'

Not only did Graham grant his blessing, he almost kissed his future son-in-law! An element of reality had miraculously brightened what until that moment had probably ranked as the most forgettable weekend of his life.

'You most certainly have my blessing,' said Graham. 'I'm delighted for the pair of you. What are your plans from here?'

'Well, actually,' said Hamish, who was studying to be a doctor, 'there's a touch of irony here, because it's my intention to propose to Catherine in Paris. And no rugby result is going to stop that!'

For the first time since Barnes had signalled full time at the Millennium Stadium, Graham laughed. A day that had been so morose had come marvellously to life. It was a timely reminder that there is life aside from rugby.

'Come on, let's go and have a celebratory drink.'

'But I don't want Catherine knowing what's going on.'

'Mum's the word.'

The others were surprised when Graham, who five minutes earlier had departed looking like a walking corpse, suddenly reappeared, smiling, and announced he was having one more wine.

'What's going on?' someone asked.

'Hamish has reminded me, because we're flying home tomorrow, we won't have the opportunity to share a drink with them in Paris. So we're going to share that wine now.'

'Wonderful,' said Raewyn. 'Wonderful,' said Catherine. 'Wonderful,' said Lynne. And wonderful it was.

Graham, accompanied by Raewyn, flew out on the Monday, finally touching down in Christchurch where several thousand people were on hand to greet the team, and that heartened him. The tone was sympathetic, not antagonistic which, given the circumstances, would have been entirely understandable. A lot of people shook his hand and wished him well. No-one spoke critically.

On the long flight through from London, Graham had permitted himself a few moments of reflection. He was realistic enough to know there wasn't a great future for All Black coaches who'd bombed out of World Cups. Not one had survived. As far as he was concerned, his All Black career was over. He'd get his report written for the NZRU and get on with life.

He'd been the International Rugby Board's Coach of the Year in 2005 and 2006. The hat trick had eluded him. Whoever wins it this year, he mused, it won't be G. Henry (New Zealand).

Obliged to front an impromptu press conference at Christchurch Airport, he continued to play a straight bat as far as the quarter-final loss was concerned. 'We didn't play as well as we hoped ... the French played better than we expected them to ... we didn't get the bounce of the ball ... we're all terribly disappointed.'

He paid tribute to his players. 'I'm proud of how they conducted themselves as people,' he said. 'They are marvellous role models for this country. They put this country on the map and touched a lot of people. They've been phenomenal. Hotel managers say they're the best young sporting team that ever stays in their hotels.'

A few hours after Graham's glowing review, one of his role models imploded. Stuck at the Heathrow Hilton Hotel with nothing to do, Doug Howlett — the team's leading try-scorer at the World Cup although a surprise omission for the quarter-final — drank himself into a mischievous state.

Around 3 o'clock in the morning, he jumped on the roofs of two cars in the hotel car park, which led to his arrest. He was booked at a local police station and released on bail pending further inquiries.

Sobered up the next day, he issued an apology. What he'd got up to represented 'tomfoolery', he said. He'd worked with the police to contact the owners of the two cars. 'I apologize to team-mates, fans and the people back home. I am embarrassed that the events of one evening have led to this situation. There was drink involved and that's not an excuse. I do take responsibility for what I've done.'

It was a real pity because Doug had always been an outstanding role model for his fellow All Blacks, but the magnitude of the situation on this occasion proved too much for him to handle.

Howlett was one of those stuck in no-man's-land. He was heading for Ireland to take up a contract with Munster. But neither he nor Munster expected him to be available until after at least the semi-finals.

And, lo and behold, who else had arrived at the Hilton Heathrow but the Wallabies, another Down Under team suddenly rendered redundant at the World Cup. Doug found he had no shortage of drinking partners!

Graham's policy regarding newspapers and radio had never changed from when he first started coaching: if his team won handsomely, he'd check out the rave reviews; if his team lost or performed indifferently, he wouldn't go anywhere near them.

And so it was in the wake of the train crash at Cardiff. He knew well enough what had transpired, that his team had inexplicably stumbled against the tournament hosts. He didn't need any armchair critic or radio talkback host to explain where things had gone wrong. He would undertake his own analysis.

But not listening to talkback radio and not knowing what was being said are two entirely different things, because other people, with the best will in the world, feel obliged to tell you: 'Graham, it's just terrible what Murray Deaker and Willie Lose and others have been saying about you. They said ... *blah de blah de blah!*'

Graham expected criticism because his celebrated team, the best team in the world going into the tournament, hadn't progressed past the quarter-finals. He knew as a coach he had disappointed the nation. What he wasn't prepared for were the vitriolic personal attacks from sections of the media.

Deaker and Lose were into Graham big time. Deaker branded the All Blacks 'chokers', and described both the team's rotation policy and conditioning as failures. 'They were no fitter than anyone else,' he asserted, as he called for coach Henry's resignation.

Lose, who also called for Graham to step aside, turned ruthlessly on Richie McCaw. 'He may be a magnificent footballer, but he's not a captain's backside,' said Lose. 'When it comes to strategy, McCaw's not there.'

Even his dear 90-year-old mother was keen to acquaint him with these 'facts'. 'Graham, do you know what so-and-so just said about you?' 'No, Mother, I don't, and I don't want to know.' 'I know that, but I'm going to tell you anyway!'

After a few days of that, Graham decided he had to get out of town.

'Come on, Raewyn,' he said. 'Book us a motel somewhere in Australia where they don't know who the All Black coach is. Somewhere nice and warm.'

Mike Cron, the All Black scrum coach, had at some stage recommended as an ideal retreat Hervey Bay, a beach resort in Queensland, a couple of hundred kilometres north of Brisbane, where he and his wife April had stayed.

And that was where the Henrys headed. It was not a place with any great rugby traditions. Graham had a feeling if he sauntered into the public bar at the local pub, not one person would recognize him. It was just the way he wanted it, because back in New Zealand four and a half million Kiwis all knew who Graham Henry was. And not a lot were blowing him kisses right at that moment.

Graham slipped into a pair of shorts and a T-shirt and he and Raewyn went for a walk along the beach in a soothing temperature of close to 30°C. When you're grieving, it's nice to be insulated.

While at Hervey Bay he had to complete his head coach's report for the NZRU. The deadline for this had been brought forward because board members had initiated a major postmortem, eager to identify as swiftly as possible why the All Blacks had failed to achieve their objectives at the World Cup. It was obviously going to be pivotal to the appointment of the new coach going forward.

Graham decided there was time for a day's fishing and relaxation before switching his attentions to the NZRU report, which was obviously going to be a depressing exercise.

Wherever you are in New Zealand, you can be in ideal fishing waters inside an hour. Graham reminded himself of this several times as the charter fishing boat carrying him and Raewyn, a most accomplished angler, chugged along for three hours before arriving at the chosen spot.

The Henrys were in the company of half a dozen hard-case Aussie males, none of whom had the foggiest notion of Graham's status, or knew anything about rugby. They did fancy themselves as fishermen, however, so when the day's big winner, by a substantial margin, was Raewyn, they were not impressed.

'Cripes,' one of them said, 'not only beaten by a bloody New Zealander, but by a bloody New Zealand sheila, to boot!'

It was a fun day, and the fish tasted bloody good, too, when they were pan-fried back at the motel. It was such a relief to be away from rugby for a day.

Rugby would be back on the agenda tomorrow morning when the video of the World Cup quarter-final would be the focus.

Graham little suspected as he dozed off that evening, wonderfully replete, that his world would be turned upside down the next day.

10

Video evidence

It was 4.30 a.m. when Graham eased out of his comfortable bed at their motel at Hervey Bay. Not a decent time to be surfacing at a holiday resort, but it was what Graham had trained himself to do. Ever since he became a professional rugby coach, Graham has risen at between 4 and 4.30 a.m. and used the next two hours, free of interruptions, to clear all his work and prepare himself for the day ahead.

And so it was at Hervey Bay. Coffee brewed, he turned his attention to his laptop and the World Cup quarter-final, the result of which had stunned not just New Zealanders but the entire rugby world.

At the time he pushed the Play button, Graham genuinely believed his time as All Black rugby coach was over. But he had a head coach's review to complete for the NZRU so he would do it to the best of his ability and then move on.

Graham's gut feeling was the video would confirm that referee Wayne Barnes and his touch judges, Jonathan Kaplan from South Africa and Tony Spreadbury from England, hadn't exactly covered themselves in glory at the Millennium Stadium, that they had missed an obvious forward pass when France scored its match-winning try — a pass so forward everyone in the stadium had witnessed it except the referee — and that Barnes had been pretty lenient on the French at the breakdowns, probably costing the All Blacks the game.

The video Graham was assessing wasn't the basic television

replay of the match, with commentary and replays. His version was made up from three different angles and featured statistical breakdowns of lineouts, scrums, penalties, tackle counts, territory, possession, etc.

The game, as Graham viewed it on screen, had been broken down into around 90 individual plays, approximately 45 per half; for example, a lineout until the finish of that play, caused by a knock-on. By analysing these, Graham could build up a picture of what had happened on that fateful day in Cardiff. It was all there, the reality, in front of him.

Graham had a different frame of reference from someone watching the game for entertainment; he knew the outcome. His job here was to focus on each segment of play and identify anything significant, anything that would account for why, on this occasion, the best team in the world, the team that almost always won convincingly, had got itself beaten.

As each play unfolded, Graham scribbled notes, recording whether a particular player had erred or committed an offence, why a lineout or scrum was won or lost, any developments at breakdowns that may have led to the scoring of, or conceding of, a try, good decisions/ bad decisions, and noting any blatant infringements the match officials might have overlooked.

Graham anticipated having the analysis completed by mid morning. Yes, it would confirm the match officials had made some blunders and probably it would show the All Blacks hadn't been quite on their game. He could wrap it all up, present his report to the NZRU, say thanks for having me, and go and find himself some fresh employment.

But what began to unfold in front of him was a rugby game off the planet, an absolute nightmare of horror proportions!

Graham couldn't believe what he was seeing. This was a match in which the French were penalized only twice in 80 minutes, implying they were absolute angels who consistently operated within the game's boundaries. But what Graham was seeing on the screen didn't equate to that at all. Quite the opposite. He was observing endless infringements by the men in blue that simply hadn't been acknowledged by referee Barnes or his touch judges.

What the hell had gone on at Millennium Stadium? The more Graham viewed, the worse it became. After 45 minutes, he started to feel nauseous. Five minutes later, by which time he'd lost count of the number of French infringements that had gone unchecked by the referee and his touch judges, he made a dash for the toilet ... and threw up.

'Are you all right, Graham?' inquired Raewyn from the bedroom.

'Yeah.'

'Are you sure?

'No, I'm not but I will get through it. I can't bloody believe what I have been watching. It's bizarre ... it's unbelievable ... we have been sawn off, big time!'

It would be three days before Graham could bring himself to resume his video analysis. He thought that after 30 years as a rugby coach, from college level to internationals, he was prepared for anything and everything. But this was unbelievable. This was rugby's showcase event, beamed out around the globe for tens of millions of viewers to enjoy, an occasion where you wanted the players and the referee to be on top of their games to promote the sport. But this game was totally different to any other game Graham had watched or been involved in. The players were doing their bit but the referee seemed to be acting out rugby's equivalent of Dr Jekyll and Mr Hyde.

Having vomited on Tuesday and not discussed the video replays with anyone since, not even his darling wife, except to say he was finding the content disturbing, Graham finally sat himself down in front of the screen again on Thursday and engaged the Play button.

Whether he wanted to believe it or not, what he was viewing had actually unfolded in a Rugby World Cup quarter-final before 71,699 spectators at the Millennium Stadium. While there had been cursory judgement of the referee, mostly relating to the missed forward pass, obviously few if any critics had taken the trouble to replay the match and identify referee Barnes's lapses. And they were monumental.

Remembering that the final penalty and free-kick count was 11 to France and two to New Zealand, here is what Graham wrote down as he replayed the quarter-final, with what Graham considers should have been the appropriate rulings shown in brackets:

First half

2m 52s: French 4 offside in maul; French 8 collapses maul. (Penalty — possible 3 points).

3m 10s: French 2 and 4 enter the side of the ruck. (Penalty — lineout).

4m 19s: French tackler does not release tackled player on the ground. (Penalty — lineout).

4m 21s: First French defender two metres offside. (Penalty — lineout).

4m 55s: Penalty against NZ for not rolling away. Was it possible the NZ player was stamped? Ignored.

7m 59s: NZ 7 can contest because no ruck called, but penalized for off feet, playing the ball.

9m 51s: France offside at ruck. (Penalty).

11m 48s: Lazy runners. (Penalty).

15m 59s: French tackler not rolling away. (Penalty).

16m 3s: French 7 ahead of last man's feet at ruck. (Penalty).

20m 4s: NZ 3 forward pass — line ball called by Kaplan.

21m 5s: French scrum wheels beyond 90 deg. Should be turnover. (NZ scrum)

23m 28s: NZ dominant and win collision but not rewarded. Penalty goes to France.

28m 1s: French 12 hands in ruck, then French 9 returns ball to ruck. (Penalty).

31m 25s: Number of French players inside 10 m circle from kick. (Penalty).

31m 31s: French players in front of last man at ruck. (Penalty).

33m 6s: French 10 and 12 offside from scrum. (Penalty).

35m 35s: NZ 4 penalized but bound into maul. Not offside. Should not have been penalized. Kick missed.

37m 39s: French 2 and 8 offside from kick. (Penalty).

37m 53s: French player joins post tackle from side. (Penalty).

38m 43s: French offside at ruck. (Penalty — lineout).

39m 35s: NZ 5 penalized but was bound and not offside. French kick the penalty goal.

Second half

42m 2s: French 14 playing ball on the ground. (Penalty).

42m 20s: French 2 and others slowing the ball down. (Penalty).

43m 39s: French tackler playing the ball on the ground. (Penalty).

43m 43s: French 9 offside at ruck. (Penalty).

45m 20s: Yellow card for McAlister. Harsh call. Three points for France.

47m 35s: French 3 pulling NZ 5 into ruck — told by ref to stop. (Penalty).

47m 41s: French 18 repeats offence. Spoken to by ref. (Penalty).

47m 48s: French 3 offside at ruck. (Penalty).

47m 55s: French 18 offside at ruck. (Penalty).

48m 12s: French 12 offside at ruck, results in turnover to French 8 m out from goal line. (Penalty).

49m 33s: French 9 and French 3 offside at ruck, one metre from French goal line. Told by ref. (Penalty). In this sequence of play there are at least seven penalizable offences. French now know they can break the law without consequences!

50m 20s: NZ scrum penalized. What for? Huge statement being made here!

51m 25s: French deliberately collapse scrum. French 7 not bound and French 9 illegal hands in scrum and offside. Signalled but ref doesn't come back when no advantage accrued. (Penalty).

52m 32s: French 10 cleaning out from side at the tackle, under ref's nose. Game changing as the French score seven points. (Penalty).

57m 50s: French 3 angles in at scrum and disrupts platform, right in front of ref. (Penalty).

58m 2s: French 11 dives on tackled play on the ground. (Penalty).

58m 20s: French 16 offside at ruck. (Penalty).

59m 33s: Ref calls ruck but French 18 off his feet and playing ball with his hands. (Penalty).

59m 52s: French 16 off his feet and playing the ball with his hands. Ref watching! (Penalty).

61m 30s: NZ 6 penalized for not binding? How does that compare with scrum at 51m 25s?

62m 4s: French 17 offside retiring in defence. (Penalty).

62m 13s: French 16 as tackler playing the ball on the ground. (Penalty).

62m 34s: French hands in ruck, slowing ball down, 8m from French goal line. (Penalty).

65m 12s: French 3 angles in and disrupts platform on NZ scrum, right in front of ref. (Penalty).

66m 5s: Repeat of previous scrum. Also, French 19 not bound. (Penalty).

67m 57s: French forward pass. Blatant, right in front of Kaplan. Results in seven points to France.

72m 31s: NZ 13 taken out chasing chip-kick. How does this compare with Luke McAlister's yellow card? Should be three points. (Penalty).

73m 32s: French offside at ruck out wide. (Penalty).

73m 56s: French 7 offside at ruck. (Penalty).

76m 29s: French hands in ruck. (Penalty).

77m: French 14 offside at ruck. (Penalty).

77m 12s: French 12 offside in front of hindmost feet on French 22. Told by ref. (Penalty).

Notes

Actuals: Lineouts — France 16, New Zealand 9; scrums — France 9, New Zealand 5; penalties — France 10, New Zealand 2; Starters — France 35, New Zealand 16.

Should have beens: New Zealand lineouts up to at least 13, scrums up to 7, penalties up to 17 (of which 11 were in kickable positions), starters up to 37.

These statistics don't include multiple offences in the same play.

The referee missed 40 penalties in total.

Also, a number of penalties against New Zealand were questionable.

The two tries France scored resulted from offences. With try No. 1 (to Dusautoir), France should have been penalized at the scrum and, later, the French 10 cleaned out the NZ 7 from the side at the tackle. Try No. 2 (to Jauzion) involved an obvious forward pass. The two tries accounted for 14 of the team's 20 points.

Take those 14 points away and say the All Blacks would have goaled 80 per cent of the kickable penalties, the final score would have been something like 42–3 or 42–6 to New Zealand.

Three decisions by match officials cost the All Blacks dearly:

The sin-binning of McAlister simply for turning and blocking the run of a French player. This reduced the team to 14, cost three points and fatigued the team over the next 10 minutes.

The referee had the whistle to his mouth for a scrum penalty against France in the 51st minute. He decided to let play run as we attacked close. After two rucks, Dan Carter attempted a dropped goal (Luke being in the bin, this was a reasonable option). The referee should have come back for the scrum penalty; instead, he let France restart at the 22 and they scored a try from this play.

France scored in the 67th minute off an obviously forward pass. The referee may have been obscured, but it would have been clear to at least one touch judge.

Summary of the statistical breakdown

First-half possession was 57% and territory 46% to NZ. Second-half possession was 73% and territory 72% to NZ.

The All Blacks had very few starting platforms in the game — 9 lineouts, 5 scrums and 2 penalties. So most of NZ's possession came from rucks, balls stolen off France, or possession kicked to NZ.

The All Blacks won 166 rucks/mauls against France's 42.

The All Blacks made 73 tackles; France, 331.

The marked increase in second-half possession can be put down to:

Luke McAlister's yellow card, meaning the ABs had to keep the ball in closer and in-hand, rather than stretch themselves.

Richie McCaw's call later in the half to keep possession in the French 22, thus exerting the pressure that would ultimately result in a try (by Rodney So'oialo).

France's ability, often illegal, to slow ball at the tackle, thus forcing the ABs to throw in extra numbers, which limited the AB's attacking options.

Loss of key decision makers in the backline, most notably Dan Carter and Nick Evans, which meant a loss of direction.

France, which was the most penalized team at the 2007 World Cup, received 85 per cent of the penalties and free kicks in the game

(11–2). The All Blacks received 15 per cent. An irony is that during the World Cup, 69 per cent of all penalties went to the team in possession.

This massive difference in the penalty count affected the AB's ability to achieve starting platforms (scrums, lineouts and penalties). Given that the All Black game plan is based on top-quality set-piece ball, explosive strikes over the gain line and in trying to keep the ball alive and score, they struggled to get their game going.

The ABs scored two tries off lineouts (a quick throw and a steal) but the team's scoring potential was compromised by the lack of starters and through being unable to accumulate points through penalty goals.

The All Blacks made 13 line breaks against four by France and 13 tackle breaks against four by France. The All Blacks had 25 off-loads compared with France's five.

By the time Graham had completed his analysis, he was in a stupefied state, and was having the greatest difficulty comprehending what he had witnessed on the screen. Few coaches in the world could match his level of experience — he'd been involved in almost 80 test matches with New Zealand, Wales and the British Lions — and never had he encountered anything remotely like this. In fact, he doubted whether in the entire history of international rugby there had ever been a game with such bizarre statistics. This game was right off the planet.

It was painfully obvious to Graham that the referee and his touch judges had effectively adjudicated on only one team, and that team wasn't France. No wonder the French official had commented to him in their dressing room that they had got away with murder. The French were under siege for more than 70 per cent of the game and kept blatantly infringing, without penalty, literally and figuratively. In the final quarter, the French threw their bodies at any part of the breakdown to halt the All Black momentum, blissfully secure in the knowledge they weren't going to be penalized.

Weird thoughts began to course through Graham's head. *Could sports betting be a factor?* he wondered. *Look at what's been going on in cricket.* But, no, he decided, this is rugby and this is the World Cup, for goodness' sake. Such things weren't possible.

Graham wasn't the only New Zealand rugby expert to scrutinize the video of the quarter-final; the NZRU also referred it to its high-performance referee coach, Colin Hawke. Hawke had been one of the country's most accomplished rugby whistlers and, intriguingly enough, had refereed Graham's Welsh team in its quarter-final clash with the Wallabies at the 1999 World Cup.

Hawke reviewed the game from both a technical and a tactical viewpoint. On the one hand, he reviewed it as if he were a match reviewer who would discuss questionable rulings with the referee; then he went over it again focusing on matters that would have a material effect on the All Blacks only.

Although Hawke's review wasn't as painstakingly compiled as Graham's, because he didn't have the same vested interest in what was going on, and in many instances he gave the benefit of doubt to the referee, his report still identified 16 occasions when the referee was remiss in not awarding penalties to New Zealand, including several critical ones in the final stages when the All Blacks, two points behind, were attacking deep inside French territory.

When Graham had flown off to Queensland he was in a depressed, frustrated state, convinced he had no future as All Black coach.

But when he flew back home, after his dumbfounding experience at Hervey Bay, he was fired up, angry, aggressive, and definitely contemplating having another crack at some unfinished business.

Often when Graham incurred criticism as a coach, he referred to a famous quote from former American president Theodore Roosevelt, an excerpt from the 'Citizenship in a Republic' speech the president had delivered in Paris in April 1910. It was timely, Graham thought, to give it a fresh reading:

It is not the critic who counts; not the man who points out how the strong man stumbles or where the doer of deeds could have done them better. The credit belongs to the man who is actually in the arena, whose face is marred by dust and sweat and blood, who strives valiantly; who errs, who comes up short again and again because there is no effort without error and shortcoming; but who does actually strive to do the deeds; who knows great enthusiasms, the great devotions; who spends himself in a worthy cause; who at the best knows in the end the triumph of high achievement, and who at the worst, if he fails, at least he fails while daring greatly, so that his place shall never be with those cold and timid souls who neither know victory nor defeat.

So following their return to Auckland, on a walk around St Heliers with Raewyn, he asked her, 'If I was to stand for All Black coach again, how would you feel?'

Graham knew he wasn't the only member of the household such a big call would involve. In some ways, it is easier for those at the pit-face than for those back home, who have to live with the aftermath when things go wrong — as they had horrendously in Cardiff. Raewyn was aware of the vitriol now being directed at her husband, largely through the media, and it was certainly impacting on the whole family.

'It's your call,' replied Raewyn. 'I'll support you if you want to go again. I know how disappointed and frustrated you were at what happened in Cardiff.'

The more Graham thought about it, the more determined he was to have another crack at winning rugby's ultimate prize, one that through the most bizarre of circumstances had been denied his team in Cardiff.

Certainly, the coaching team's performance hadn't been perfect — he acknowledges that the conditioning window had been a mistake and it was obvious that many of the players hadn't demonstrated the appropriate mental toughness in adversity in the final stages of the game — but he was now assessing things from a different standpoint, aware that with an even playing field at Cardiff, his team would have unquestionably progressed to the semi-finals.

Shag and Smithy's futures were also a factor. He knew if Robbie Deans was appointed coach, and he was the obvious successor if the NZRU chose not to reappoint Graham, almost certainly Shag and Smithy would not be part of the back-up staff.

No All Black coach who'd lost a World Cup had ever survived. Grizz Wyllie and John Hart were replaced by Laurie Mains after crashing out in 1991; Mains gave way to Hart in 1996 after his team agonizingly dropped the final in extra time in South Africa; Hart resigned immediately his team exited the 1999 tournament at the semi-final stage; and John Mitchell (and his assistant Deans) were dispensed with after losing in Sydney in 2003. That's when Graham entered the scene.

While there was no guarantee the board of New Zealand Rugby would reappoint him, Graham was now beginning to feel there were compelling arguments for Shag and Smithy and himself to continue their work, if that was at all possible.

With all the blood-letting, anguish and, from aspects of the media, hysteria that had been associated with the hugely disappointing loss to France, Graham had somewhat lost his perspective.

With help from Smithy and Shag and the back-up brigade, he had built a team of proud young men that over four years had enhanced the All Black legacy of being the most successful sporting team in the world across a hundred years.

The All Blacks in those four years had won 43 of their 49 matches, claimed three successive Tri-Nations titles, retained the Bledisloe Cup, completed the first Grand Slam of the UK in 27 years, were unbeaten at home, and had won all 12 matches played on end-of-year tours of Europe. As a consequence of all those successes, the All Blacks had stamped themselves most emphatically as the No. 1 team in the world — until matters unravelled in 80 minutes at the World Cup.

Graham and his management and coaching team had constantly sought to upgrade the All Black environment and tried to ensure the team didn't just win but won with quality. One of the requirements was that players fronted every test both mentally and physically, and gave 100 per cent. Playing up to 15 internationals a year placed huge demands on these players: they were continually putting their bodies on the line.

In fact, because he had demanded such an awful lot of his players, Graham didn't feel he could just walk away. The players were watching and waiting. It was *his* time to stand up and be counted, time to put *his* body on the line.

At this difficult time, with the media still banging on about the ridiculousness of the rotation policy, the team's apparent 'gutlessness' in the final quarter, and McCaw's failure as a leader, Graham took encouragement from the calls and messages he received from friends and colleagues, and even from individuals he'd never met before.

One who phoned was Peter Leitch, the Mad Butcher (now Sir Peter), a man renowned for his unquenchable support and backing of the Warriors. He was a league man through and through, whom Graham couldn't ever recall meeting.

'Graham, it's Peter Leitch here, mate,' he barked down the phone. 'I just wanted to tell you I'm ashamed of the crap that's being talked about you and the All Blacks. You guys have built a fantastic record and New Zealand should be proud of you. One game doesn't undo that. Good luck for the future — I hope they reappoint you.'

Graham and the Mad Butcher would ultimately become close friends after finding themselves neighbours on Waiheke Island in Auckland's Hauraki Gulf, where they purchased adjoining holiday home properties.

Graham also had a call from Grant Dalton, head of the country's America's Cup syndicate. Dalton commiserated with Graham, saying he understood exactly how he felt, because it wasn't that many years since Team New Zealand had been copping it in the neck from the media and disgruntled fans after the Swiss boat *Alinghi* wrested the famous trophy from New Zealand's grasp.

Two total strangers who phoned out of the blue to not only offer encouragement but to extend invitations to head out on the briny were Geoff Thomas, one of New Zealand's foremost fishing writers and commentators, and Eddie Brooks, who runs charter fishing boats out of Paihia and who is affectionately known as Eddie the Fisherman. 'Any time you want to come up, just call,' said Eddie, 'and I'll guarantee you'll catch your dinner.'

Not only would Graham take both Geoff Thomas and Eddie Brooks up on their offers, he would become hooked, if you'll excuse the pun, on the sport. These days he fishes more than he runs rugby coaching sessions. And he has been quoted as saying, 'The simple act of dropping a fishing line over the side of a boat is the only thing that enables me to forget about rugby.'

Graham's closest friends, who were collectively aghast at the World Cup outcome, all encouraged him to put himself forward for reappointment. And Graham was particularly heartened, as the date of the fateful NZRU board meeting drew closer, at the number of messages of support he received from the All Black management and players, which mirrored many of the All Black management and players' reports in the official reviews — both independent and the NZRU's — conducted after the World Cup.

Another individual who was stunned by the referee's performance was Auckland businessman Kent Baigent. Because he'd watched the game from the sanctity of his home, he was in a position to replay it several times, courtesy of My Sky.

Most New Zealand rugby fans were so gutted by the outcome, so shocked at the result, he believes, they never revisited it to fully understand what actually went on. But Baigent did, and was so outraged by the refereeing performance — he identified 27 offences committed by the French that had gone unpunished (Graham had come up with 40) — that as someone with expertise in film-editing, he wanted to bring it out in the open by producing a video highlighting the referee's mistakes.

But because the television authorities would not release the alternate camera angles material to him, he eventually had to give up on the project.

Because Baigent maintained a close association with Ali Williams he received an invitation to a function involving the All Blacks, and finished up sitting next to coach Henry.

He naturally told Graham of his video plan that had failed to come to fruition.

Baigent told Graham he was determined to have justice served for his beloved All Blacks. Graham convinced him the most appropriate course of action was through the NZRU and that he personally would be encouraging the national body to institute an inquiry through the International Rugby Board.

Graham's report certainly caused a stir among board members, none of whom had fully appreciated the one-sided nature of the officiating until Graham took them through the video replays, stage by stage.

He told them he believed, given the graphic video evidence available, that the NZRU should pressure the International Rugby Board to institute an inquiry. He also emphasized that it was incomprehensible that the IRB did not have strategies in place to investigate bizarre matches. And when it came to bizarre, this World Cup quarter-final was an absolute doozy.

But the IRB didn't: cricket's controlling body, the ICC, and football's, FIFA, certainly have processes in place but rugby, which every four years hosts one of the three largest sporting tournaments in the world, didn't. And that's obviously because with its amateur background it has always been seen as a game played by gentlemen. Rugby had always been perceived as squeaky clean — but was it?

Before appointing the All Black coach for 2008, the NZRU commissioned an independent report into New Zealand's World Cup campaign by the law firm of Russell McVeagh. The individual entrusted with this important research was Michael Heron, a man in his thirties and a partner in the company which specializes in health and safety, media and entertainment, sports law and telecommunications. The document he presented came to be known as the Heron Report.

Heron's report was referred to Graham and his fellow coaches before it was presented to the board. Aspects of it irritated Graham because he felt the report had jumped on the bandwagon being promoted by the media, namely that there had been a lack of composure on the field, a lack of quality opposition, a lack of leadership, a questionable rotation selection policy, and an unsatisfactory conditioning process.

Even though the conditioning process had got the players into excellent physical condition, it had been driven by the management instead of via a consultative process with the players, and it had antagonized pretty much everyone from individual players to Super 14 franchises and Super 14 coaches. And so Graham acknowledges the conditioning window was a mistake, never to be repeated.

The so-called rotation policy, however, was an entirely different issue, and Graham will argue that without it the All Blacks would not have won the World Cup in 2011. The policy allowed the coaches to build a healthy base for New Zealand rugby that would sustain the team through the years ahead.

Graham disputed the criticism of Richie McCaw's leadership because of the freakish circumstances of the quarter-final. In the near-80 test matches in which he had been involved as a coach, never had he experienced such a game. Graham and his captain both knew that if you controlled possession and territory, and pressured the enemy relentlessly, tries and/or penalty goals inevitably followed. That's how it had been with this All Black team over several seasons and it's what should have happened at the Millennium Stadium. But when the match officials decline to award penalties for the most blatant of infringements by the opposition, what can you do?

Graham and his fellow coaches were able to have parts of the report modified before it was officially presented to, and accepted by, the NZRU. But they weren't able to influence either Michael Heron or the board to push for a full-scale inquiry into the officiating of the All Blacks' match against France.

As far as Graham was concerned, the major reason the All Blacks had lost was not because of conditioning or rotation policies or decisions by his captain, but purely and simply because the officials had refereed only one team, to a degree unprecedented in the history of the sport.

He knew if a comparable situation had occurred in other sports, it would be investigated. But there existed a blissful purity about rugby, or at least that's how everyone wanted to perceive it. It wasn't politically correct to even suggest the match officials might have favoured one team. That isn't how rugby operates. Not very sporting at all, old chap! This is the game played in heaven, after all.

It was obviously the Rugby World Cup refereeing panel's call to give Barnes, very much a greenhorn on the international scene, a quarter-final of modest stature. When he was appointed to the 6 October quarter-final in Paris, it was logically presumed the game he would be controlling was New Zealand against Argentina, a safe fixture for him to advance his international experience. But of course

Coaches usually pump their fists before major contests, but Graham is demonstrating what the semi-final victory over the Wallabies in the 2011 Rugby World Cup means to the team. And are they delighted! *TRANZ / ACTION IMAGES*

Graham flanked by Piri Weepu, left, Keven Mealamu and Owen Franks after the All Blacks' quarter-final victory against Argentina at the 2011 World Cup. *TRANZ / ACTION IMAGES*

Go, Beaver! Stephen Donald went from forgotten man to national hero in just over 40 minutes during the World Cup final. Here he takes the attack to France. *PHOTOSPORT*

'Teabag, you beaut!' Tony Woodcock is embraced by Piri Weepu after scoring the All Blacks' only try in the World Cup final, from a move kept on ice for four years. *TRANZ / ACTION IMAGES*

No All Black was more emotional following the World Cup win than 36-year-old Brad Thorn. His contribution to the team's success was massive. *TRANZ / ACTION IMAGES*

Happiness is wearing a World Cup gold medal around your neck. Graham and Keven Mealamu share the moment after the nailbiter at Eden Park. *PHOTOSPORT*

They call it Bill, the Webb Ellis Cup. And beer drunk from it never tasted sweeter, as Graham is discovering. *TRANZ / ACTION IMAGES*

Mission accomplished: Wayne Smith, Graham, Richie McCaw and Steve Hansen join
the 1987 All Blacks as world champions. *TRANZ / ACTION IMAGES*

Showing off 'Bill' during the street parade through Auckland the day after defeating
France in the World Cup final. *TRANZ / CORBIS*

Graham admitted to 'finding peace' after winning the Rugby World Cup. This photo, taken during the Auckland street parade, suggests he also found great happiness.

Rugby coaching duties behind him, Graham is looking forward to spending more time with his grandchildren — and what delightful grandchildren they are.

Kate, the youngest child of Matthew and Marie. *Henry Family Collection*

Olivia, the eldest child of Matthew and Marie. *Henry Family Collection*

Jake, the younger child of Catherine and Hamish. *Henry Family Collection*

Finn, the middle child of Matthew and Marie, and Sofia, the elder child of Catherine and Hamish. *Henry Family Collection*

After the agony of 2007, Graham and Raewyn bask in the glory of a successful Rugby World Cup campaign four years on. *TRANZ / CORBIS*

Marvellously, Graham's 96-year-old mother, Ann, was able to attend the investiture at Government House in Wellington. The family, from left: Marie, Matthew, Lady Henry, Sir Graham, Catherine, Hamish and Andrew. *DOUG MOUNTAIN / PHOTOGRAPHY BY WOOLF*

the Pumas wrecked that plan by defeating France. Suddenly, Barnes was right in the spotlight. Pass the Parcel had landed him a biggie. Was he up to it?

The irony of the whole issue is that if the NZRU hadn't swept the controversy under the carpet, and instead had backed Graham's powerful push for a full-scale inquiry, the international uproar that would have ensued would have made it virtually impossible for the NZRU to even consider reappointing him as All Black coach.

The date was set for the NZRU board meeting at which the All Black coach for 2008 would be appointed: 7 December. Surprise was expressed in many quarters that Graham was even seeking re-election, given his team's 'worst ever' World Cup performance.

There were four candidates — Robbie Deans, Colin Cooper, Ian Foster and Graham — with the bookies installing Deans as the favourite. It's extremely rare for the bookies to be far off the mark in such matters. Few critics gave Graham much hope of survival, despite the All Blacks' 87 per cent win record under him. Deans, whose Crusaders team had finished only third that year in the Super 14 after winning in 2005 and 2006, was considered an overwhelming favourite to take over the men in black.

Cooper and Foster were the first eliminated, leaving it to Messrs Deans and Henry to present their cases to the interviewing sub-committee: Mike Eagle (who chaired the meeting after Jock Hobbs again stepped aside because of his relationship to Deans), Chris Moller (CEO), Steve Tew (deputy CEO), Kirsten Patterson (General Manager Corporate Services), Darren Shand (All Black manager) and board members Ivan Haines, Graham Mourie and Paul Quinn.

One individual who sat in judgement that day describes Deans as being 'not compelling' and Graham as being 'extremely nervous and not at his best'. Graham himself considers his presentation the worst he has ever made to any panel at any time.

So after Graham had left the boardroom and located Raewyn, he told her, 'I've blown it.' Then he phoned Smithy in Christchurch and conveyed the gloomy news that he thought they were history. 'I don't think we'll get the job,' he said.

Yet even if he hadn't articulated himself well, Graham did manage to convey that in his four years the All Blacks had achieved the best results of any team since the game went professional and the best results since Fred Allen's All Blacks in the 1960s. While the All Blacks were winning 87 per cent of their games, no other international team had achieved even 70 per cent. He said the team had pushed out the boundaries of how the game can be played. 'So many good things have happened since 2004,' he said. 'We have an All Black culture and we have changed a lot of people.'

He and his fellow coaches, Wayne Smith and Steve Hansen, he assured the board, had the support of the All Black players and captain, the support of the All Black management team, the support of the NZRU management and staff, the support of New Zealand Rugby's commercial partners, and the support of the union's media partners, Sky Television and TV3.

'We would desperately like to continue coaching and managing the All Blacks and to put into practice the learnings of the last four years to further strengthen this team and New Zealand rugby. We have certainly learnt some lessons and are better prepared to meet those challenges. From our viewpoint, the job is not finished.'

From all reports, the board did not take long to make a decision. By six votes to one, they reappointed Graham Henry coach of the All Blacks for a two-year term. Ted and Shag and Smithy were back in business.

Eagle, as chairman, said the board followed a thorough process which reflected the importance of the position to New Zealand Rugby. 'The board considered Graham Henry was the best candidate for the position,' he said. 'The appointment was based on his remarkable results over a four-year period.'

It's fair to say not everyone in the Land of the Long White Cloud (a cloud that had been depressingly dark since the World Cup) supported the decision. Former All Black Richard Loe, for example, writing in the *Herald on Sunday*, was extremely critical of Graham's reappointment:

> Our coaches were substandard just like the result they led us to, so why would I pay to go and watch the All Blacks now? The prospect

just doesn't excite me. Henry has made it clear he won't be sticking the best team on the field, as has Steve Tew. So we'll get more of last year, will we? We'll be playing rotated teams against France B, Canada and South Africa B.

People are sick of it. They are disillusioned. Cockies are swearing away, saying if Henry is back, they won't be.

Mark Peters, one who voted for Graham, would later say in an interview:

When you are there interviewing someone and you look in their eyes, you can see a burning window right through to their soul. It was clear to me that Graham had to be given another chance. He knew exactly where things had gone wrong and no-one had ever, ever had a chance to rectify things after previous failed World Cup campaigns. He hurt, we all hurt. Graham knew and I knew he deserved a second crack at it.

Peters would survive on the board but Warwick Syers would be dumped early in 2008 in what was interpreted as a protest vote from the provinces against the reappointment of Graham in the wake of the World Cup failure.

In defending the board's decision, Syers said there were issues around refereeing at the World Cup that were unfortunate. 'They have not been spoken about by the NZRU,' he said, 'because it is not politically expedient to do so.'

Within a week of Ted and Shag and Smithy being reinstated, Robbie Deans was appointed coach of Australia, contracted for four years.

'As a Super rugby manager and coach for 11 years, I feel I can't afford to forgo the position offered me in Australia,' he declared.

Reinstated, Graham believes he was fortunate to have two such outstanding CEOs as Chris Moller and Steve Tew administering New Zealand rugby throughout his term as head coach. Both extremely capable administrators, they were hugely supportive after his reappointment, which he much appreciated.

11

Media mayhem

Graham always applied a simple philosophy to the media once he became a top-level rugby coach: if his team won handsomely, he would read the newspaper reviews and listen to the radio, but if his team was defeated — and that didn't occur very often — or performed indifferently or there were controversies, he wouldn't go anywhere near the papers or the air waves. It was called controlling your environment.

He recommended this policy to the players he coached and he knows it was adopted by several of the sensible senior members. However, he also appreciated that the younger, more impressionable, individuals often felt compelled to read what the critics and commentators were saying about them.

Over the near-40 years Graham had been coaching, initially at college and club level, then with representative teams before moving on to the international stage, the media scene had altered dramatically.

When he was guiding Auckland's fortunes in the good old amateur days — while simultaneously running Kelston Boys' High School — he'd had to contend with only a handful of genuine rugby correspondents and radio and television broadcasters. It was rare for an individual who didn't have a thorough grounding in rugby to attend press conferences or media briefings in those days. Questions were relevant and largely astute, and because his teams consistently won, Graham seldom came under fire. A couple of rare exceptions, though, were when Auckland was beaten in the first NPC play-offs by Waikato in 1992 and then lost the Ranfurly Shield to the same opponent the following year. Graham was grumpy enough with himself at those reversals without requiring the critics to ask embarrassing questions.

He rebounded from those setbacks to become the most successful Auckland coach in history, even recapturing the Ranfurly Shield. (Although, to be honest, since taking up virtually permanent residence in Auckland from 1985 to 1993, the Shield had rather lost its lustre in the Queen City.)

By the time the 1990s rolled around, a new phenomenon had emerged, talkback radio, and it wasn't long before Radio Sport came into existence, affording the nation's unofficial critics boundless opportunities to expound their theories on why certain sporting teams were or weren't performing up to scratch. They were goaded into action by talkback hosts such as Murray Deaker, who were smart enough to know that nothing boosted ratings more than issues of controversy. State that the All Blacks were a tad unlucky to lose but they're about to come right, and few listeners would react. But toss in that the coach was biased against Aucklanders or that Jimmy so-and-so was the team's weak link, and the phones would run red hot.

As professional rugby developed, Graham's press conferences began to attract larger attendances as more and more radio stations and publications found the need to present items on rugby. This inevitably led to individuals blissfully ignorant of what had gone on out in the middle of the field attending press conferences and asking such penetrating questions as, 'Graham, who did you think played well for your team today?' Graham, to his credit, never answered with 'What have you been looking at for the last 80 minutes?' Instead, he always gave a sincere answer.

When he forsook Auckland and took over the reins of the Welsh national team, becoming an international celebrity overnight, Graham quickly appreciated what the media was all about. At his first press conference in the UK, he found himself confronted by more than 100 journalists. And probably twice that number were in attendance at the Crowne Plaza Hotel, Heathrow Airport, when the British Lions team was announced in 2001, with Graham famous for being the first 'foreigner' to win the Lions coaching appointment.

He survived the challenging couple of months of the Lions tour in Australia, where his team lost the series 2–1, suffering more embarrassing moments from a couple of his own players, who fancied themselves as columnists, than from the media. While disappointed that the Lions hadn't won the series, the UK media were largely sympathetic and understanding, given the closeness of the series — the teams scored seven tries each — and the horrendous number of injuries sustained by the Lions.

None of the media ever attacked Graham personally, either when he was in charge of the Lions or when he was coaching Wales. They identified issues that he might have handled better, occasionally chipped him for not selecting a particular player and, in assessing match or series outcomes, branded him a success or a failure. Which is what you've got to expect when you're a high-profile coach.

What Graham wasn't prepared for as a rugby coach were the personal attacks upon him after the All Blacks exited the 2007 World Cup after losing to France.

Because the expectations — created by the All Blacks themselves through their stunning achievements across four years — were so high, an entire nation was overcome with grief when the seemingly impossible happened: their team beaten in the quarter-finals.

If there were extenuating circumstances, such as a referee who turned in a performance unparalleled in World Cup sporting history — and we're not just talking rugby here — the media, certainly those in the most influential positions, chose to ignore them.

Only one individual was responsible for the All Blacks losing to France, in their assessment. No, it wasn't the referee, or either of the touch judges, or any of the players wearing black jerseys. It was Graham Henry, he who had introduced conditioning windows and rotation policies and generally buggered up a champion team.

Deaker, who was in Paris for the quarter-final, laid the blame for the loss squarely at Graham's feet. He said the conditioning, rotation and selection policies had failed, and the choice of Mils Muliaina, the world's best fullback, at centre was a mistake.

He claimed if the All Blacks of 2005 and 2006 had continued they'd have beaten France by 30 or 40 points but, because of the conditioning and rotation policies, they had gone backwards.

'We choked,' said Deaker. 'There's no other word for it — choked, choked, choked.' He called for Graham to resign.

Of course, everybody is entitled to their own opinion, but Deaker may have been a tad jaundiced at the time: he had written nine-tenths of a book called *Henry's All Blacks* — a book he wanted Graham to be personally involved in, but Graham had declined — to be completed and released, with great fanfare, when the All Blacks, for the first time in 20 years, claimed the Webb Ellis Cup. Despite the ABs' premature exit from the tournament, the book still got published (with at least one chapter rewritten), but it never threatened the bestseller's list.

The All Blacks had, well in advance of the 2007 World Cup, received media training from former television news presenter and current affairs journalist Ian Fraser.

He warned them they would find some of the media mean-spirited. There existed old hacks, he explained, whose own lives were uninteresting, and who would find satisfaction in chopping down tall poppies. There were quite a number in New Zealand journalism, he warned.

The World Cup misfortunes certainly promoted mean-spiritedness among the New Zealand media, with Chris Rattue of the *New Zealand Herald* supreme among them. Ever since Graham had written to his editor saying how Rattue had angered and embarrassed New Zealanders and the All Blacks while they were on tour in Wales by describing the Welsh as the village idiots of world rugby, Rattue had taken an obvious dislike to the All Black coach.

Predictably, Rattue condemned the All Black management after the quarter-final loss to France but, when Graham was reappointed, he became positively apoplectic, announcing that from that moment forth, whenever the Bledisloe Cup was at stake, he would be supporting Robbie Deans's Australian team.

Rattue's distaste for Graham as a coach was never more crudely expressed than after the first squad for 2008 was named:

As divided as my loyalties remain while Graham Henry is at the helm, you have to fight off post World Cup bitterness and try to find some reasonable ground. The trouble is the squad is playing for a coach I can't stomach and under an administration which I loathe, not only for allowing Henry's one-trick excuse act to find a receptive audience but also its determination to ruin the game like a secret society that almost encourages a state of fear.

OK, Chris, we understand where you're coming from!

Graham could never understand why the *New Zealand Herald* continued to promote a writer who never seemed to attend matches or press conferences, and who certainly never once contacted Graham for a comment. He remains the embodiment of Ian Fraser's 'disgruntled hack' who interviews his own laptop and indulges in violent knee-jerk reactions to pretty much every result. His sensationalism and personal attacks on Graham seem an incongruous fit in the country's largest selling daily newspaper, which had always been essentially conservative. The great Sir Terry McLean, whose eloquent writings graced the paper for four decades, would turn in his grave at some of Rattue's raves.

If Rattue belonged, and still does belong, to the 'chopping down tall poppies' brigade, then Murray Deaker and Willie Lose, two of Newstalk ZB and Radio Sport's talkback hosts in 2007, definitely, in Graham's mind, slotted into the king-making category. Deaker revelled in the king-maker role and Lose became his clone.

Deaker is a man whose obsessiveness, which almost ruined his personal life, tends to spill over into his radio programme. He'd gone completely overboard, figuratively speaking, after Russell Coutts and Brad Butterworth abandoned Team New Zealand to sail for the Swiss, and now he turned on Graham, dramatically, after the All Blacks' loss to France.

Because he was in the UK, where replaying videos of the match to identify what had really gone on would have been difficult, Deaker probably never had the opportunity to assess whether there were extenuating circumstances in the All Blacks' loss. So he went straight for the jugular — Graham's!

Nothing short of Graham's resignation was going to satisfy him. An 87 per cent win record across four years and a referee who had overlooked as many as 40 infringements by the French that could have been penalized — all this counted for little. Graham's team had lost. The All Blacks had choked again. The coach had to go!

Deaker hosted the top-ranking radio sports programme on Newstalk ZB at weekends, syndicated throughout New Zealand, ran nightly midweek talkback programmes on the same station and presented his 'Deaker on Sport' programme Wednesday nights on Sky TV, so he was in a position to influence an enormous number of people.

Most New Zealanders were so nauseated by the events at the Millennium Stadium that only an infinitesimal number of them would have replayed the game in an attempt to understand just what had gone on. Most would have adopted the damn-and-blast attitude, grizzled and groaned after the final whistle, and confined the video, if indeed they had access to it, to the don't-ever-want-to-go-there-again heap.

So when Deaker heaped all the blame for the outcome in Cardiff on coach Henry, most people who tuned into his programme probably presumed he was right: the All Blacks had lost, and coach Henry had completely buggered them up with his conditioning and rotation policies to such an extent they had choked under pressure.

Graham didn't listen to any of this, which was his way of controlling his own environment, although friends and colleagues inevitably felt obliged to pass on some of Deaker's juicier comments.

Raewyn, however, did listen to some of the rants. She accepted that following a loss there had to be debate and analysis, but she was horrified that Deaker, in her opinion, had become so horribly personal.

This was a person Graham had known for more than 30 years. He had assisted Deaker during the challenging years when alcohol threatened to tear his (Deaker's) life apart and, in turn, he had turned to Deaker when he needed direction before he quit New Zealand to become coach of Wales. Prior to events at the World Cup, Graham would have labelled Deaker a friend.

Raewyn couldn't stand Deaker's attacks on her husband any longer, so she emailed him, without telling Graham. It was a private email, and as far as Raewyn is concerned, it remains private. But to her surprise its existence became a news item in the *New Zealand Herald*. She certainly didn't publicize the fact she'd sent the email — she didn't even let on to Graham — and to this day doesn't know how the *Herald* learnt of it.

All Raewyn is prepared to concede more than four years on is that in the email she reminded Deaker of the meaning of friendship. She has never had a reply or spoken to him since.

Here's the story the *New Zealand Herald* ran:

The wife of reinstated All Black coach Graham Henry has gone on the attack on behalf of her husband, sending a critical personal message to one of his biggest critics, Murray Deaker.

Raewyn, who her husband has dubbed the All Blacks' fifth selector because of her rugby knowledge, had been incensed about the marketing of Deaker's anti-Henry book in which he pulls apart the All Black coach over his World Cup failure.

The book has been heavily advertised on Newstalk ZB with Deaker saying he and Henry have been mates for 40 years but 'this is not a mates book'. The book lays the blame for the All Blacks' dismal World Cup performance squarely at Henry's feet.

Sources say Raewyn corrected Deaker on any misconceptions he might have about a friendship but the broadcaster wasn't willing to go into specifics.

'She just reacted about something,' says Deaker. 'Someone asked me the other day if I was going to do something about it and I said I was going to do nothing. Sometimes giving things time is the best way to go.'

Asked if he had contacted Raewyn since she sent him the email, he said, 'The content was such I don't think she wants me to get in contact.'

For Smithy, the loss at Cardiff was devastating after the disappointments of the 1999 and 2003 World Cup campaigns. His son Nicholas was in the grandstand and his wife, Trish, was about to fly across for the semi-final and final.

The months after the World Cup disaster were extremely challenging for all the coaches and management. Smithy spoke at a rugby club function at which a club member stood up and said the team of eight-year-olds he coached demonstrated more passion and commitment than the All Blacks against France.

In Akaroa, where Smithy often holidayed, the butcher had written on a blackboard outside the shop: 'Good luck in Aussie, Robbie — stick it up the NZRU!'

Smithy asked the butcher, 'Does Robbie shop here?'

'No.'

'Well, I do, and I've spent a lot of money in this shop. And unless you rub that message off the blackboard, I won't be spending any more!'

Smithy, Shag and manager Darren Shand, all good Christchurch men, were targeted by disgruntled fans, some of whom had spent tens of thousands of dollars getting to Europe with supporters groups only to find the men in black heading back Down Under about the time they were arriving in Europe.

However, not everybody agreed with Deaker. On a visit to Auckland, Smithy was invited out to a dinner where there were a large number of people in attendance. Smithy called the host aside. 'I just want to say I've got huge respect for Graham Henry,' he said, 'and I'd prefer there was no criticism of him tonight.'

'That's all right,' the host bounced back. 'We're all fans of Graham Henry here!'

Graham also found that the vitriol being directed at him by sections of the media didn't equate to how most of the public were interpreting things. Indeed, only one individual confronted him personally. It happened in a supermarket after the new season was under way. This random individual came up behind Graham and said, 'I know who you are and I know you are doing OK this year, but you should have got dropped after the World Cup.'

'Oh, thank you for sharing that with me,' said Graham, whereupon the accuser turned and took off.

The 2008 and 2009 seasons were particularly challenging ones for

Ted and Shag and Smithy for a number of reasons. After crashing out of the World Cup, they knew they would be under heavy scrutiny from the media, in particular, and the public. Also, the game itself, through the incorrect interpretation of the laws, particularly at the breakdown, had deteriorated and was tending to reward teams that played kick-and-chase rugby.

In addition to this, the All Blacks had lost their front row colossus Carl Hayman, who had found an offer from the UK club Newcastle too good to resist. Other World Cup campaigners who'd succumbed to lucrative offers were Byron Kelleher, Nick Evans, Anton Oliver, Jerry Collins, Aaron Mauger and Luke McAlister.

Hayman's departure represented a massive loss for the All Blacks. Throughout Graham's first four years, he was decisively the best prop in the world. However, he was sick of the constant scrutiny and the commitments to the media and sponsors that went with being a high-profile All Black. He also wanted to fulfil his dream of being able to purchase a dairy farm in the Taranaki, and Graham understood that.

The loss of all these experienced players, however, opened the door for such exciting players as Ma'a Nonu, Richard Kahui, Rudi Wulf, Adam Thomson, Jerome Kaino and the great workhorse who'd recommitted himself to rugby, Brad Thorn. The future looked bright, but the coaches knew it was still going to be a demanding season.

With Richie McCaw leading the charge, the All Blacks defeated Ireland once and World Cup champions England twice to get their season off to a positive start. When they then defeated the Springboks in Wellington, led by Rodney So'oialo because McCaw was nursing an injury, the win extended Ted and Shag and Smithy's record to a remarkable 26 straight home victories in four and bit seasons.

Unfortunately, that demonstration of invincibility on home soil was about to come crashing down. An audacious try scored by halfback Ricky Januarie in the 75th minute gave the Springboks a 30–28 win at Carisbrook — at Carisbrook, for goodness' sake, where the Springboks hadn't won in 87 years. Carisbrook had been regarded as the ultimate fortress against overseas raiders.

Rugby's laws as they existed in 2008 were made for the Springboks, who consistently drove off their lineout giants Victor Matfield, Bakkies Botha and Andries Bekker, putting players in front of the ball, making it almost impossible for defending teams to get at the player with the ball.

Referees were also being lenient on tacklers, allowing them to (illegally) play the ball when they were on the ground.

Graham found it a particularly frustrating time to be coaching because the interpretation of the laws was militating against attacking teams. Because possession couldn't be guaranteed at breakdowns, teams were finding it smarter to kick rather than risk a turnover; as a consequence, rugby was suffering not just as a spectacle but as a game to coach and play. Even Graham's own sons told him they were having difficulty understanding the tackle-ball rulings and were finding a lot of games boring. Like many others, they had stopped going to watch matches live.

A fortnight after the Carisbrook setback, the All Blacks headed to Sydney and a clash with the Wallabies that was, not unnaturally, built up massively as a personal duel between Robbie Deans and Graham Henry.

A decision by the All Black management to delay their journey to Sydney until the Thursday was about to backfire. Horrendous weather in Wellington had meant the team had had to train indoors and their late arrival meant they'd missed out on the host city's test-match hype.

To Graham's chagrin, the man he'd beaten for the All Black coaching role emerged the victor, his team romping home by 34 points to 19. The All Blacks, still minus McCaw, played adventurous rugby and contributed handsomely to a spectacular contest, witnessed by 78,944 fans — more than had attended the State of Origin league decider at the same venue — but the Wallabies, lethal at the breakdown area, romped away in the second half. It was the first time since 2000 that the All Blacks had lost two Tri-Nations matches in succession.

It was now Deans one, Henry nil. Graham, Steve and Wayne acknowledge they had been out-thought and out-played in Sydney.

They had a week to turn things around before the replay at Eden Park.

The All Blacks' hefty defeat had Graham's greatest critic, Chris Rattue, positively salivating. He wrote in the *New Zealand Herald*: 'Sydney was such an Aussie triumph and All Black disaster that it has proved already that the Deans supporters were absolutely right, no matter what happens from here on in.'

It wasn't just Rattue getting into Ted that week; the Deans sympathizers were also in full flight. The All Black coach and the NZRU board who'd reappointed him were all copping it in the neck, placing immense pressure upon Ted and his team to get it right at Eden Park.

Fortunately for Graham, McCaw was back to lead the side. In other significant changes, Jimmy Cowan replaced Andy Ellis at halfback, Richard Kahui came in for Anthony Tuitavake on the wing with McCaw replacing Daniel Braid at No. 7. And Rodney So'oialo and Jerome Kaino swapped positions, Kaino moving from No. 8 to blindside flanker, the position in which, by 2011, he would stamp himself the best player in the world.

Graham considered the All Blacks had been tactically naive in Sydney. They had endeavoured to play too much rugby and had not kicked intelligently, too regularly gifting the ball back to the Australians.

Graham identifies a handful of watershed matches in his international coaching career, contests that just simply couldn't be lost. And this rematch with the Wallabies was one of them. He can't ever remember working harder, and hardly slept.

There would be no benevolence towards Robbie Deans's team this time. The men in black played a far more astute game. Kicks, when made, went no more than 20 metres and were contestable, the reverse of Sydney.

Loosehead prop Tony Woodcock had two nicknames: one, predictably, was Woody; the other Teabag. Graham always called him Woody, although many of his team-mates preferred the alternative.

Teabag would come to have enormous significance, and would even help win a World Cup. It was the code name given to a lineout ploy devised by Steve Hansen. Perfected at training, it had its first airing against Deans's men at Eden Park.

'Teabag,' announced hooker Andrew Hore as he prepared to throw to a lineout deep inside the Australian 22. For the move to succeed, it required his throw to lock Ali Williams to have pinpoint accuracy. It did. Half the All Black lineout squeezed forward, the other half filtered back, creating a cavernous zone through which good old Teabag sauntered, after taking Ali's delivery from the peak of his jump, for a ridiculously easy try.

Woodcock amazingly scored another try three minutes later, but it was the Teabag move that brought the whole team immense satisfaction. For a secret move to be executed with total precision in the heat of battle, completely dumbfounding the opposition, was a source of huge satisfaction to the whole team.

'We'll put that one on ice,' said Hansen later. It wouldn't be used again until the World Cup final in 2011 ... 1177 days away!

The All Blacks demolished the Wallabies 39–10, scoring four tries to one. A slight smile returned to Graham's face. Although there were still a couple of massive challenges in front of the team — the Springboks in Cape Town in a fortnight's time and a further rematch against the Wallabies in Brisbane — they'd rediscovered the winning way.

Skipper McCaw described their relief at the press conference: 'The boys have been hurting all week and wanted a good performance. When you lose two in a row, it's a question of how you get back on the horse.'

The odds were still heavily stacked against the All Blacks retaining the Tri-Nations trophy but, thanks to the victory at Eden Park, it was at least achievable.

McCaw had been criticized, quite mercilessly in some quarters, for his part in the All Blacks' World Cup downfall. Most critics found it easier to ignore the match officials' influence and instead apportion all the blame to, in no particular order, the coach, the players and the captain.

McCaw was vilified for failing to implement a Plan B when, with time running out, Plan A patently hadn't succeeded. What the critics conveniently overlooked was that neither Plan A nor Plan B, nor Plans C through to Z, had the remotest chance of succeeding on this freakish occasion — even if Richie or anyone else had chosen to activate them, there was a greater likelihood of Halley's Comet being sighted through the Millennium Stadium roof than there was of referee Barnes awarding the All Blacks a penalty in those critical closing stages.

McCaw, although utterly perplexed, followed his coach's lead and declined to blame the referee or anyone else for the defeat. That's Richie: stoic, honest, loyal.

To best prepare the team for the Springbok challenge, it was decided to give the players eight days in Cape Town. After assembly in Auckland, they faced an early morning departure for Sydney from where they would fly through to Johannesburg.

Graham, always an early riser, did a double-take when he surfaced in Auckland to prepare for the big day of travel. The players were at a meeting in the team room, and it was only 4.15 a.m.

'What the hell's going on?' Graham asked team manager Darren Shand.

'Richie organized a team meeting for 4 a.m.'

'Really!'

At his own initiative, McCaw had set up a players' meeting. Management were not involved. At the meeting McCaw spelt out his expectations in terms of behaviour — starting with the long, gruelling flight through to South Africa — as well as preparation and performance for the week ahead. After the disappointments of the World Cup and the recent losses to South Africa and Australia, he wanted the players to reassert themselves as the best team in the world.

Graham was convinced from the moment he learned of McCaw's inspirational rev-up that the players would deal to the Springboks. McCaw's initiative epitomized what the black jersey meant to the All Black skipper. Some critics claimed to have identified poor leadership and a lack of mental toughness at the World Cup. Well, McCaw was displaying that toughness right now. Mentally, he was the strongest man Graham had had the pleasure to coach.

The All Blacks never let the Springboks into the game at Cape Town. With McCaw turning in one of his finest performances — he was named Player of the Match — the ABs kept the Springboks scoreless for only the fourth time in 75 contests (and the first time ever in South Africa), winning 19–nil. The winning margin could have been even bigger but Dan Carter experienced a rare off-day with his goal-kicking, missing five of seven attempts.

The drawn-out nature of the Tri-Nations Championship in 2008 meant there was a full month before the All Blacks tackled the Wallabies in Brisbane in what would now become a winner-take-all contest. The NZRU helped the team prepare by arranging an international against Samoa in New Plymouth, which turned into a try-fest for McCaw's men. They won 101–14, bagging 15 tries.

Having learnt their lesson from the Sydney experience, the All Blacks altered their modus operandi. Instead of flying across the Tasman on the Thursday — the original plan — they gave themselves a full week in Brisbane to acclimatize. And it paid off.

Again brilliantly led from the front by McCaw, the All Blacks came storming back from 7–17 down early in the second half to establish a commanding 28–17 lead before conceding a late try. Final score: 28–24. No shortage of mental toughness this time. Game, Bledisloe Cup and Tri-Nations trophy to New Zealand.

Afterwards, Graham sat contentedly in the Suncorp Stadium dressing room; in fact, he was positively purring.

'Well done, guys,' he said to his players. 'You have been outstanding under extreme pressure since Sydney. Thanks for your efforts. You can be enormously proud of yourselves. They were three great wins — Auckland, Cape Town and now here.'

A side issue to the Brisbane game resulted in Steve Hansen firing off an angry missive to the Australian Rugby Union, alleging Wallabies coach Robbie Deans had received secret footage of All Black trainings while they were in Brisbane. Hansen alleged an Australian television station had filmed All Black practices and handed the tapes to the Wallabies.

He never received an answer.

One of the obvious secrets to success for the All Blacks in 2008 was that the coaches had settled on a regular line-up — no rotation, dare we say it! — fielding the same starting XV in Auckland, Cape Town and Brisbane: Mils Muliaina, Richard Kahui, Conrad Smith, Ma'a Nonu, Sitiveni Sivivatu, Dan Carter, Jimmy Cowan, Rodney So'oialo, Richie McCaw, Jerome Kaino, Ali Williams, Brad Thorn, Greg Somerville, Andrew Hore, and Tony Woodcock. The substitutes used were Isaia Toeava, Anthony Tuitavake, Stephen Donald, Piri Weepu, Adam Thomson, Anthony Boric, John Afoa and Keven Mealamu.

It's interesting to note that of the 23 players who featured in those matches, only three, Sivivatu, So'oialo and Somerville, would not be part of the 2011 World Cup campaign three years on.

In 105 years of test-match rivalry, the only occasion New Zealand and Australia had engaged each other beyond their own boundaries was in 1991 at the Rugby World Cup when they squared off in the semi-final at Lansdowne Road in Dublin, the first occasion the All Blacks had ever lost a World Cup fixture.

The opportunity for the two great rivals to clash offshore again came at the beginning of November 2008, at the exotic destination of Hong Kong, a novel and convenient stopover for both teams heading to the UK. In an enterprising gesture, the Hong Kong Rugby Union had bid for the game, to promote the sport in the ex-colony while hopefully making a few dollars for New Zealand, Australia and itself. It turned out a win-win situation with 40,000 fans packing the Hong Kong Stadium.

With the Bledisloe Cup secure, Ted and Shag and Smithy used the occasion to try some fresh combinations. Hosea Gear and Cory Jane (who came on as a sub) made their All Black debuts, Stephen Donald played at first-five with Carter switching to the No. 12 jersey, Isaia Toeava took over at fullback and Neemiah Tialàta slotted into the front row.

To Graham's relief, his team came from 9–14 down at half-time to win 19–14. The organizers were thirsting for a spectacular contest but the combination of slippery surface and a finicky referee (Alan Lewis) meant the game never exploded into life. And the win came at a hefty cost, with hooker Andrew Hore invalided out of the tour. In just the fourth minute he suffered a high ankle sprain, finishing up on crutches. It didn't prevent him being selected as the New Zealand Rugby Player of the Year, though.

Then it was off to the UK in search of another Grand Slam. Because of the All Blacks' continuing great record in the UK, some of the media were becoming blasé about Grand Slams, which annoyed Graham.

Well, Henry's All Blacks not only pulled off the feat for the second time in three years but this time managed it without conceding a solitary try, a remarkable achievement. Scotland landed two penalty goals, Ireland one, Wales three and England two while the All Blacks recorded scores of 32, 22, 29 and 32.

A virtual second XV was fielded against the Scots, affording the opportunity for Jamie Mackintosh, Kieran Read and Liam Messam to make their All Black debuts, with Ted and Shag and Smithy using pretty much their strongest XV in the three other internationals.

There was one other highlight. In this modern professional rugby era, the All Blacks rarely get to play against club or provincial teams; their rugby diet is almost exclusively test matches now. So it was a rare delight to have a fixture slotted in at Limerick against Munster, the red-shirted lot who in 1978 had pulled off a stunning victory against Graham Mourie's team that would go on to complete New Zealand's first Grand Slam. It remains the only occasion any Irish team has downed the All Blacks in more than 100 years of trying. The 2008 game was arranged to commemorate the 30th anniversary of Munster's famous win.

For a long time at Thomond Park, it seemed history was going to repeat itself. Playing with ferocity, as they always do, the men of Munster — featuring a cluster of Kiwis in the backline, including Doug Howlett at fullback — led 16–10 at half-time and were still three points ahead with four minutes to play. But a well-taken try to Joe Rokocoko allowed the All Blacks, captained on this occasion by Piri Weepu, to escape victorious.

It was while he was in Ireland that Graham received the news that the International Committee for Fair Play had awarded him the

Pierre de Coubertin Trophy for his 'exemplary attitude' following the All Blacks' World Cup quarter-final loss to France. The award had come rugby's way on only three other occasions: Welsh rugby hero Gareth Edwards was the recipient in 1978, the French club team Paris Club de France won in 1991 and Graham's first All Black captain, Tana Umaga, had been acknowledged in 2003 for going to the assistance of Welsh forward Colin Charvis when he'd been knocked unconscious during a test in Hamilton and Umaga had been concerned the Welshman might have swallowed his tongue.

Other winners have included Czech long-distance runner Emil Zátopek, who won three gold medals at the 1952 Olympic Games, legendary English soccer player Stanley Matthews, and former South Africa president Nelson Mandela.

The award was presented at a ceremony in Istanbul, Turkey, in January 2009. Because of its prestigious nature, Graham made the effort to attend, along with Raewyn.

Graham's rugby adventures had taken him to countless destinations around the globe, but Turkey was somewhere completely different. It certainly didn't feature on any rugby map. But fortunately, Graham and Raewyn were regulars at their local Kahve Turkish Café in St Heliers and had befriended the owner Sudar. He was overjoyed when he learnt they were journeying to Istanbul. 'You must call my friend Buland. He is a football fan like myself — we know nothing about rugby — but he will look after you.' And that's how Graham and Raewyn came to explore the exotic city of Istanbul, with their own eager chauffeur. He was prepared to drive them the 210 km to Gallipolli but unfortunately time did not permit.

12

Sharing the ownership

A perception probably exists among New Zealand's rugby faithful that as a former headmaster with an impressive record preparing school, club, provincial, Super and international teams, Graham is a powerful personality who operated throughout his time as All Black head coach pretty much the same way he started: as the boss. Sure, he would have modified his methods, sharing his coaching responsibilities with Shag and Smithy, but essentially he would have been responsible for team tactics, preparation and planning, tweaking here, tweaking there, directing operations like the conductor of an orchestra. The players would be waiting breathlessly at the beginning of each week to find out how Ted wanted them to prepare for the upcoming opponent. After all, that's a head coach's role, isn't it?

Well, nothing could be further from the truth. The Graham Henry who prepared the Auckland representative team in the 1990s, when rugby was delightfully amateur, of course, bore no resemblance to the Graham Henry who guided the fortunes of the All Blacks through the final few seasons leading up to World Cup glory in 2011.

Graham would tell you he wouldn't last five minutes now coaching the way he had in the 1970s and 1980s when he was a total autocrat. It's how things were done in those days, when coaches like Fred Allen banged the table with a clenched fist and bawled out individuals who weren't paying attention. Graham concedes he enjoyed the coaching style at the time, but that was when rugby was amateur, when teams trained twice a week before fronting up for a match on the Saturday.

Afterwards, the players would go back to being bankers or builders or labourers or students, and Graham would return to teaching.

All that changed when rugby became professional. For the most talented players, and coaches, rugby was no longer their pastime, their sport; it was their profession, their seven-day-a-week job.

Although Graham modified his methods, he continued to function very much as The Boss. He nominated the battle plan for the upcoming contest, organized the training schedules, delivered the team talk, gave directions and, if necessary, changed personnel at half-time and generally oversaw the entire operation.

Nothing much changed until he was appointed coach of the British Lions in 2001 when he suddenly found himself with three assistant coaches. That took some adjusting to, because Graham wasn't accustomed to delegating too many of his coaching responsibilities. It was an important learning curve. So, too, was being technical adviser to Wayne Pivac and Grant Fox with Auckland for two years upon his return to New Zealand. He emerged from that phase of his career, as third in charge, a wiser and far more understanding coach.

By the time Graham stepped up to the All Black coaching role in 2004 his philosophy had broadened. He came with a back coach (Wayne Smith), a forward coach (Steve Hansen) and a scrum guru (Mike Cron), leaving him to mastermind operations. Collectively, the four of them, with Graham in the role of facilitator, determined the match tactics and training strategy, and on match days Graham delivered the inspirational team talk.

Well, if Graham thought that was the way forward, he was to receive a couple of important wake-up calls. Like all other NZRU employees, he was subjected to 360-degree performance evaluations, the process in which individuals are assessed by their peers, bosses and workmates. When the results of the first one came out, Graham felt sick for a week! But he was astute enough to realize that if those around him were identifying shortcomings in his methods, then he had better modify them if he wanted to become a better coach and manager.

Also, Tana Umaga, his first All Black captain, had stopped him in his tracks by suggesting that the team talks which Graham deemed such a fundamental part of the game were essentially a waste of time. When other senior players confirmed that they never listened to Graham's match-day talks because they were already focused on the events ahead, he felt obliged to discontinue them.

It was part of an evolutionary process that would help bring Graham, if not exactly screaming, into the 21st century and make him a more effective head coach.

The most spectacularly effective part of that evolutionary process would be in passing ownership of the All Black team on to the players.

This handing over wasn't something that happened overnight. It was an evolving process which management were always trying to get better. It had its origins in 2004 but because it wasn't right, not every player bought into it. The process started to show real progress in the 2008 and 2009 seasons, after the board of the New Zealand Rugby Union — God bless them — reappointed Graham, along with the coaching and management teams. And it became solid and highly effective in 2010 and 2011.

Shandy, Ted, Shag and Smithy, using Gilbert Enoka as their facilitator, had embraced the shared leadership concept, but hadn't got it quite right. They'd essentially left it to the players to choose their own leaders, initially implementing the concept with a group of nine, a number that proved a little cumbersome.

What came to work so brilliantly — indeed, Graham goes so far as to suggest that without its implementation the All Blacks would not have won the World Cup in 2011 — was the appointment by the coaches of the Magnificent Seven.

Richie McCaw, Dan Carter, Mils Muliaina and Andrew Hore became the on-field leaders and Conrad Smith, Brad Thorn and Keven Mealamu the off-field leaders, although they all effectively led on the field.

The on-field leaders would get together on Sunday nights with Ted and Shag and Smithy. They would review the previous game and formulate the plan for the upcoming contest. The players always had a major input into the game plan and the intensity required at trainings; collectively, they would identify what had to be nailed in the week coming up.

Enoka the facilitator, or Bert as he was popularly known, would summarize proceedings, type them up and circulate copies to all those who'd attended the meeting.

The Monday training was always light, with the main, physically intensive session coming on the Tuesday. That's when the set pieces — scrums, lineouts and defensive alignment — became a major focus.

The on-field leaders would talk again with the coaches at lunch on the Tuesday to make sure everything was coming together satisfactorily.

Wednesday was a day off. It hadn't always been that way; indeed, the change didn't come until after the 2007 World Cup campaign. It was on Graham's initiative that the week was dramatically restructured, after he concluded that the game plan lost its clarity some time between training on Wednesday morning and match kick-off on Saturday evening.

So Wednesday became a free day, a recovery day, one when the players could relax, physically and mentally, before cranking up again with two sessions on Thursday. The morning session was usually indoors and light, with the players walking and jogging, and talking as they sought to increase clarity on what they were planning for match day. The afternoon session was short but high-paced. Having talked the talk in the morning, now they executed the moves to ensure everyone was on the same page. It was, as Graham would describe it, about technical alignment.

Friday featured the traditional Captain's Run at the match venue, unless exceptional circumstances prevented access to the ground. It provided an opportunity for the kickers to familiarize themselves with angles, wind draughts and the match surface, while skipper McCaw reappraised match tactics from his perspective.

The off-field leaders, Smith, Thorn and Mealamu, who worked closely with manager Darren Shand, had two primary roles: to organize the team's social schedule and to help ease new players into the All Black environment.

It was their responsibility to ensure the newcomers were enjoying themselves. They did this surreptitiously, slotting their mentoring roles in over breakfast or at lunchtime or over a coffee. Graham describes them as 'three very special guys' who achieved a massive amount in terms of team morale.

The shared ownership arrangement didn't stop with the Magnificent Seven: Tony Woodcock worked closely with scrum guru Mike Cron in helping make the All Black scrum one of the most feared units in the game, Kieran Read operated as the lineout organizer, and Ma'a Nonu, with others, had a major input into the team's defence planning.

The leadership group, who were much admired by their peers, could easily have been expanded but the team's management felt that would have been counterproductive. Seven was just the right number.

Their work wasn't confined to the boundaries of the rugby season, either. They usually got together a couple of times in high summer, along with the three coaches, plus manager Shand, strength and conditioning coach Nic Gill and facilitator Enoka — who represented the glue that bound everyone and everything together — to set objectives for the year ahead.

In 2009 Wayne Smith came up with a concept that was adopted and proved nothing short of brilliant: the All Black Club, which was embraced wholeheartedly by the whole team.

One night per week the team room became the All Black Club room. Players and management were obliged to attend wearing their club jerseys — Graham always fronted in his Auckland University colours — and there were fines for any infractions. Sessions lasted one hour, no longer.

Each meeting one or two players would speak about their clubs and what they were famous for, always with humour.

Shag (Steve Hansen) was the club captain and Dan Carter his assistant, and their resourcefulness and sharp wit ensured there was a lot of laughter, providing a valuable release valve before and after high-pressure international fixtures.

The club gathered momentum as it went along with a notice board and impressive honours boards being created. The honours boards featured all the players' names, the number of tests they had played, and the year they had been part of a Tri-Nations winning team, retained the Bledisloe Cup, or featured in a Grand Slam triumph. There was space for the Rugby World Cup, but it was blank!

A Life Members board was instituted onto which were inducted the fourth selector, Sir Brian Lochore, and NZRU chairman Jock Hobbs. Joining them was Graham Henry, on the pretext of his age.

No rugby club would be complete without the obligatory raffles and these also featured. Product from the team's major sponsor, Adidas, were always a popular prize, and sometimes there'd be a dinner for two on offer; other times booby prizes — unmentionables — were handed out.

While the All Blacks Club usually functioned in the team's hotel team room, occasionally the event was taken 'on tour', notably to Richard Kahui's Te Rapa club in Hamilton and Andrew Ellis and Kieran Read's University club in Christchurch.

Smithy will tell you that his All Black Club idea was germinating for a couple of years before being implemented. By popular consent it was one of the best things ever introduced into the team environment.

Having something to laugh at was important in 2009 because it became a particularly challenging and frustrating year. There were a couple of obvious reasons for this: injuries to key players, most notably Dan Carter, who'd torn his Achilles tendon while on 'sabbatical' in France, and the game itself which continued to reward conservative teams with accurate goal-kickers ahead of attack-conscious sides.

Statistics certainly bore this out, with international scoring patterns showing an alarming trend. The nine Tri-Nations matches produced 69 penalty goals at an average of 7.7 a game, but only 27 tries. The IRB's continued rejection of the differential penalty goal had promoted a game of 'aerial ping pong'. This played into the hands of the Springboks, who controlled the set pieces through their awesomely efficient lineout, allowing them to dominate territory. When the penalties inevitably came, they kicked them. The Springboks won five of their six matches and waltzed off with the Tri-Nations trophy. Morne Steyn flourished, with his boot accounting for 90 of the team's 158 points. He banged over eight penalty goals against the All Blacks in Durban and seven against the Wallabies in Cape Town.

Complicating matters for the All Blacks in 2009 was the fact that the experimental laws being trialled by the IRB, known as ELVs, operated in Super 14 matches but not in the Tri-Nations fixtures where global laws still applied. This meant the All Blacks had to adapt to lineout drives that couldn't be pulled down and a slower game that didn't have the flow or momentum offered by free kicks. It was like playing a totally different sport and proved difficult to master with just 10 days' preparation.

The All Blacks, and also the Wallabies, strove valiantly to adhere to their attacking principles, but the law interpretations in 2009 were stacked against them. The Wallabies scored more tries than any other team during the year, which included end-of-year tests against England, Ireland, Scotland and Wales, yet finished up losing more than 50 per cent of their matches.

And the All Blacks dropped five games — the season opener against France in Dunedin, all three Tri-Nations clashes against the Springboks, and the end-of-year romp against the Barbarians at Twickenham — making it decidedly the least successful of Graham's years as head coach. The solitary comfort was that the Bledisloe Cup was retained.

The All Blacks' leading playmaker, Carter, was never going to be available till well into the season and injuries sustained during the Tri-Nations took out a cluster of experienced individuals, most notably Richie McCaw, Conrad Smith, Ali Williams and Andrew Hore.

What that did, of course, was seriously deplete the group of on-field leaders; indeed, the only 'survivor' as the international season got under way was Mils Muliaina, who was handed the captaincy.

What should have been one of the highlights of Muliaina's celebrated career became a rather painful experience. His first post-match speech was a losing one after the All Blacks crashed to defeat against France at what used to be the All Blacks' greatest fortress, Carisbrook, and a week later he had to hand over the Dave Gallaher Trophy to Thierry Dusautoir. Even though his team had won the rematch 14–10, the French had finished with a superior points aggregate.

When the All Blacks then laboured to a 27–6 win over Italy, an opponent they traditionally hoisted half a century of points against,

Graham glumly reflected that the team had never played so poorly throughout his time as head coach as they did that June. He felt sorry for Muliaina — three tests as captain, three rubbishy performances.

The All Blacks had lost their way, and Graham is the first to concede that. With three of the on-field leaders missing, instead of giving new captain Muliaina unqualified support and developing other on-field leaders and passing on that responsibility, the coaches had reclaimed ownership of the team and sought to captain it from the bench.

'Sorry, Mils,' Graham said to him after his stint as captain had concluded, with McCaw back for the Tri-Nations. 'You deserved better than that. We stuffed it up for you.'

The Tri-Nations provided a weird mix of results for the men in black — three wins over Australia and three losses to South Africa.

Was there a common factor in these results? Well, most definitely yes as far as the successes against Australia were concerned: the Bledisloe Cup is the trophy the All Blacks value most highly after the Webb Ellis Cup — and there was also a bloke called Robbie Deans. Fact is, the players didn't want to get beaten by Robbie. His name was never mentioned by the coaches in match preparations but a good few of the players had a Crusaders connection and most certainly did not want to lose to a Robbie Deans coached team.

What a pity Deans wasn't involved with the Springboks as well! But the South African team was truly awesome in 2009, creating huge pressure on opponents at the set pieces. Coming off a stimulating series against the British and Irish Lions, the Springboks were an experienced, game-wise team. They devised a smart game plan, one assisted by the existing laws, which they executed with clinical efficiency. It eliminated the All Blacks' strengths and exposed their deficiencies.

The Boks took the high ground, mentally and physically, effectively bullying the All Blacks. They broke the All Blacks down in the set pieces, allowing them limited quality set-piece ball. They attacked through lineout drives and demonstrated huge physicality at the breakdown. Graham was so impressed with the Springbok tactics, he wrote in his season's review to the NZRU that 'there is no substitute for physical dominance — it is the number one pillar in the game'.

The Springboks limited their own use of the ball so opportunities for turnovers were kept to a minimum, consistently attacking through aerial bombardment and hard chasing.

To the Springboks, field position was gold. Whenever penalties were awarded to them within 60 metres of the goalposts, they had the players ready to place the goals. In their six Tri-Nations fixtures, five of which they won, they scored only 10 tries but slotted 29 penalty goals and three dropped goals. Morne Steyn almost never missed and if the distance was sometimes a tad excessive for him, his namesake Francois would step forward and astonish onlookers with prodigious kicks from his own half.

Victor Matfield stamped himself as the best lineout player in the world and loosies Juan Smith and Pierre Spies were irresistible as they drove opponents back.

It was a formula that proved too much for the All Blacks, who were left to survive on crumbs, spending an excess of each game in their own half. They were accused of naivety by some critics for endeavouring to launch attacks from deep in their own territory, but Ted and Shag and Smithy defended their tactical approach. They weren't prepared to abandon their attacking policy just because the laws militated against them. They had a profound belief the law-makers would, sooner rather than later, amend the laws to encourage tries to be scored rather than goals to be kicked. If they didn't, the game was doomed.

Outgunned in Bloemfontein and Durban, the All Blacks made a valiant attempt to retrieve some prestige in the third Bok clash at Hamilton's Rugby Park but once again they yielded to the lethal goal-kicking of the Steyn boys, ultimately going down 32–29, two tries apiece. They'd made progress but not enough.

While losing to the Springboks wasn't a great experience, and certainly not three times in the one season, mingling with them in the changing rooms afterwards and socializing with them on the rare occasions that became possible was always a highlight.

Graham drew a parallel between John Smit, the Bok leader, and his own captain, Richie McCaw. Both were extremely intelligent, charismatic, focused individuals who led by example while wielding a significant influence on any game in which they participated. They knew games were won by the combination of an inspirational culture and environment off the field as well as correct execution of the game plan on the field.

To win a Rugby World Cup, you need a strong, inspirational captain. Graham had always known that: it hadn't escaped his attention that the leaders who had held the Webb Ellis Cup aloft in 1991 (Nick Farr-Jones, Australia), 1995 (Francois Pienaar, South Africa), 1999 (John Eales, Australia), 2003 (Martin Johnson, England) and 2007 (John Smit, South Africa) were all dynamic, hugely inspirational personalities. Graham was relieved that in Richie McCaw, he knew his All Black team possessed a leader of that calibre. Richie was critical to the World Cup campaign coming up in just over two years' time.

From their conversations with Smit and Co, the All Black management came to appreciate that the current Springboks, as a multiracial team, saw it as their destiny to be role models for the Rainbow nation and lead their country by example, both in terms of on-field success and off-field harmony. Plainly, this represented a massive motivation for the team; it was their emotional button.

A lacklustre season for the All Blacks finished on a high when they hammered the Wallabies 33–6 in Wellington in a contest in which no trophies were at stake (the Bledisloe Cup had already been secured and the Tri-Nations trophy had taken up residence in South Africa).

The Wellington contest was notable for the introduction of the 2.00-metre tall Otago player Tom Donnelly as Brad Thorn's locking partner. Isaac Ross had been preferred until then and while he possessed extremely good athletic skills, he had been found lacking in the tight stuff. With Ali Williams (who had torn his Achilles tendon again) and Anthony Boric injured, the selectors took a punt on Donnelly.

The 27-year-old had been knocking on the door but the selectors remained unconvinced he was genuine test material. Well, he answered that most emphatically in Wellington. Such was his impact, it left the selectors wondering whether, had they used Donnelly in the Tri-Nations series, they might have to some extent been able to neutralize Matfield.

Anyway, Donnelly was in and Ross was out (ostensibly left behind to bulk up) when the All Blacks headed to Tokyo to take on the Wallabies.

For this end-of-year tour, Ted and Shag and Smithy swapped coaching roles. Ted took charge of the forwards, Shag was responsible for the backs and Smithy organized the defence. This was done to give each coach a greater awareness of the others' roles and to provide a change of voice for the players.

At the final training run in Tokyo, Graham was whisked away early to fulfil media commitments. While he was absent, the New Zealand prime minister, John Key, who was in Japan on Government business, dropped in, joining the players in the dressing room and offering words of encouragement.

When Graham rejoined the team, he was advised that in his absence the players had discovered a new leader, someone who was hugely motivational. Best not to go away too often, Ted, or we might take this individual on board permanently!

Prime Minister Key would develop a close relationship with the team, often bringing his son into the dressing room after matches. PM Key would chat with the players while his son acquired a selection of extremely valuable autographs.

A repeat Grand Slam wasn't an option for the All Blacks in 2009 because this time they didn't play Ireland or Scotland. They produced rugby of only modest quality in putting away Wales, Italy and England. While they didn't concede a try (matching their achievement of the previous year), they scored only three themselves, relying on the accurate goal-kicking of Dan Carter at Cardiff and Twickenham, and Luke McAlister in Milan, for survival.

Then they moved on to Marseilles to deal with the always troublesome Tricolores who had so embarrassed them at the World Cup two years before and again in Wellington six months earlier.

It had been a challenging year for Graham and his fellow coaches. There had been frustrating losses to the Springboks and more than a few unconvincing performances, including those on the current tour.

'Right-ho, guys,' Graham said at a team meeting in Marseilles, 'let's see if we can't finish on a high. We've been winning but playing conservatively, almost too scared to play. This time, let's go out and express ourselves.'

And that's precisely what happened. The All Blacks produced a near-perfect performance, running in five tries (as many as they'd managed in their four previous outings) to win 39–12, allowing them to reclaim the Dave Gallaher Trophy. Having one of the world's best referees controlling the game, Alain Rolland, had certainly helped.

It was a significant performance that would set the scene for the next two years, featuring the bulk of the players who would guide New Zealand to World Cup glory in 2011: Dan Carter, Ma'a Nonu and Conrad Smith combined with devastating effect along the backline, sparked by Mils Muliaina from fullback; Cory Jane showed dash on the wing; Kieran Read, Richie McCaw and Jerome Kaino were in the process of stamping themselves as the most lethal loose forward set in world rugby; Brad Thorn and Tom Donnelly were effective in the lineout; and Tony Woodcock, Andrew Hore (in the absence of Keven Mealamu who was injured) and Owen Franks (who came on as a substitute) were strong in the front row.

Two others who came off the subs bench at Marseilles and would go on to play heroic roles two years on were Stephen Donald and Andrew Ellis.

The curtain drop on 2009 followed a game at Twickenham against a potent Barbarians team featuring several of the Springboks who had beaten the All Blacks in all three games that year. Victor Matfield captained the team from lock, Bryan Habana and Jaque Fourie were in the three-quarters, Fourie du Preez was at halfback, Schalk Burger wore the No. 7 jersey and Bismarck du Plessis was the hooker with Tendai Mtawarira (the Beast) and superboot Morne Steyn coming off the reserves bench. The team also featured Wallabies Matt Giteau, Drew Mitchell, George Smith, Stephen Moore and Will Genia, a couple of Italians, and a dashing winger 'on loan' from the All Blacks, Joe Rokocoko. The side collectively boasted more than 900 international caps, making it arguably the most experienced rugby team ever fielded anywhere, any time.

As far as the All Black coaches were concerned their year had effectively concluded in Marseilles. The Barbarians game was about entertainment. For probably the only time in their eight years running the All Blacks, winning wasn't a major priority. So they made 14 changes from the team that played France, retaining only skipper McCaw (who was subbed at half-time).

Three players who'd made their All Black debuts on tour, Ben Smith, Zac Guildford and Tamati Ellison, were in the starting XV with the other new chum, Mike Delany, coming on as a substitute.

The All Blacks were competitive but it was the Barbarians who won the game, 25–18, all three of their tries going to Habana.

It's fair to say Ted and Shag and Smithy were pleased to see the end of 2009. The year hadn't been a write-off but nor, by their extremely high standards, could it be termed overly successful. Five losses made it their worst year by some distance.

Naturally, it provoked criticism from sections of the media. One who jumped to the All Blacks' defence was Bryan Gould. In an article published in the *New Zealand Herald*, under the heading THE ALL BLACKS — JUST ANOTHER TEAM? Gould wrote:

Given the success of rugby and its importance to New Zealand, how surprising it is to find at least in some quarters that in recent times rugby is denigrated, the All Blacks diminished.

Yes, of course we should celebrate sporting success in other areas but we can surely do without demeaning our achievements in rugby. It is almost as though some journalists and commentators resent our rugby success or (reflecting their profession's constant quest for novelty) have grown bored with it.

They seize upon the chance offered by success elsewhere to compare rugby unfavourably with the latest (usually transient) triumph. The All Blacks and rugby's administrators make their fair share of mistakes and should not be immune from criticism for doing so.

But do the carping (and sometimes sneering) critics realize what a national taonga they so carelessly demean? Do we have to do ourselves an unnecessary injury by thoughtlessly devaluing something we might appreciate fully only when we have lost it.

The aura of the All Blacks means not only that they are the best known and admired team in the world — the one the others most want to play and beat — but they are probably the most famous national team in world sport.

One consequence of this is that the All Blacks are hugely important to New Zealand's national identity. For millions of people around the world, the All Blacks are what they know best about New Zealand.

To their pleasant surprise, the All Blacks returned home ranked No. 1 in the world again. While they had been registering five test victories on tour (against Australia, Wales, England, Italy and France), the Springboks had crashed to defeat against Ireland and France.

Given that one of their major goals for the season was to establish themselves as the No. 1 team in the world, that outcome was most satisfying. However, Graham wasn't getting carried away. 'The team understand the IRB rankings are an ongoing process and we rank ourselves No. 2 behind the Springboks after what went on in 2009,' he reported to the NZRU.

That would be turned around emphatically in 2010.

13

Follow the leader

When the All Black management decided to implement their shared ownership policy, working towards the 2011 World Cup, it was critical the best leaders were identified and installed.

As it turned out, in selecting Richie McCaw, Dan Carter, Mils Muliaina and Andrew Hore (for the on-field role), and Keven Mealamu, Brad Thorn and Conrad Smith (as the off-field leaders), they couldn't have done better.

It was the task of Mealamu, Thorn and Smith to help the new internationals establish themselves in the team, and they had a swag of fresh faces to work with when the 2010 international season kicked off with a game against Ireland in New Plymouth — no fewer than five players would make their All Black debuts in that contest: Israel Dagg, Aaron Cruden, Benson Stanley, Victor Vito and Sam Whitelock.

Smith was one of the least experienced, at international level, of the seven team leaders but he ranked as one of the most team-oriented individuals Graham had ever encountered. A highly qualified person — having graduated with LLB (Hons) from Victoria University in Wellington and been admitted as a barrister and solicitor in the New Zealand High Court — he rates success more on how the team performs and how it is progressing, not predominantly on how he personally might have played. He possesses the rare ability to produce close to 100 per cent effort every test, which speaks volumes for his personal preparation. He's an outstanding team person.

Thorn, by comparison, was the most experienced international player in the team, across two codes. He'd enjoyed NRL success with the Brisbane Broncos and represented the Kangaroos. New Zealand-born, Thorn had always harboured a passion to represent the All Blacks and that had finally come about in 2003. After another stint playing league, he was now totally committed to rugby.

He told Graham he didn't like himself as a young man, so had drastically altered his lifestyle. Thorn now embraced religion, although his team-mates would never have known that, and seldom touched alcohol, which had caused some of this dislike in his youth. This self-awareness combined with his ability to lead by example and relate to others meant that Thorn could provide massive support to the young All Blacks.

Thorn was also committed to getting the best out of himself as a player. At the age of 35, he was pumping bigger weights in the gym and working harder on his core skills than he had been a decade earlier.

Graham found Thorn compared strongly with Martin Johnson who had captained his 2001 British Lions team and who, when England won the World Cup in 2003, had stamped himself as the best lock in the world. Johnson and Thorn were classic examples of players who through their commitment and dedication continued to improve well into their thirties.

Mealamu, whose All Black career dated back to 2002 and who by 2010 had claimed more than 80 test appearances, was a highly respected, totally good man. If a vote was taken on leadership, he'd score 29 out of 30, missing 30 because he wouldn't vote for himself.

Like Thorn, 'Kevey' has a great wife and family of which he is enormously proud. He's a leader by example, a do-as-I-do man rather than a do-as-I-say. Like the others, his ability to put the team first was an outstanding example to the rest of the team. His work with Andrew Hore and Corey Flynn, who were both trying to get better even though competing for the same position, was a classic example of what makes great teams.

Smith, Thorn and Mealamu were outstanding role models. All appeared to have their lives in perfect balance, allowing their sporting careers to flourish. They were classic examples of Sir Brian Lochore's creed that better people make better All Blacks.

Besides providing guidance and encouragement to the team's newcomers, Smith and Thorn and Mealamu, with other leaders, were also responsible, when the team was in match mode, for setting the tone for Saturday nights. Relevant to what lay ahead, they might decide the team should meet at their hotel for drinks with a curfew of, say, 2 a.m., or they might select a nightclub for the players to attend with a curfew of, perhaps, 4 a.m.

The on-field leaders' role, with assistance from the off-field leaders, was to help ensure the All Blacks were ready to fire every time they took the field. Towards this end, they had their regular meetings with coaches Ted and Shag and Smithy. They had a wealth of experience regarding game knowledge and an understanding of what was required each week to be able to perform to a high standard come Saturday.

McCaw and Muliaina were on their way to becoming the two most experienced players in the history of All Black rugby. They were the best players in their positions in world rugby, much admired and followed as leaders. They were the role models the young players frequently turned to.

McCaw, having served his apprenticeship under Tana Umaga, had developed into one of the great captains of all time. He was promoted to the leadership probably a year or two earlier than originally intended after Umaga stepped down at the end of 2005. Graham had wanted Umaga to commit to the 2007 World Cup, which would have allowed McCaw two more years' valuable training, but it wasn't to be.

When John Smit was at his peak as a leader, around 2007 when the Springboks won the World Cup, McCaw, while unrivalled as an openside flanker, was still in the development stages as a captain. Captains are made, not born. His greatest years as the team's leader were still ahead of him.

Extremely intelligent — he's in the top two per cent of New Zealanders for intelligence — McCaw's attention to detail is immense while his desire and motivation to win is total. He's a warrior, brave in the extreme, the player you want leading your team when the going is toughest. Inspirational was a word invented for McCaw. The players play for him.

Muliaina, like his skipper, was a veteran of the 2003 and 2007

Rugby World Cup campaigns and brought vast experience to the team. He had for many years been the best fullback in the world. The way he has overcome his numerous injuries is a great example to others.

He is a quality person, highly respected by his peers. Young players relate well to him and find him the ideal person to engage in conversation regarding challenges and how to handle pressure.

Dan Carter and Richie McCaw have been, probably since about 2005, quite simply the best rugby players in the world. When Carter's on song, as the British Lions discovered in 2005, opponents dance to his tune. A perfectionist with an extreme knowledge of the game, he is the navigator. He became to the All Blacks in the 2000s what Grant Fox had been in the 1980s, except he's even more complete. Tackling was never a special strength of Foxy's but Carter is fearless and possessed of a classic technique that can lower a 120-kg prop as easily as a pint-sized fly-half. By the age of 29, Carter had eclipsed Fox's aggregate of test points for the All Blacks, a mark many believed would never be threatened: Fox amassed 1067 points in 78 tests, at an average of 13.6 points per game, whereas Carter racked up 1188 points in 79 tests, at an amazing average of 15 points per game.

Graham soon came to appreciate that there was no point in expecting things to happen unless he was on the same page as Dan, who has always been possessed of a superb game knowledge.

Tactical preparation became a stimulating challenge for both of them. Graham, having been involved in the business of rugby coaching for four decades, thought he knew a thing or two about tactical awareness, but he was constantly being extended by Carter. Dan the Man would tutor his fellow All Black backs on tactical options. Like the others, he is a hell of a good man, modest, grounded, but also the perfectionist who has the confidence of the group to let him lead them around the track.

Andrew Hore might appear, to some, to be the odd man out in this seven-strong group of leaders, but he is bright and, in a rugby context, knows exactly what is required. A confidant of McCaw's, Hore is a good southern man who cuts straight to the chase. There is no camouflage with him.

It was important to have someone like Hore in the group, someone who always says it the way it is. Being 'PC' was never part of his make-up. Possessed of a good sense of humour, which he often uses, Hore often takes the heat out of tense situations to get to the right conclusion.

Graham recalled how back in the amateur days, when players were so infrequently together, many of his most stimulating moments, when tactics or a battle plan to defeat a particular opponent were formulated, often came in sessions back at the clubrooms or in a bar on a Saturday night in the company of such wise men as a Grant Fox, a Sean Fitzpatrick or a Zinzan Brooke. Come Monday and they would all be back at their real jobs focusing on what earned them their salaries.

Professionalism changed all that and allowed coaches like Graham to plot their time so much more meaningfully. As the 2010 season approached, he knew that the key to the All Blacks getting better was to have a total alignment between the coaches and the leaders. Towards this end, he regularly linked with his two most influential player/leaders — as far as the game plan was concerned — Richie and Dan, during the Super Championship. He made regular trips to Christchurch where they met, over some Thai food and a Steinlager Pure, to discuss tactics and trends to ensure they were consistently on the same wavelength.

Graham often thought how fortunate he was to have two players of the calibre of Richie and Dan, quite emphatically the best in their positions in the world, inspirational leaders and true match-winners. Oh, that anything should happen to them before the World Cup in 2011!

The greatest boost Ted and Shag and Smithy could have received came when the IRB announced that in 2010 the new law interpretations that had been trialled experimentally in the Super 14 competition would apply to all rugby. The All Black coaches' prayers had been answered.

They felt vindicated at having determinedly adhered to their attacking principles in 2009 even though this had rebounded on them in the Springbok contests.

Smithy put it best: 'We could see if the laws didn't change, no-one was going to watch rugby. It was becoming a kick-fest. Although we played some headless rugby against South Africa in 2009, it stood us in good stead for when the changes were made. Coaching at that level was about positioning yourself in the crow's nest and seeing where the game was going.'

Suddenly, attacking teams were going to be rewarded.

The experimental law variations (ELVs) introduced were:

- At the scrum, all backs except for the two scrum-halves must be at least 5 metres behind the hindmost foot of the scrum.
- Either side can use as many players as they like in the lineout, providing they fit between the 5-metre and 15-metre line.
- The opposing hooker in a lineout no longer has to stand between the 5-metre line and touchline; he can stand anywhere he wishes.
- On a quick throw-in, the ball can be thrown straight or back towards the defenders' goal line.
- Where touch judges are trained referees, they are now referred to as assistant referees, with responsibility for policing the offside lines.
- Penalty kicks are generally to be given only for offside and foul play. Most other penalties have become free kicks, with the option of taking a scrum, which cannot be used for a kick at goal or a dropped goal.
- If the ball is passed or run back into the 22 and then kicked out on the full, the resulting lineout is taken from where the kick was made.
- The maul can be collapsed by defending sides without incurring a penalty if the forward momentum of the attacking side has been neutralized or reversed.
- The corner flag is now part of the field of play.

There was a buzz about the All Black camp right from the start of 2010. The new laws, essentially fresh interpretations, created excitement and there was a determination to make up for the disappointments of the previous year; in particular, to avenge the three losses to the Springboks.

The coaches and the team leaders had, for a couple of years now, divided up their season. And that's how it was in 2010, with fresh objectives being set for each part of the campaign. First came the midyear warm-up fixtures against Ireland and Wales; next were two Tri-Nations home games, followed by home-and-away Bledisloe Cup contests against Australia; then, after a three-week break, came two challenging Tri-Nations matches in Johannesburg and Sydney; and at season's end was a Grand Slam opportunity in the UK with a game against Australia in Hong Kong en route — a total of 14 matches.

Although the players naturally wanted to win every game, their principal goal was to retain the Bledisloe Cup. That's the trophy that brings the greatest satisfaction — put it down to good old-fashioned trans-Tasman rivalry with spice added by the Robbie Deans factor. The Tri-Nations trophy and the chance for a rare Grand Slam both ranked highly, but they weren't on the same level as the Bledisloe Cup.

Individual contests aside, the team pledged to become the best rugby team there had ever been. Now that the law interpretations favoured them, they believed this was an achievable goal. No-one outside Team All Blacks would know of this; an internal aspiration, it was their secret goal.

With an eye on the 2011 World Cup, the selectors introduced several exciting young players during the June contests against Ireland and Wales — Israel Dagg, Aaron Cruden, Rene Ranger, Sam Whitelock and Victor Vito. Dagg and Vito got starts, with the other three getting involved off the bench.

Ireland was hammered 66–28. In this bizarre game, refereed by Wayne Barnes, Ireland played the final 65 minutes with 14 men and, for 10 minutes, operated with just 13 men. The All Blacks then went on to play Wales, twice, comfortably putting them away 42–9 and 29–10.

The All Blacks' rip-roaring form extended into the Tri-Nations series. The Springboks, against whom the All Blacks had been almost powerless 12 months earlier, were dissected 32–12 in Auckland and

31–17 in Wellington while the Wallabies were swept away 49–28 in Melbourne.

Even though their draw had been favourable, with two home games against South Africa to start with, the All Blacks had unquestionably stepped up several notches on their 2009 form.

They eked out a 20–10 win over the Wallabies in a ho-hum contest in difficult wet conditions in Christchurch before heading to South Africa. If the Christchurch game left a bit to be desired, the result didn't, for it meant the Bledisloe Cup was secure in New Zealand for another 12 months, and that was cause for great celebration.

The Tri-Nations trophy was pretty much in the bag also when the All Blacks flew out to South Africa, but the players knew that, after the events of 2009, unless they could defeat the Springboks on their own territory they weren't true champions worthy of the world No. 1 ranking.

It was the first occasion FNB Stadium, a massive venue created for the FIFA World Cup in the heart of Johannesburg's black township of Soweto, had ever hosted a rugby international and an incredible 94,700 fans crammed in for the All Black game. And there were other records being made that night: it was Smit's 100th test and McCaw was equalling Sean Fitzpatrick's record as the All Blacks' longest-serving captain with 51 tests.

The 94,200 who were cheering for the home team were on particularly good terms with themselves as John Smit's men built on a narrow half-time advantage to lead 22–14 with a dozen minutes to play. But then Carter narrowed the gap to five points with a penalty goal, setting up an epic finale. The rarified air that exists at 6500 ft on the high veldt had brought about the undoing of many previous All Black teams, but not this one. McCaw and his men were possessed of enormous self-belief and were full of running.

It was McCaw who went over in the corner to level the scores, with about three minutes remaining. But it was no sure five-pointer. The TMO replayed it an agonising number of times — Graham's hopes sinking with each replay — before the try was confirmed. Carter's difficult conversion missed, leaving the teams locked at 22–all.

Only about 90 seconds remained, surely not enough time for another score. But these All Blacks were on fire. They knew they had the legs on the Springboks and they weren't prepared to settle for a draw.

'All-out attack,' ordered McCaw, as they prepared for the restart. 'We want the win.'

From the restart the All Blacks created a turnover to set in motion the game's final attack. The ball was quickly in the hands of Ma'a Nonu, who powerfully fended off a defender. In a cruel twist of fate, it turned out to be the Springbok captain Smit, who was left sprawled on the turf.

Nonu burst clear and threw a perfectly judged pass that found replacement winger Israel Dagg, who sprinted in for the winning try. Dagg went alarmingly close to the dead-ball line before grounding the ball, an unnecessary act of bravado that later incurred the wrath of the coaches.

'You do that again and you'll be looking for a new team,' he was told. 'We didn't need the conversion, just the five points.'

With Carter's conversion, the All Blacks emerged victorious: 29–22. Three losses against South Africa in 2009 had become three wins in 2010.

Up in the coaches' box, Graham simmered with pride. Any victory over South Africa was satisfying but this one was special. In the white-hot atmosphere of Soweto, with 90,000-plus fans cheering them on, Graham knew this was the best the Springboks were going to be. And the All Blacks had still beaten them, coming from behind to do so. The mental strength of the players was superb. He saw this as a precursor to what could be achieved at the World Cup.

Smit was devastated. At the final whistle, he sank to his knees in anguish, later saying, 'I thought we'd done enough to win. I can't think of anything worse than losing your 100th test by missing a tackle at the death.'

One of the mantras that had been promoted among the All Blacks was that it only takes 20 seconds to score a try, so no matter how far behind, you can still win ... if you maintain belief in each other.

It was a philosophy that skipper McCaw would adhere to, and

ultimately it would help win a World Cup.

The All Blacks had built a close association with, and developed a deep respect for, the South African players and were welcomed into their dressing room. Graham admired the fact the South Africans also involved their families on these occasions.

Smit, who was probably the opponent the All Blacks respected most in Graham's eight years as head coach, held one of his children as he chatted away, disguising what must have been the immense disappointment he felt at that moment.

The All Blacks' Tri-Nations heroics didn't end at Soweto. Three weeks later, at ANZ Stadium in Sydney, the All Blacks found themselves 9–22 down against the Wallabies with 15 minutes remaining. With the Tri-Nations trophy and Bledisloe Cup already secure, this time there weren't the same emotions driving the team. But, nevertheless, they were playing Australia, the opponent they most wanted to deal to!

On this occasion, the ABs were without their superstar playmaker/goal-kicker Carter, who was carrying a minor injury. Cruden started in the No. 10 jersey but by the time all the drama unfolded in the final quarter he'd given way to Colin Slade, who worked closely with Richie on tactics and whose booming boot helped turn the game. The goal-kicking duties on this occasion were with the versatile Piri Weepu.

Mighty McCaw ... that man again ... scored with 15 minutes remaining, from a move cunningly conceived by Graham, who had analysed the hell out of the Wallabies.

Graham's painstaking video research had identified a flaw in scrum-half Will Genia's play. He'd noted that when the opposition fed the ball into attacking scrums, Genia quickly retreated behind his own scrum, to get into position to nullify his opponent running right.

A move taking advantage of Genia's absence had been practised till it was perfected, then filed away for an appropriate moment, which came in Sydney when the All Blacks were awarded a scrum about 30 metres out from the Australian goalposts.

Halfback Piri Weepu faked to run wide with an imaginary ball, attracting the attention of both the Australian openside flanker David

Pocock and Genia. Kieran Read picked up and in-passed to McCaw who had an outrageously easy run to the goalposts. Never had a pre-planned move worked with such ruthless efficiency!

Up in the coaches' box, Graham beamed. 'That worked OK?' he observed drolly to Shag and Smithy.

Weepu's conversion brought the All Blacks within six points. Then, eight minutes from time, after a period of sustained pressure, Read was over, himself, beside the posts. Weepu's simple conversion had New Zealand ahead 23–22, and that was how it finished. This was the All Blacks 10th straight win over Deans's men.

It was fitting that two Canterbury men should score the crunch tries in this thrilling victory to bring some cheer to the people of Christchurch whose city had been shattered by a massive 7.1 earthquake seven days previously.

The mental toughness that would be required to win a World Cup had brought the All Blacks through from desperate situations twice in a fortnight, allowing them to create history by becoming the first team to win all six Tri-Nations matches in one season, another important milestone in the All Black legacy.

The All Blacks had been branded chokers after their failure to win the 2007 World Cup. Well, the 2010 results, particularly the performances in South Africa and Australia, had demonstrated a mental strength. These were no chokers. Throughout Graham's term as head coach their win record now stood at 86 per cent.

While the critics were lauding the All Blacks' achievements, particularly in turning the tables on the Springboks, Ted and Shag and Smithy weren't getting too carried away. They were mightily heartened at the resolve and mental toughness demonstrated by their players, but they also recognized that the Springboks were without their crack halfback Fourie du Preez, who as a match-winner was in the same class as Dan Carter, and there had been the important home advantage in two of the three South African contests.

When the All Blacks flew out for Hong Kong in late October, they were without Israel Dagg and Piri Weepu, victims of dreadful injuries. Dagg had torn the muscles off his thigh while Weepu had fractured his tibia, fibula and ankle playing for Wellington against Taranaki just a few days before the All Black team assembled.

After the heroic come-from-behind performances in Soweto and Sydney, it was frustrating for the All Black coaches to see their team get run down by the Wallabies in Hong Kong. Twelve points clear going into the final quarter, they conceded late tries to Drew Mitchell and James O'Connor to lose 24–26.

Though there was nothing tangible at stake, the result ended the All Blacks' hopes of creating a record test-winning sequence. For the second time during Graham's reign as head coach, the All Blacks had tripped up after 15 straight test wins, three short of the world record of 18 created from 2006 to 2010 by that notable rugby nation Lithuania!

The luckless individual who would cop much of the blame for the Hong Kong loss was Stephen Donald, who replaced Carter in the 59th minute — the coaches not wanting Carter on the field for the full game because he was still recovering from injury — at which point the All Blacks led 24–12. It was his first international appearance in 12 months.

Things couldn't have gone worse for the man they call Beaver. He missed a vital penalty attempt from close range, then in the dying moments failed to put a clearing kick across the touchline, setting the Aussies up for O'Connor's winning try.

Graham backed his embattled first-five, saying he would bounce back. 'He had a difficult twenty minutes. He knows that, we know that, but I think he's good enough to overcome that. Some guys hadn't played international rugby for some time and found the pace of the game and skill requirements pretty demanding.'

Smithy offered some words of encouragement also. 'With Stephen, we all love him. Everyone's got belief in Stephen. He's got real character. It's not easy at a time like this — you go to a dark place. I've been there myself! That's the accountability of the All Black jersey. He'll get another opportunity.'

The events at Hong Kong Stadium took their toll on Donald, who clearly held himself responsible for the loss. It was a long time before Beaver's bounce returned.

Although the coaches expressed confidence in him, they reserved the No. 10 jersey exclusively for Carter in the four Grand Slam fixtures in the UK. Donald got 30 minutes' action against Scotland, coming on when the score was 35–3, and a token three-minute appearance against Wales.

With Aaron Cruden and Colin Slade coming through as understudies to Carter, many wondered whether Donald would ever represent his country again. Beaver probably thought the same as he flew back to New Zealand.

But fate deals some intriguing hands at times. And Beaver might just have one more card to play!

This would be Graham's last European tour with the All Blacks. What a record he and Shag and Smithy had fashioned on five previous tours: 19 wins from 19 tests. They'd beaten Wales five times, England and France four times each and Ireland, Scotland and Italy twice each, achieving Grand Slam successes in 2005 and 2008. The solitary blemish on their European test scorecard had come in the quarter-finals of the 2007 Rugby World Cup, courtesy of France.

Henry's men had to deal with Martin Johnson's improving England team first up, an occasion that drew 80,500 fans to Twickenham. The game marked Sonny Bill Williams's All Black debut and, interestingly, he found himself opposing another league recruit, Shontayne Hape.

The All Blacks romped away to a 17–3 half-time advantage, then withstood a strong fight back by the home side in the second half. They played the final 10 minutes with Jerome Kaino in the sin bin. Later, Keven Mealamu was cited for a dangerous tackle, receiving a four-game suspension that, on appeal, was trimmed to two weeks, allowing him to play against Wales.

Scotland was swept aside 49–3 and Ireland put away 38–18 in a game in which the All Blacks didn't get ahead until right on half-time.

That left Wales standing between the All Blacks and a third Grand Slam in five years. To remind the players of the significance of the occasion, photos of the 1978, 2005 and 2008 Grand Slam-winning teams were displayed in the team room. Next to them was a blank sheet of paper headed 2010 followed by a large question mark!

It had the desired effect, the All Blacks scoring five tries to Wales's one and winning 37–25.

Disappointingly, some writers back home deprecated the All Blacks' achievement, implying a clean sweep of the four home unions no longer represented anything special. One even branded it a Grand Sham.

The facts speak otherwise. Until Graham's team came along, only six Grand Slams had been achieved collectively by South Africa, Australia and New Zealand in more than 100 years of trying and no team had managed it since 1984.

South Africa had done the Slam in 1912/13, 1931/32, 1951/52 and 1960/61, Australia just once in 1984 (when the Ella brothers were in full cry), and New Zealand in 1978, 2005, 2008 and now 2010.

Graham is the only coach to claim a Grand Slam more than once, and he's now done it three times!

The most tries scored by an individual during a Grand Slam is five. It's been achieved twice, by brothers, believe it or not. Quite amazingly, Rico Gear touched down five times in the 2005 Sweep and Hosea Gear matched him in 2010!

The top try-scorer in the 2008 Sweep, when the All Blacks kept their own line intact, was Ma'a Nonu with three.

As the All Blacks winged their way back to New Zealand, Graham reflected on a year of considerable achievement. There had been that one hiccup in Hong Kong, otherwise every box carried a large tick: the Bledisloe Cup, Tri-Nations trophy, a hat trick of wins over South Africa, and another Grand Slam.

Not too bad ... not too bad at all.

But the box he wanted to be ticked more than any was coming up in 2011: the Rugby World Cup. Now *that* presented an entirely different challenge.

14

Operation World Cup

So now it's Rugby World Cup year 2011 and the All Blacks are raging hot favourites to win, which is perfectly understandable. They are the No. 1 ranked team in the world, they are in possession of every achievable trophy, they have lost only one of their previous 20 internationals, they are Grand Slammers, and their average winning score throughout 2010 was 35–15.

Might as well present them with the Webb Ellis Cup now and save everyone else the expense of travelling Down Under for the tournament.

But, hey, haven't we been here before? Like, in 1991 and 1995 and 1999 and 2003 and 2007. Well, OK, probably in 1995 and 1999 the All Blacks weren't the favourites going into those World Cups, although the New Zealand public believed they would do the business on both occasions. But in 2003 in Australia and 2007 in France, they most certainly were, only to crash out in the semi-finals against Australia in Sydney and then, horror of horrors, four years on in the quarter-finals against France in Cardiff.

Those disasters proved that world rankings and favouritism count for nothing at World Cups. The All Blacks came away from those two tournaments not only red-faced but branded chokers. The cold, hard fact is that the All Blacks haven't won the Webb Ellis Cup in 24 years.

So why should 2011 be any different? Answer: because the New Zealand Rugby Union had the courage in late 2007 to reappoint

Graham Henry, Wayne Smith and Steve Hansen as selector/coaches of the All Blacks.

It was a ballsy decision, given that there was a fresh candidate with outstanding credentials, Robbie Deans, waiting in the wings. No coach had previously survived a losing World Cup campaign, and all Graham's predecessors had progressed to at least the semi-finals, with Laurie Mains making it through to the grand final in 1995. Graham's team had embarrassingly exited at the quarter-final stage, a notably worst performance.

The nation was shattered at the outcome, the media generally unsympathetic, with sections of them positively vitriolic. Graham's prospects of reappointment were rated so low the bookies installed Deans as warm favourite, and it's rare for bookies to be wrong in such circumstances.

But on this occasion they were. Messrs Henry, Smith and Hansen, bruised but not bowed, were reinstated. The NZRU board members, to their enormous credit, had looked beyond one calamitous World Cup contest — in which the referee had influenced the outcome to an unbelievable degree — and acknowledged what Graham and his fellow coaches had achieved over four years.

Given their national body's vote of confidence, Ted and Shag and Smithy now had to make it work. They had to maintain the high standards they had set from 2004 to 2007 *and* win the World Cup. No other outcome would be acceptable.

There had to be a reason why the All Blacks had bombed out in the last three World Cup tournaments when everyone had expected them to succeed. To say they choked on each occasion, as some of the media kept insisting, was to imply New Zealand rugby players lacked mental fortitude, which Graham knew was patently not true.

In 2010, his team had fronted up before 94,000 South African fans at Soweto, where the atmosphere had been positively electric. Against a highly motivated Springbok opponent, the All Blacks had produced a spectacular finish to steal victory in the dying seconds. If that didn't demonstrate that the All Blacks are possessed of mental fortitude, nothing would.

So if it wasn't a mental thing that kept causing New Zealanders anguish at World Cups, what was it?

The dual management team comprising the seven player leaders and the three coaches plus Shandy, Bert and Nic Gill, with assistance from Ceri Evans and Renzie Hanham, formed the MAD Group (Mental Analysis and Development), and made it a major project of theirs to analyse why the All Blacks hadn't won the World Cup in 24 years. And they came up with some startling answers.

Ceri, a former New Zealand football captain, is a psychiatrist and both he and Renzie are highly respected and ranked at the top of the tree in martial arts. They understand pressure and the skills required to handle extreme pressure in a physical contest. Their knowledge was special for the group.

The All Blacks' first mistake, they now realized, was that they had applied a Tri-Nations/Grand Slam mentality to their 2007 World Cup campaign, i.e. concentrating on one game at a time. That formula works just fine for tournaments such as the Tri-Nations, where you can lose a test and still be the champion, and Grand Slam tours, three of which the All Blacks had won in five years, but not for rugby's major challenge — the World Cup.

At a World Cup, once you progress beyond pool play, it's sudden death; there are no second chances. The one-game-at-a-time mentality hadn't worked in 2007. A change was needed, the development of a World Cup mentality, one that acknowledged the uniqueness of the tournament, embraced it and wasn't inhibited by it. The team needed to be normal, not obsessed. They needed to be prepared, organized — and relaxed. Then bring it on!

The group's analysis also revealed that most top-ranking teams performed better at World Cups than in normal test matches and that form going into World Cups counted for nothing. The All Blacks, for example, had won 19 of their last 20 matches going into the 2007 tournament whereas the French team that defeated them had lost 10–61 to the All Blacks in Wellington four months earlier. And in 2003 the Wallabies defeated the All Blacks in the World Cup semi-finals in Sydney four months after losing to them 21–50 at the same venue.

The other important factor that came out of the research was the need to cater for the unexpected. Nothing new there, of course, but if coaches and players understand the unexpected will happen, then they are better prepared mentally to deal with worst-case scenarios.

A couple of worst-case scenarios had arisen in 2007, and the All Blacks hadn't dealt with them adequately at all. The first was losing both specialist first-fives, Dan Carter and Nick Evans, plus others, to injury during the quarter-final. The other was a referee who obviously let the opposition get away with murder. That's a difficult one, of course, and extremely hard to mentally adjust to.

There had actually been quite a catalogue of worst-case scenarios involving All Black teams at World Cups, from 'Suzy's' food poisoning episode in Johannesburg in 1995 to Stirling Mortlock's early intercept try in Sydney in 2003 and then the challenging events of 2007.

What would be the worst-case scenario in 2011? Losing both Dan Carter and Richie McCaw to injury? Surely not possible!

The coaches had observed that in the second half of the quarter-final against France in 2007, when the players became stressed because suddenly things were going horribly wrong, a number of them appeared to lose focus. They couldn't handle the extreme pressure. It was a 'possum in the headlights' situation. Their minds became blank. It probably was one game where some players actually did choke. Given that the referee refused to penalize the French regardless of how blatantly they infringed, there were extenuating circumstances. But if you want to win, you have got to handle the unexpected. That's the reality at that level of competition.

What happens when players' minds go blank is that they lose focus and their ability to perform diminishes significantly. They get into a flight/fright/freeze mode and they don't trust their mates. In other words, they choke. All those things happened at Cardiff on that terrible afternoon in 2007 when many didn't handle the unexpected.

In the years since, the All Blacks had done a lot of work, led by those special members of the MAD Group and facilitated by Bert, on how the mind functions under extreme pressure, to help players identify when they were coming under stress and how to combat that.

In 2007, it was apparent that some of the players, confronted with such extreme circumstances, had walked away from adversity. The coaches wanted the team to develop a knowledge and understanding of the mind so that, instead, they would be able to embrace pressure and the unexpected in 2011. Graham would like to explain more about this strategy but feels because it involves a methodology adapted exclusively for the All Blacks, it would be inappropriate to reveal further details. The All Black ethos is important and some things All Black you don't talk about!

It was manager Darren Shand who reminded the coaches at one of the World Cup planning sessions that World Cup finals were won on penalty goals and dropped goals, not tries. But at the suggestion that the All Blacks would probably need to adopt a more conservative approach when they reached the final, Graham retorted: 'That's not our mentality. Why change because it's a Rugby World Cup; hell, we have won 86 per cent of our games since we have been together.'

Statistics, however, certainly backed up Shand's claim. The five World Cup grand finals since 1991 had produced just five tries against 36 penalty goals and four dropped goals. Two of those dropped goals (Joel Stransky's at Johannesburg in 1995 and Jonny Wilkinson's at Sydney in 2003) were last-gasp match-winners.

Graham noted the statistics but reminded those present that he not only wanted to win the World Cup in 2011 but he also believed the team could do that with explosive high-skilled rugby that opponents would not be able to handle. After all, that was the successful game they had developed and the guys enjoyed playing. It was what the media termed 'winning in style'.

Nevertheless, the coaches had noted that winning in style had become just a little bit harder as the 2010 season progressed. Not through a lack of endeavour on the part of the All Blacks but because their opponents were getting smarter. They were analysing and tracking the All Black moves and patterns and starting to shut them down.

French coach Marc Lièvremont was quoted as saying he believed his team was capable of containing the All Blacks at the World Cup because their style of play was now well known. No doubt Robbie Deans was thinking the same. And Smithy came up with the stat that

42 of the All Blacks' 59 tries in 2010 had come from turnover ball.

But Ted and Shag and Smithy didn't get to be some of the world's premier rugby coaches by resting on their laurels. If the world was catching up to the All Blacks, then the All Blacks needed to keep ahead. It's what Smithy refers to as 'being up the crow's nest' — planning ahead for individual players and the game to stay ahead. These game-changing strategies and the individual development plans were a major focus. Changes like having the best-prepared players, physically and mentally, in world rugby; highly explosive, quick athletes who could handle the pressures of the unexpected; a back three who could snuff out the high ball, could counter and kick; tight forwards who could pass under pressure and thereby create space; unconventional kickers who could put recoverable kicks down a wide channel; better and varied use of the ball from the breakdown; and so on.

The Super 15 coaches were supportive in promoting some of these changes. Ted and Shag and Smithy discussed these trends in the game with Pat Lam (Blues), Ian Foster (Chiefs), Mark Hammett (Hurricanes), Todd Blackadder (Crusaders) and Jamie Joseph (Highlanders) and received 100 per cent backing for the initiatives.

Four years earlier the All Black management had encountered some resistance when they tried to sell their conditioning programme to the Super coaches, because it meant they were denying the franchises their finest players for the first seven weeks of the competition. The programme had been considered essential at the time, but the All Black coaches weren't going down that path this time. They had learned and were prepared to allow the All Blacks to participate in the Super 15 competition; they just wanted the Super coaches to indulge them a little in some of the tactics and player welfare and development needs that were part of the big picture for the Rugby World Cup later in the year. Between seasons Ted and Smithy had spent a lot of time watching videos of rugby matches. Graham scanned more than 60 games, a variety of contests from the Heineken Cup, Six Nations and Tri-Nations championships; even a few vintage All Black tests.

The purpose was to generate ideas for improvement, identify situations that made a difference, such as the 'crow's nest' examples, events that caused a momentum change. Graham found a couple of classic examples in an England-Australia match at Twickenham in 2010. The English have a reputation for being staid but in this match, they scored two remarkable tries from turnover ball in their own 22. One was initiated after the Australian halfback Will Genia lost the ball diving for a try. England launched a counter-attack and scored at the opposite end of the field.

Both tries came after extensive periods on attack by Australia. Graham used them as prime examples of momentum swings. Controlling the momentum of the game and regaining momentum control after losing it are huge issues in test-match rugby.

He married these examples up with Smithy's best clips and ran them past his trusty team leaders, Richie and Dan. They put together a motivational clip and filed away several of the best examples of how to effect momentum swings.

Having the All Blacks involved in the majority of games was great for the promotion of the Super 15; it's what all stakeholders in the game wanted. But the Crusaders, the competition's most successful team — they've won it seven times and been runner-up on three other occasions — were confronted with major challenges. The massive earthquakes that had fractured Christchurch in September 2010 and February 2011 had caused irreparable damage to the team's home ground, AMI Stadium. With no other suitable venue in the city, it meant the Crusaders were obliged to play every one of their 2011 matches effectively on the road.

The earthquake damage also eliminated Christchurch as a World Cup venue. To the massive disappointment of local fans, all its Cup games were reallocated, the pool matches to Dunedin, Invercargill, Nelson and Albany, and the two quarter-finals to Eden Park in Auckland.

The only matches that resembled home games for the Crusaders were those hosted by their franchise partners — four in Nelson and one in Timaru. Another so-called 'home' game, against the Sharks, was played at Twickenham in London (and won 44–28). There was also a 'home' game played in Napier.

If that wasn't challenging enough, the team's captain and star performer, Richie McCaw, was carrying a stress fracture in the fifth metatarsal on his right foot. This required surgery, sidelining him for the first two months of the season. 'I wanted to get stuck in for the Crusaders,' he said at a press conference, 'but the foot needs to be repaired, so it's best to have it done now and get it out of the way.' He didn't feature in the starting XV until the ninth match of the competition, against the Force in Perth.

Being unable to play any matches in Christchurch should have eliminated the team from championship contention. But the Crusaders are the Crusaders: if they were asked to play all their matches on an ice floe, they'd still be competitive.

They finished the round-robin section in third place, downed the Sharks in Nelson in the quarter-finals before overcoming the Stormers in Cape Town in the semi-finals. Their globetrotting finally caught up with them, with their energy levels dipping in the second half of the grand final against the Reds in Brisbane. They lost 13–18 but won admiration for their amazing performances against the odds.

The heroic efforts of the Crusaders helped set the scene for what would become an epic year in New Zealand rugby.

Obviously, the World Cup represented the major priority on the 2011 calendar for the All Black coaches. That didn't mean Ted and Shag and Smithy and the player leaders were prepared to sacrifice matches — they wanted to win everything — but it did mean there were more important fixtures on their agenda than the Tri-Nations clashes with Australia and South Africa.

The coaches devised a pathway for each player. Some, like the Crusaders players, had had too much rugby and needed rest. Others, like Tony Woodcock, Israel Dagg and Richard Kahui, were coming off injuries and needed game time. Ted and Shag and Smithy sat with each player to define the pathway.

The South Africans patently didn't give a hoot about the Tri-Nations in the year of a World Cup. In 2007, they had finished a clear last in the Tri-Nations Championship and gone on to win the Webb Ellis Cup, and obviously that's how they had set their priorities for 2011.

The squad they despatched for matches in Sydney and Wellington read more like a development team. Coach Peter de Villiers insisted more than 20 of his World Cup candidates were carrying niggly injuries and couldn't be considered for selection. Yeah right.

The Wallabies put the inexperienced Boks away 39–20 and the All Blacks dealt to them 40–7. Only two of the eight forwards, skipper John Smit and Danie Rossouw, would feature at the World Cup. The others were a right mix of no-names.

The All Black coaches gave all their leading players an outing in the opening two Tri-Nations fixtures, with excellent results. The romp against the anonymous Springbok side was followed by a handsome 30–14 win at Eden Park over an Australian team that had been humbled by Samoa in a warm-up fixture.

The Aussie result brought great satisfaction to the All Black camp because it meant they retained the Bledisloe Cup — for the eighth straight year during Graham's time in charge — the only trophy other than the Webb Ellis Cup that they genuinely yearned for in 2011.

Because the Crusaders had spent their whole campaign on the road, and peaking for each individual at the World Cup was the objective, key players were spared the long trip through to Port Elizabeth for the return match with the Springboks, who were suddenly bolstered by all their superstars.

Dan Carter, Richie McCaw, Brad Thorn, Kieran Read and Owen Franks, as well as Conrad Smith, Ma'a Nonu (who toured but didn't play) and Mils Muliaina, were missing as the All Blacks crashed to a 5–18 loss, but they were restored to the starting XV for the Tri-Nations decider against the Wallabies in Brisbane; indeed, the team fielded there was pretty close to the strongest All Black team available.

So there was disappointment when the men in black trailed 3–20 at half-time and eventually lost 20–25. However, they had stuck to their major objective for players to peak during the finals of the World Cup. Taking them to South Africa was not part of that big picture, which resulted in rust showing early in the game in Brisbane. Also, there were two serious injuries to loose forwards Kieran Read and Adam Thomson that hadn't helped the cause, especially with Kaino rested. So the game was lost but, hey, the Bledisloe Cup was in the cabinet at head office in Wellington!

David Long would write in the *Sunday News* that the nation's hopes that the All Blacks would at last win another World Cup were seriously dented as they were humbled by Australia. 'The wave of enthusiasm the country has enjoyed for the past few years has been reduced to a ripple and it's a sobering fact the All Blacks will enter the World Cup on the back of two straight defeats. This is the most significant loss since that defeat to France in the World Cup quarter-final four years ago.'

Graham told reporters, 'We didn't turn up in the first half. I wish I knew why. We'll be better going forward, which can only be a good thing.'

An incident late in the game would come back to haunt the perpetrator, Quade Cooper, and the Wallabies. Putting a knee into the head of New Zealand's favourite son Richie McCaw, vividly captured by the television cameras, wasn't the smartest thing to do. Although Cooper avoided a citing, his cynical behaviour would lead to him becoming Public Enemy No. 1 at the World Cup and his mere presence certainly added an edge to the All Blacks' performance when the two nations clashed in the semi-finals.

Anyway, the Wallabies claimed the Tri-Nations title for the first time since 2001. Following on from the Reds' triumph in the Super 15, it was obvious the Australians, with a cluster of exciting young attackers, were going to be a threat at the World Cup. But did anyone tell them that the World Cup has never been won by the Tri-Nations champion?

The All Black and Wallaby selectors wanted to delay the naming of their 30-strong World Cup squads until after the Tri-Nations Championship was completed, but the World Cup organizing committee made them comply with the date set.

So four days before doing battle with the Wallabies in Brisbane, the squad was released and, as with every All Black team announcement, there were surprises.

The biggest shock was the omission of winger Hosea Gear, who in 2010 had been labelled by Graham as the best wing in the world; a specialist left-winger, he lost out to the more versatile Zac Guildford. Also missing the cut was Sitiveni Sivivatu, a veteran of 45 tests dating back to 2005, while Victor Vito was preferred as a loose forward to Liam Messam, and Colin Slade became Carter's deputy ahead of Aaron Cruden. Otherwise, the selection was predictable.

All the players who had helped make the All Blacks the dominating team in world rugby, apart from Tom Donnelly, who had suffered a serious injury on the 2010 Grand Slam tour, and Joe Rokocoko, who had signed to play in France, were involved and ready to do the business.

Kieran Read, who was such an integral part of the team, was selected despite having sustained painful high-ankle ligament damage against the Wallabies. To everyone's relief, X-rays had revealed no broken bones. An intensive rehab programme would have him back in action at least for the play-off games. He was such an important player, the selectors were prepared to carry him for the first month of the tournament.

The only All Black triumph at a World Cup had come in 1987 when Brian Lochore's team romped to victory, so it was natural Graham and his management team should turn to the survivors of that magnificent campaign to provide enlightenment and motivation for the team of 2011.

Grant Fox and John Kirwan, the leading point-scorer and equal-top try-scorer, respectively, from that inaugural tournament, spoke to the players. So also did Jock Hobbs, who would undoubtedly have captained that champion World Cup team of '87 had not recurring bouts of concussion forced his premature retirement, and Brian Lochore (now Sir Brian).

Fox and Kirwan were able to present contrasting experiences because as well as sharing in the glory of 1987 they had been members of the 1991 team that was blown out of the water by the Wallabies in their semi-final in Dublin.

The players had great empathy with Jock Hobbs, who they knew was fighting leukaemia. He had confronted great personal challenges and he likened these to the mountain now confronting the All Blacks. He told them they needed to give their best every day and not become distracted.

'Each day you get out of bed in the morning and you try to be world-class,' he told them. 'You give your all for every second of every minute of the seven games you'll play. You can do no more than that. Guys, never let the music die in you.'

Jock, with the support of NZRU CEO Chris Moller and others, had secured the World Cup for 'the stadium of four million' and he described how the country was responding, which gave the players a great kick. Because they were in camp, they weren't aware of the sea of flags that were flying or how many Kiwis were decked out in All Black gear or how the entire nation had linked arms and got in behind the team.

Jock was an outstanding man whose passion for the game, combined with his integrity, had saved New Zealand rugby in 1995 and, with others, had secured the rights to the 2011 Rugby World Cup. His words to the team reflected how he lived his life, even in the most difficult days near the end. He tried to be world-class every day. And in the eyes of the All Blacks, he was world-class — a man of great empathy, a special New Zealander.

Another special New Zealander who had great empathy with the team was Sir Brian Lochore. He talked about how those squad members who didn't make the 22 for any particular match still had an important role to play. A couple of the 1987 team, Frano Botica and Bruce Deans, didn't get on the field at any stage of the tournament. 'Yet they trained harder than the others,' he said. Total commitment to the team from those not in the starting 22 had been questioned at times in 2007. It couldn't be a question mark in 2011.

Sir Brian also emphasized how he and his team were desperate to share the mantle of Rugby World Cup champions. It was time, he said, and that time was now.

The selection attitude in 1987 was the antithesis of the so-called rotation policy adopted by Ted and Shag and Smithy. Of course, rugby was amateur back then and it was rare for the All Blacks to play more than half a dozen test matches in a full calendar year. Even in 1987, the World Cup year, the All Blacks took to the field only seven times.

Sir Brian and his fellow selectors, Alex Wyllie and John Hart, had effectively used only 15 players throughout the entire World Cup. The only occasion they'd relented was for the pool match against Argentina when half a dozen players (including Zinzan Brooke who would star at the next World Cup) made their solitary appearances. Seven players appeared in all six matches and another seven played in five of the six.

The 2011 team eventually got to lunch with the 1987 champions, which was a delightful occasion for all concerned.

One other famous Kiwi who addressed the team, over dinner one night, was Willie Apiata, the only living recipient of the Victoria Cross for New Zealand. The team was entranced as Willie spoke of his experiences in Afghanistan. They heard about his going into the eye of the storm, and how he'd had to flush the enemy out to rescue his buddies. It was a team thing, about looking after your mate. Except that in Afghanistan, if you got it wrong, you got shot.

The players found his talk hugely inspirational. Graham described it as 'incredibly special' and said the All Blacks took a lot out of their night with this remarkable soldier.

By the time 9 September rolled around, New Zealand was enveloped in World Cup rugby fever. Every second car, it seemed, carried a flag and every fifth person appeared to be wearing an All Black jersey. The main topic of conversation in offices, at schools, in bars and in coffee shops was rugby.

The seventh Rugby World Cup was launched with a spectacular opening ceremony at Eden Park and a dazzling fireworks display on Waitemata Harbour. Organizers had anticipated that in addition to the 60,000 who packed Eden Park, probably 50,000 would throng to Rugby Party Central on Auckland's waterfront — but they miscalculated by at least 50,000. While it ended in transport chaos, it certainly got the event under way with a bang.

Now it was time for the on-field action.

15

Doing the business

Refereeing aside, there were several factors that were considered to be responsible for the All Blacks' downfall at the 2007 World Cup: rotation, the conditioning window, injuries, players negotiating their career futures prior to and during the tournament, the team's leadership model, and the fact the All Blacks hadn't faced any serious competition until they met a fired-up French team in the quarter-final.

The All Blacks scarcely raised a sweat in disposing of Italy 76–14, Portugal 108–13, a depleted Scottish team 40–nil, and Romania 85–8. In these four outings they scored 46 tries (16 more than any other team), and conceded only four.

The All Blacks have always breezed through pool play, to the extent that their average winning score in pool matches across six World Cups coming into 2011 was an extraordinary 63–11! Three times they'd hit the century, which included the World Cup record score of 145 against Japan in 1995.

So Graham was delighted when he saw that the draw for 2011 presented pool matches against Tonga, the surprise package of the 2007 tournament and a team that is always physically challenging, and France, the opponent that was fast becoming New Zealand's World Cup nemesis. The others in the pool were Japan and Canada.

On a night when the occasion was greater than the rugby, the All Blacks opened their campaign with a comfortable win over Tonga, the first try of the tournament going to Israel Dagg. The scorer of the first try at the inaugural tournament at the same venue in 1987, Michael

Jones, has been immortalized in a magnificent bronze sculpture that sits behind the ASB Grandstand.

One of Jones's illustrious team-mates back in 1987, John Kirwan, coached New Zealand's second opponent, Japan. Knowing his team was on a hiding to nothing, JK fielded a virtual second XV in Hamilton, reserving his best players for the upcoming winnable contests against Tonga and Canada. The All Blacks coasted to an 83–7 victory.

Twenty-four hours after the All Blacks' game against Japan came the contest that set the 2011 Rugby World Cup alight. Against all odds, the Irish, who in six World Cup tournaments had never topped their pool or progressed beyond the quarter-finals, knocked over the Tri-Nations champion, Australia. It represented one of the greatest upsets in World Cup history.

The men in green turned on a breathtaking performance, never allowing the Wallabies into the game. They were inspired by the mass of green in the grandstands and the fact all the New Zealand fans were cheering for them. 'It felt like a home game,' a delighted Irish captain, Brian O'Driscoll, declared afterwards. Never before had so many New Zealanders become so passionately involved in a game not involving the All Blacks.

The result had major repercussions for the All Blacks because now the Wallabies, who had been perceived as their most likely opponents if they progressed to the final, were on their side of the draw. And barring further upsets, it meant the Wallabies and the Springboks were on a quarter-final collision course, after which one of them would be heading home.

While the result certainly favoured the All Blacks, it wouldn't count for much if Graham's men couldn't get past the French, the ever enigmatic French, the most difficult of all opponents to predict — Graham wondered if even the French themselves under-stood where they were going at times! They seemed to operate on a higher emotional plane that any other nation. The challenge for any opponent was to diffuse that emotion, which, for a variety of reasons, hadn't happened at Cardiff in 2007.

Controversy raged when Marc Lièvremont named his starting XV. Morgan Parra, a proven scrum-half, was at fly-half with Imanol

Harinordoquy, one of the finest loose forwards in the game, relegated to the bench.

Some critics suggested Lièvremont was sacrificing the All Black game following Australia's loss to Ireland, because suddenly the 'other' side of the draw presented a seemingly easier path to the final. Given that the southern hemisphere powerhouses, New Zealand, South Africa and Australia, were now all grouped on one side of the draw, there was a degree of logic in that strategy.

Of course, Lièvremont denied the charge and the manner in which his team exploded into action on Eden Park scarcely suggested they were handing the game to the All Blacks; indeed, for the opening eight or nine minutes, as Graham looked on uncomfortably from the coaches' box, it was all the All Blacks could do to keep their line intact. Parra and Maxime Mermoz made dangerous incursions and Parra struck the uprights with a dropped goal attempt.

The All Blacks had resolved to attack the French in the set pieces and that's ultimately where this game was won. The game turned on a defensive scrum. The All Blacks jolted the French pack into reverse and won a penalty. Next instant Ma'a Nonu was careering off downfield and, from a quick recycle, Adam Thomson (the player who was keeping the No. 8 jersey warm till Read returned) scored.

Ted, Shag and Smithy along with the player strategy group had identified the back of the lineout, in Harinordoquy's absence, as one zone where the French would be vulnerable. Because of Parra's inexperience, Graham also saw the inside channel from set pieces as another vulnerable area, one which Carter would exploit quite mercilessly.

With Carter directing operations majestically, and setting up further tries for Cory Jane and Israel Dagg, the All Blacks opened up a commanding 19-nil lead, coasting to a 37–17 victory.

Forward coach Steve Hansen was beaming afterwards because the All Blacks had scored four tries off set plays, three off the lineout and one off their own kick-off. 'When your set piece is operating well, it gives you a platform,' he said.

A poignant and delightful postscript to the victory came when Jock Hobbs, battling the leukaemia that was sapping his energy, made it onto the field to present a special cap to Richie McCaw. The All Black skipper was making his 100th test appearance, the first New Zealander to achieve this milestone.

The good people of Christchurch know how on the most tranquil of days events of earth-shattering proportion can strike out of the blue. The 6.3 earthquake of 22 February which devastated their city remains vivid in their memory. Seven and a half months on, it was a similar gentle day in Wellington as the All Blacks, a day out from their final pool match against Canada, went through their Captain's Run routine. In addition to heeding the wise words of their skipper, in the Captain's Run the players cover the main themes of the game plan and spend time building mentally as individuals and putting an edge on their personal skills.

Canterbury rugby followers, following the World Cup from afar after having all their matches transferred to other venues, were chuffed because one of their favourite sons, Dan Carter, for the first time in his illustrious career, was captaining the All Blacks. Their other favourite son, Richie McCaw, was taking a well-earned rest.

Usually, Carter wrapped up his Captain's Run outings with about 15 place kicks at goal. On this occasion, because he was the captain and the demands upon him were greater than normal, he settled for just four kicks.

Four place kicks, that's all. The fourth was a simple one straight out from the goalposts. He swung through the ball as he had done thousands of times in his career. Only this time pain seared through his left leg. He dropped to the ground, clutching his groin.

Manager Darren Shand was standing about 10 metres away and was startled by what he'd just witnessed. *It must be cramp, surely*, he thought. *Couldn't be anything else, just gently kicking the ball like that.*

Or could it? Graham knew from 30 metres away that, from DC's reaction, the Rugby World Cup was now over for the greatest No. 10 in the game.

Graham realized the worst case scenario he and his management team had talked about and prepared for, after their 2007 experience, had just occurred.

Manager Shand will tell you that Graham never functions better than in a crisis. He had admired the way Graham had handled the desperate situation in the wake of the quarter-final disaster in 2007, when a lesser man would have gone to pieces. Now he was in control again.

Graham first had to reassure his players, who were in various states of shock after seeing their match-winning first-five and goal-kicker crumpled on the ground, in obvious pain.

'We need to be strong and confront adversity,' Graham said to them. 'Well, we've lost Dan. It's a hell of a blow, but we've just got to get on with doing the business.'

At a hastily-arranged press conference, Graham broke the terrible news, emotionally expressing his sympathy for Dan.

'It's a tragedy for Dan,' he said, 'a tragic situation for a highly talented young sportsman. This was his scene, the scene he had been preparing for for life. He's been a world-class player for a long time — probably one of the greatest New Zealand has ever produced. The World Cup was going to be his pinnacle, where he was going to show the world he was the greatest of all time.'

Through the simple act of kicking the ball, Carter had torn his adductor longus tendon off the bone. He had never had trouble with that muscle in his life. That it should tear when it did was inexplicable. The chances of it happening roughly equated to a 6.3 earthquake flattening Christchurch.

As a result of Carter's mishap, Aaron Cruden, the 22-year-old who was so unlucky to miss selection in the first place, was introduced to the squad with the captaincy for the Canadian game passing to Andrew Hore.

The All Blacks swept aside Canada 79–15, with four of the team's 12 tries going to Zac Guildford, who'd been on the mat after it was revealed he had indulged in a drinking spree the evening of the Tri-Nations match in Brisbane, and two to Jerome Kaino, who was steadily emerging as the standout performer of the tournament. In Carter's absence, Slade stepped up to the mark, turning in an accomplished performance. The fact the Canadian scrum was in rapid reverse most of the afternoon meant he was able to operate under almost no pressure.

Once they had defeated France, the All Blacks were assured of a place in the quarter-finals, but they had to wait another 24 hours before they knew whether their opponent would be Argentina or Scotland. And it wasn't till the final whistle blew to an enthralling contest in the rain in Wellington that the answer was provided.

The All Blacks had three times engaged Scotland at the quarter-final stage in World Cups, in 1987, 1995 and 1999, but on this occasion they would be doing battle with the Pumas, who had scraped through with a 13–12 win over Scotland, courtesy of a brilliant solo try by Lucas Amorosino.

Up to the quarter-finals, the All Blacks' behaviour had been exemplary. The gossip magazines were doing a starve. Not only were the boys doing the business on the field, they were angels off it … until the Thursday night before the quarter-final. Suddenly, a big oops, which broke in a Sunday newspaper.

Cory Jane and Israel Dagg had treated themselves to a rather wild night out at Mac's Brewbar in Takapuna. Witnesses described them as being 'under the weather', which was probably a stretch, and said Jane lit up a cigarette, which was contrary to the smoke-free ban in pubs in New Zealand.

They didn't cause any damage or get involved in any trouble, but their behaviour fell below the high standards set by the All Black management and team leaders.

When the pair arrived late back at their hotel, the Spencer on Byron in Takapuna, they were targeted by fans until Piri Weepu intervened, ushering them away and guiding them safely to their rooms.

Manager Darren Shand expressed his disappointment and said they would face the consequences because 'they will be known as the guys who let the team down'. He said it was not what was expected from team members. 'We have no policy regarding drinking,' he said, 'but we expect team members to make good decisions.'

Their joint misdemeanour was dealt with, not by manager Shand or the coaches, but, as was team policy for acts of ill-discipline of this nature, by the seven player leaders. It was with great trepidation that Dagg and Jane had to front their peers, who took a dim view of their 'front page' shenanigans and ordered them to apologize to the whole squad and explain their behaviour.

Dagg and Jane were given the message that they had made very poor decisions and, in so doing, they had let down the country and their team-mates. And the speaking to by the seven player leaders certainly worked. The two disgraced players went on to become two of the standout performers in the semi-final against Australia: Dagg would create the game's only try and Jane would brilliantly defuse Australia's aerial attacks.

This is a classic example of the potency of the dual management structure operating within the team: a lecture from a grumpy manager wouldn't have had half the same impact on the two players as facing their peers had had. Young men hate letting their peers and team-mates down, on or off the field. And if they do, which was clearly obvious in this case, they will be desperate to make amends.

The All Black coaches welcomed the Pumas as a quarter-final opponent because they knew their powerful forwards would give their side the physical workout they needed at this stage of the competition.

And that's exactly how it panned out. However, with grim memories of what had happened at the quarter-final stage four years earlier, Argentina's 'physical workout' raised the anxiety levels of the New Zealand supporters, including Graham's wife, Raewyn.

When Argentina hit the front 7–6 after a well-taken try by Farias Cabello in the 31st minute, memories of Cardiff 2007 came flooding back and Raewyn, who was viewing the game with some of the other All Black management wives, felt positively nauseous. 'I didn't enjoy that game at all,' she admitted later. 'The memories of 2007 were still too vivid.'

Her husband wasn't anxious at all. Graham could see that the All Black game plan was working well and that sustained pressure would ultimately break down the Pumas' defence. Mind you, that's what he thought would happen at Cardiff in 2007 but when the referee appeared to ignore one team's infringing, things went seriously awry. Well, that certainly didn't happen this time: Welsh referee Nigel Owens was extremely vigilant on breakdowns and offsides and the

Pumas suffered, allowing Piri Weepu to land seven penalty goals, an All Black World Cup record.

There had been secrecy over who would handle the goal-kicking without Carter. When Graham was quizzed about this on the Friday preceding the game, he replied, 'Hell, we've got to keep something quiet from the opposition!'

He chose well because Slade, the other option, suffered the first-five's curse, going down, after half an hour, with a similar injury as Carter — a groin tear.

Weepu emerged the hero. Not only did he kick the goals, he directed operations brilliantly from halfback and, after Slade's departure, handled the kick-offs and re-starts as well. His heroics even inspired a T-shirt proclaiming KEEP CALM — PIRI'S ON, which became an instant best-seller.

Down in their changing room, the All Blacks had been so focused on their game, no one was aware of the drama unfolding at Westpac Stadium in Wellington where a late penalty goal by James O'Connor allowed the Wallabies to defeat the Springboks.

It meant the Springboks were on their way home while the Wallabies were into the semi-finals where they would do battle with the winner of the New Zealand-Argentina game.

Graham heard the result but didn't reveal it until after the All Blacks had won their game. Personally, he would have preferred the Springboks as the semi-final opponent, partly because he was a traditionalist but also on this occasion because he regarded them as less potent than the Wallabies in 2011.

'Hey, guys,' he announced in the dressing room to his match-wearied warriors, 'we are playing Australia in the semis next weekend. They just beat South Africa in Wellington by two points.'

If Graham had announced that the team ticket had just won Lotto's first prize, he wouldn't have got a more positive response — the players were stoked. They couldn't wait to play the Wallabies; it was just what they wanted.

Graham was surprised. There was no question about whom the players wanted to be taking on in the semi-final. Were they fired up! So much for old fogies like Graham romanticizing about a clash with the old foe and whom he considered the less potent opponent — the young players didn't see it that way at all. To them, the Australians were the prime foe, the best in the world at so many sports, and they wanted to go after them.

Right there and then, Graham was as certain as he could be in these situations that the All Blacks were going to beat Australia and go through to the final.

The victory over Argentina came at a cost. Slade had done in his groin muscle while Mils Muliaina survived only 40 minutes of his 100th test appearance before suffering a fractured shoulder. Mils, a world-class player and critical member of the team for many years, was presented with a commemorative 100th test cap by Jock Hobbs, like Richie had been two weeks earlier. It heightened the hype among the All Blacks to have two players like McCaw and Muliaina, who had given so much to their country and the All Blacks, to be recognized in this way.

Their replacements were Stephen Donald — Beaver, who'd been on the outer since his shocker at Hong Kong in 2010 — and Hosea Gear, who'd been desperately unlucky to miss selection in the first place.

Donald was whitebaiting on a remote part of the Waikato River when Graham tried to phone him. After three attempts, when he still hadn't got through, Mils Muliaina took possession of Ted's phone and fired off a txt to Beaver: *Answer the phone, you idiot!* That finally prompted a response and, in the terminology that had suddenly become fashionable, 'nek minnit' coach and whitebaiter were talking.

'Beaver, it's Graham Henry here — what are you up to?'

'I'm whitebaiting, Graham.'

'Have you caught any?'

'Yeah, I've got about three kilograms so far.'

'Well, if you bring it to my room at the Heritage Hotel in Auckland, you'll be in the All Blacks!'

And so it was that 27-year-old Donald, who had last played rugby six weeks earlier for Waikato and who was contracted to join the Bath club in England in the season ahead, became the team's fourth-choice first-five. If it hadn't been for the team's rotation policy, where would they be now?

What is Graham Henry most renowned for as a rugby coach? What is it that has consistently given him the edge? The answer, or one of the answers, is video analysis of opponents. It's what he's done since he first became a serious rugby coach. When he coached the Auckland representative team, he used to analyse videos on the VCR — stop, start, stop, start — until the wee hours of the morning.

Graham was always searching for natural weaknesses in opposition teams, with his game plans always revolving around the exploitation of those weaknesses. If an important opponent couldn't kick off the left foot, or was a weak tackler, or a loose forward was slow off the scrum, Graham would know about it, and ruthlessly exploit that weakness.

You'd think when you came to assess an opponent for a World Cup semi-final, there wouldn't be too many frailties showing. Teams surely wouldn't have advanced that far on rugby's most important stage with glaring shortcomings.

Yet this Australian team that had eliminated the defending champion, South Africa, just might have a glaring weakness — someone who was not only a poor tackler but who had difficulty fielding high balls under pressure. Hmmm, he definitely needed to be exploited.

But the individual who focused Ted and Smithy and Shag's attention as they reviewed the Australia–South Africa quarter-final — a game which bore a striking resemblance to the All Blacks' fateful quarter-final four years earlier, with the winning team spending only 20 per cent of the game in opposition territory and making 147 tackles compared with their opponents' 35 — was not a weak link; rather, he was the standout player. Openside flanker David Pocock had unquestionably won the game for Australia with his mastery at the breakdown. The South Africans claimed Kiwi referee Bryce Lawrence had let him get away with murder but whether their cries of foul play were justified or not, Pocock had wielded a massive influence on the outcome.

So how to negate Pocock in the semi-final? Keep him occupied making tackles would be a good start. Take the play to him. Don't give him an even break that would allow him to match Richie McCaw at the breakdowns.

And if Pocock represented the greatest threat, then Quade Cooper was plainly the weakest link. Coach Robbie Deans had taken him out of the front line, as had the Queensland Reds, because he was a suspect tackler. He doesn't lack heart but defending is not his area of strength.

Dropping him back produced a weakness in Australia's back three, not only on aerial skills but in a positional sense as well. The Irish took advantage of that; New Zealand could, too. When the All Blacks attacked, they looked for areas of natural weakness among the opposition. They didn't need to employ the world's greatest detective to identify this one!

Cooper made his first blunder at the kick-off, pushing the ball across the touchline and yielding a scrum back on halfway to the All Blacks. From there they swung onto attack, exerting relentless pressure until Ma'a Nonu scored what would become the game's only try in the sixth minute, brilliantly set up by Israel Dagg.

Funny that the All Blacks should challenge Australia — well, Cooper, especially — in the air because that's the game plan the Wallabies adopted in the Tri-Nations game in Brisbane. Their aerial tactics had exposed the All Blacks, most notably Zac Guildford. But so brilliantly did the All Black back three, and Cory Jane in particular, deal with the aerial bombardment at Eden Park, Deans was forced to change tactics at half-time.

'We weren't getting our hands on the ball and clearly possession was the key,' admitted Deans after the game, 'so we changed our game plan.'

Deans paid a glowing tribute to the New Zealand defence, saying most teams would have leaked a try or two, but the All Blacks hadn't.

Apart from some indifferent goal-kicking, which could have put them beyond reach earlier, the All Blacks produced near-perfect semi-final football, never giving the Wallabies a sniff.

Tactically and physically, Graham would rank it the best performance by the All Blacks in his eight years as head coach. 'Doesn't get much more satisfying for we coaches than that,' he observed to Shag and Smithy at the final whistle. 'We played them out of the game.'

New Zealand had never beaten Australia in a World Cup contest, losing the two previous meetings in 1991 and 2003, so that was an added bonus.

McCaw had heroically survived another 80 minutes on the park. Given his troublesome foot, there was a temptation to sub him once victory was assured. But McCaw deserved to be there at the final whistle. Four years earlier, to the weekend, he'd had absolutely nothing to smile about, for on that occasion his team had been shockingly eliminated by France; but now, at least five minutes before that final whistle, he was smiling.

Now they were through to the World Cup final where, most unexpectedly, their opponents would be the French, who had edged out Wales 9–8 controversially in the previous evening's semi-final.

The Welsh, under Kiwi coach Warren Gatland, had emerged as one of the finest attacking teams at the tournament and looked to have the measure of the French but, tragically, in the 17th minute their outstanding captain Sam Warburton effected a tip tackle on winger Vincent Clerc and was shown a red card. The surviving 14 Welshman demonstrated great courage and determination but found the handicap of operating a man short for the final hour just too much.

Which left New Zealand and France, who had each participated in two previous finals, to contest the Webb Ellis Cup for 2011.

16

One point's enough

While it's accepted that in sport nothing is ever guaranteed, there was surely no more obvious outcome to the 2011 Rugby World Cup final than that the All Blacks would defeat France.

It was truly a no-brainer. The All Blacks, operating on their beloved Eden Park where no team had defeated them since 1994, had swept aside every opponent, including France in pool play, while amassing 39 tries.

The French for much of the tournament were a team in turmoil, many of the players seemingly at odds with the coach. After being crushed by the All Blacks they had suffered another humiliating loss, to Tonga, one of the greatest upsets in World Cup history. In four outings they had scored just 13 tries. After scraping into the play-offs, they regrouped to defeat the under-achieving England team, then edged Wales out of the tournament, thanks to the referee adhering to the IRB directive on the spear tackle.

It was Jonathan Davies, the great former Welsh fly-half, who raised the first smidgeon of doubt about the outcome, writing: 'The All Blacks would write France off at their peril. There is a chance, however small, France could become the most outrageous party poopers. Mr Unbearable Tension could be their 16th man!'

The French had been written off by everyone — well, everyone except perhaps Jonathan Davies — and history reveals there is no greater motivation for a team than to be written off. It was to prove a powerful catalyst once again.

While nothing short of amputation would have stopped captain Richie McCaw playing, there was ongoing concern about his troublesome foot. With one of the team's iconic stars, Dan Carter, grounded, the All Blacks could ill afford to lose the other. McCaw hadn't trained with the team for three weeks. He was maintaining his aerobic fitness in the gym but at team sessions he just walked behind the team, not wanting to inflame a foot that patently required surgery to fix it. At least being there, he was able to take a vital part in team discussions on various technical or tactical aspects regarding the final.

Then there was the mysterious case of Piri Weepu, the team's Mr Fix It, who had so magnificently answered the call when the team needed a reliable goal-kicker against Argentina after Carter dropped out. During the warm-up session, Weepu's goal-kicking was erratic and he seemed to be favouring one leg.

'What's the matter with Piri?' Graham asked Wayne Smith.

'I think he's all right, Ted— I'm not aware of anything wrong.'

'I'll check with Deb Robinson [the team doctor].'

What was wrong with Weepu was that the previous day he had taken himself off for an extended goal-kicking session — not ordered by any of the coaches — and returned with a tender adductor such as had already put Carter and Slade out of the tournament. A simple case of doing the extra because it was a final when it was important to keep things normal.

The muscle had settled down by the time he arrived at Eden Park on match night — but Weepu was feeling it again during the warm-up, after his practice kicks.

Dr Robinson reported this to Smithy, saying that Weepu was confident the leg would be fine once he'd thoroughly warmed up and got into the game.

Yeah right.

The unfancied French demonstrated their intentions by lining up in a V formation to confront the All Black haka, before advancing menacingly towards it.

One of the reasons this game became a dogfight was because the All Blacks failed to nail any of the scoring opportunities that came their way early in the game. Piri was struggling with his adductor and missed every kick, and they didn't have Dan Carter to taunt the French and to navigate the ship the way he had in the pool game. Both of these factors were impacting seriously on the team's confidence.

If penalty goals weren't an option, the All Blacks would have to score tries. Time to recall the Teabag move, last used on this ground against Australia in August 2008. It had worked a treat on that occasion and then been put on the back burner, reserved for the 'big one', the final. No reason why it couldn't produce the same result again this time.

As the All Blacks gathered for a lineout near the French 22, skipper McCaw decided it was the perfect move for that position on the field.

'Teabag,' he whispered to his fellow forwards, not too loud in case any of the long-standing English-speaking French forwards recalled the move from encounters a few seasons previously.

It required Keven Mealamu to throw accurately, which he did, and Jerome Kaino to gather the ball safely, which he did. And the French are still trying to fathom what happened next! One half of the All Black lineout eased back while the other half crowded forward, creating a chasm through which Woodcock, having received the ball from Kaino, charged for the goal line and a try, a try he, and the All Blacks, will never forget.

'We've been keeping that move up our sleeve for the final,' he said later. 'I scored it, but it was a great team effort.'

Weepu couldn't convert and at half-time, after a tense, tight and surprisingly even 40 minutes of action, the All Blacks led 5–0. Graham had been warned World Cup finals were low-scoring affairs usually won by a penalty or a dropped goal — and he was beginning to believe that now.

In their pool match a month earlier, the All Blacks had several times ripped the French defence to shreds in the first half to be comfortably ahead 19–3 at half-time. So what was different this time?

The French forwards got into the All Blacks early and didn't allow them to set a platform, which was the key to the game. Also, psychologically, the All Blacks couldn't help feeling that they'd played their final the week before, against Australia. And it hadn't helped that everyone had assured them the outcome was a forgone conclusion. They certainly weren't as fired up as they had been against the Wallabies. They were 10 per cent off. Furthermore, this was their 12th test match in 14 weeks and fatigue was possibly starting to become a factor.

There was also the disruption of losing Cruden with a knee injury after half an hour. What was it with these All Black first-fives? They were dropping like flies. They were now down to No. 4, good old Stephen Donald. He'd joined the squad so late there wasn't time to outfit him with his own jersey. He had to borrow Cruden's back-up jersey, which was at least two sizes too small.

The camaraderie that existed among the All Blacks was evident the moment Donald ran on the park. Brad Thorn gave him a welcoming slap on the back. 'Great to have you back, Beaver!'

Despite the closeness of the score, Graham wasn't unduly concerned at half-time. He had great faith in his players and was confident they would do the business in the second half. 'Stick to the game plan, keep talking — you'll come through,' he assured his troops.

His optimism lasted only six minutes. First, Donald, who at half-time had been instructed to assume the goal-kicking responsibilities — even though he hadn't had any kicking practice for six weeks — banged over a super penalty goal to give his team an eight-point buffer.

But from the restart, the All Blacks defences became confused, for probably the only occasion in the entire World Cup campaign. Weepu's desperate hack at the ball went awry and Thierry Dusautoir, France's inspirational captain — who would go on to win the Player of the Match award — scored beside the posts. With the conversion there was only one point in it, with 33 minutes still to play.

Now it was worry time … for Ted and Shag and Smithy … for the entire management team … for the 'stadium of four million' who had been championing the All Blacks every step of the way. The All Blacks had twice before had their World Cup dreams shattered by the French. Surely, it wasn't going to happen again, not here at their fortress of Eden Park.

The French had given a false impression of their talent in the pool game. This was the real French team now, being led from the front by Dusautoir and his partner in crime, Harinordoquy. Their confidence was up, they were taking the game to New Zealand, playing in New Zealand's half, playing superbly. It was desperate stuff.

There should be a book written on how All Black supporters handled that final half hour of pulsating action. Some couldn't handle it at all and either turned their backs on the game or went outside. Some prayed. Most fell deathly quiet.

Up in the All Black coaches' box, anxiety reigned. Ted and Shag and Smithy were beside themselves. This wasn't how they perceived the final unfolding at all!

What sustained them was they knew their players were mentally strong. They knew there would be clear and intelligent communication on game tactics and a trust in each other to get the job done. They knew Richie would be in control and would have great support from Conrad, Brad, Horey, Kevy and the rest of the boys, which was enormously reassuring. They had prepared them for worst-case scenarios and that was pretty much what was unfolding right now. Although they were prepared for the unexpected, it didn't need to be this bad, though — with three No. 10s (Carter, Slade and Cruden) and two on-field leaders (Carter and Muliaina) out of the World Cup and out of the final.

Because Ted and Smithy tended to become too emotional during matches, Shag was the individual responsible for coolly passing messages down to the manager Shand and the management team on the touchline.

Concerned that all the play was happening in the All Blacks' half — not a good thing when one penalty goal could wipe out your advantage — and prompted by Messrs Henry and Smith, Steve issued instructions to kick deep for position. 'Play the game in their half, their 22. Get the ball in behind the French, great chase, turn it over, get the next set piece, score points … get us out of the heat, boys!'

The message was received by the All Blacks, comprehended — and ignored. The players on the field had decided they wouldn't kick because they feared that might spark a strong counter-attack by the French. Look what had happened in Hong Kong the previous year: when the clearing kick missed touch, the Wallabies launched a counter-attack and scored the winning try.

No, the All Blacks were perfectly happy doing what they were doing. They had confidence in the referee (Craig Joubert), and they had supreme confidence in their own ability to contain the French raids.

The introduction of Andrew Ellis, Ali Williams and Andrew Hore to the game straight after Dusautoir scored his try, and earlier Stephen Donald, injected a wealth of experience and additional clarity onto the field. And this was an occasion when experience counted for everything. Thank God for rotation!

Under captain McCaw's directions, to ensure they had the numbers on their feet to defend, the All Blacks were committing only enough players to each ruck to contain the French, and by constant communication they were ensuring no-one ventured offside or gave referee Joubert any cause to issue a penalty.

At one stage, Kaino reached through and went to secure the ball. He was probably within his rights, but because it involved an element of risk, Ellis suddenly barked out, 'No, JK, leave it alone!'

Ted and Shag and Smithy couldn't understand why their instructions were being ignored. But they could see their players appeared to have things under control. So they fell silent.

Graham admits that with about 15 minutes to play, when the French were racking up about their 16th phase deep in All Black territory, he endured a terrible 'What if ...?' moment. 'It was the only time in the entire World Cup I was stressed and I had a momentary anxiety attack. How would I handle it, and, more importantly, how would Raewyn and the kids and Mum handle it, if we lost?'

But out of the 2007 wreckage had emerged a team with the mental strength to survive. Everything the coaches and the players had talked about for four years was coming together.

Richie and the boys weren't letting this one get away. They

frustrated the life out of the French until eventually they forced the turnover with about five minutes to play. You knew then the trophy was won. The All Blacks had the ball and they weren't letting the French get it back.

There was time for a rock-solid demonstration of scrummaging and a masterly lineout take by Brad Thorn before referee Joubert finally blew for full time. To the immense relief of an entire nation, after 24 years New Zealand was the rugby world champion again.

Skipper McCaw had played himself to a standstill. With foot fractured and seriously inflamed — when he finally removed his boot in the changing room the foot was so swollen he would never have got the boot back on again — he had no right to even be on the park, yet he had survived the full 80 minutes and directed his team to an epic victory.

Richie would say to Graham later that the final 30 minutes were the best 30 minutes of his life. Graham would say to Shag and Smithy that if Richie hadn't played, he doesn't believe they would have won the final.

McCaw didn't win the Player of the Match award, which probably deserved to go to Dusautoir, but if there had been a special trophy for most courageous performer in the final, he would have bolted in.

Far more important than being best player of the night, the All Black captain went forward to receive the Webb Ellis Cup, the first Kiwi to take possession of it since David Kirk 24 long years ago.

Kirk has done all right for himself since. One imagines McCaw will, too.

He would be paid a delightful tribute by Robert Kitson in the *Guardian*:

Richie McCaw is required to be a simultaneous mix of Sir Edmund Hillary, Colin 'Pinetree' Meads and Mother Teresa. He has done a sterling job — you could travel to the furthest corners of the North and South Islands and still not find a soul with a bad word to say about him. Because McCaw is the embodiment of how most Kiwis like to see themselves — uncomplaining, modest, durable and resourceful. 'He's very very bright, he's brave and he's talented,' said Graham Henry, 'not a bad combination; we would not have won the final without him.' Wayne Smith said, 'Probably the same things characterize him as a player and a leader. He's bright, humble, comes from a rural background, so he's tough and never gets too far ahead of himself. He's hugely resilient.' McCaw on one leg is better than most players on two.

Four years earlier, when Graham unenthusiastically fronted the media following his team's shock loss to France, he went to extreme lengths to say nothing. A two-point loss had left him numb, so diplomacy ruled. It was the start of the worst weekend of his life. But now after rugby's ultimate goal had been achieved, Graham overflowed with quotable quotes.

At the official press conference, he lavished praise on his skipper. 'Richie is an inspiration to the whole team and management. He can hardly walk — how he played today, I don't know. It was down to heart and determination. He is the best leader this country has ever had. Richie has gained strength through experience and he got his reward today.'

Of his own reappointment in 2007, he said that a number of good coaches had been sacked before their time. 'Look at Sir Alex Ferguson and Wayne Bennett. They are great examples of the reward patience brings. You are evolving, getting better. You learn from your experience and mistakes you may have made along the way. It takes at least two years to know what it's about, to get your feet under the table, to feel comfortable in the job.'

In seeking to place the World Cup win in context, he said it was the aspiration of the team — both players and management — to add to the All Black legacy. 'The All Blacks have always been the winningest sporting team in the world over a hundred years and we saw it as our job to add to that legacy. It was extremely important we won the Tri-Nations, the Bledisloe Cup and achieved a Grand Slam or two, but the ultimate was always going to be winning the Rugby World Cup. That's the Holy Grail. That's what gives you peace.'

And to a radio interviewer who inquired how he felt right at that moment, he replied, 'I'm just so proud to be a New Zealander. I've got huge pride in what New Zealand has achieved as a nation and great personal pride for what those young men achieved at the death.'

To the same interviewer who asked how he felt during the closing stages of the final, he said, 'It was the only time I was stressed during the whole World Cup — the last 30 minutes almost killed me!'

The difference between 2007 and 2011 was just three points — a one-point win compared with a two-point loss — but to Graham, the difference felt like a million points. The All Blacks were not only the No. 1 ranked team in the world, they were champions, champions of the rugby world. It doesn't get any better than that.

17

After the ball

On the Friday following the World Cup triumph, Graham went fishing. The offer had come from fishing guru Geoff Thomas to Graham and any of his World Cup champion players who fancied a relaxing day out on the water. So Ted was accompanied by Richie and Dan, Ali Williams, Andrew Hore, Tony Woodcock, Anthony Boric and one or two others, and off they went in Geoff's superbly well-equipped boat out into the Hauraki Gulf.

In terms of fish landed, it was an average day, but it was a wonderfully relaxing occasion. A few bottles of the sponsor's fine product Steinlager Pure were consumed as the men reflected on the achievements of the past seven weeks while waiting for the fish to bite.

When Richie removed his shoes, Graham cast a glance at his feet and couldn't believe what he was seeing: one foot was normal; the other was the size of a balloon.

'Jeez, Richie, look at that foot — it's bloody enormous!'

'Yeah, Ted. Pleased there are no more games. Don't think I'd get the boot back on!'

Graham could only marvel at the man in front of him. How he'd got through 80 minutes of grand final rugby on that foot, goodness only knows. And there was Dan Carter, almost mobile again after an operation in Melbourne had repaired his torn adductor tendon.

Graham's worst nightmare as the All Blacks were preparing for the World Cup had been that Carter and McCaw, the two best players in the world, would be taken out by injury — and Dan had gone down in a heap on the eve of the Canadian game. Now, looking at Richie's fearfully swollen foot now, Graham realized it was a minor miracle his skipper had kept going.

Only Richie and the team doctor, Deb Robinson, had known the extent of the problem. The captain hadn't trained for the past month, merely walked around behind his team-mates at training, because once he began exercising the foot it increased the inflammation and the swelling.

Graham knew it was a delicate situation but was prepared to go with whatever would allow his captain to play the final three matches. Looking down at the mess that was Richie's foot, he realized he was in the company of a most remarkable human being.

Not many players would have survived on that foot. Through sheer guts and determination, Richie had played out the 80 minutes of the semi-final against Australia, and then repeated that effort against France in the final. Only in the quarter-final against Argentina, knowing victory was secure, did he permit himself to be replaced, eight minutes from the finish.

The tenacity he had demonstrated in leading from the front was testament to his character. Ted knew that without him it was extremely unlikely the All Blacks would have won.

Back in 2007, Richie had been panned after the quarter-final loss to France. Now he was being hailed as one of New Zealand's greatest leaders. Everything the team, the player leaders and the management team had plotted and planned and talked about for four years had come together when it mattered.

'Cheers, Richie,' said Ted, raising his glass to his amazing captain. 'And cheers to you too, Dan. You guys are very special.'

Graham couldn't believe how Dan had handled his crushing injury. The World Cup meant everything to him and prior to the injury he'd been in sublime form. He had given a virtuoso display against France the previous weekend, navigating the side to a stunning victory. Yet while the injury would have personally devastated him, Dan had remained buoyant and positive around the team. He'd carried on his leadership role, assisting Colin Slade and Aaron

Cruden and, ultimately, Stephen Donald.

If there were down times, and there must have been, he'd kept those to himself. Around the team he had been as positive as he had ever been. He was always upbeat, confident the boys could do the business. Graham thought his input over the final three weeks had been nothing short of phenomenal. He was certain if Dan had played the final the All Blacks would have won comfortably. But he couldn't play and Graham and all the others had endured 30 minutes of sheer hell before victory was secured.

Spending this day in the company of Richie and Dan and the other All Blacks, especially those who had shared the journey that had started way back in 2004, was wonderfully special for Graham.

What a memorable week it had been. The Monday following the grand final happened to be a national holiday, Labour Day, and the mayor of Auckland's super city, Len Brown, brilliantly decreed that this provided the perfect occasion for a victory parade down Queen Street for the World Cup heroes.

Given the short notice, the turnout was amazing. Crowd estimates varied wildly from 30,000 to well over 200,000. The actual number would have been closer to the former but, whatever, it was a mind-boggling experience for the All Blacks and their management. The World Cup had captivated the entire nation and the All Blacks had supplied the perfect climax by winning the final.

'It's when you see this number of people cheering the team, you realize what winning this trophy means to New Zealand,' said skipper McCaw.

On the Monday evening the International Rugby Board hosted its glitzy annual awards function at the Vector Arena. Not surprisingly, the All Blacks waltzed off with the Team of the Year award, France's awesome leader Thierry Dusautoir claimed the Player of the Year trophy (the other finalists were three All Blacks, Piri Weepu, Jerome Kaino and Ma'a Nonu, and Wallaby David Pocock) and the man who'd secured the event for New Zealand, Jock Hobbs, was awarded the Vernon Pugh Award for distinguished service to rugby.

Oh, and yes, there was one more trophy: Graham Henry was named Coach of the Year, the fifth occasion in eight years he had been so honoured. No other coach had won the award more than once!

Graham was genuinely embarrassed that he alone received the trophy. He was the head coach, for sure, but so many others had contributed mightily to the World Cup success. He tried to acknowledge them all in his acceptance speech — his fellow coaches, Shag and Smithy; Mike Cron, the scrum coach; Mick Byrne, the skills coach; Nic Gill, the strength and conditioning coach; Shandy, the manager; Gilbert Enoka, the facilitator (the man who was the 'glue'); Deb Robinson, the doctor (who'd had her hands full over the past month); Peter Gallagher, the best rehab physio in the world; George Duncan, the massage therapist; Alistair Rogers, the analyst; Joe Locke and Jo Malcolm, who looked after the media; Bianca Thiel, the fabulous executive assistant; and Errol Collins, the baggageman who had a great feel for the need to make a clown of himself for the benefit of the team. Many of these people were world class in their respective fields and collectively Graham knew they represented the best 'team' in the world.

On the Tuesday, the team was off down to Christchurch, the shattered city, for another parade. This one was especially poignant given that the good folk of Christchurch had been denied their share of World Cup action after AMI Stadium was rendered unplayable.

The earthquakes have left central Christchurch looking like a war zone, so this second parade moved around the perimeter of the city and on to the Fanzone at Hagley Park, where tens of thousands of fans had followed much of the World Cup action on giant screens. Banners acknowledged Canterbury's great contributors — Richie McCaw, Dan Carter, Brad Thorn, Kieran Read, Andy Ellis, Israel Dagg, Zac Guildford, Corey Flynn, Sam Whitelock, and the Franks brothers. Intriguingly, there were also banners for the unlikeliest of World Cup heroes: Beaver! In a little over half an hour on Eden Park, Stephen Donald had been transformed from one of New Zealand's abandoned rugby men into a cult hero.

He and Brad replied on behalf of the All Blacks after Christchurch mayor Bob Parker had welcomed the team and congratulated them on their mighty efforts.

The All Blacks had based themselves in Christchurch for four days prior to their pool match against France. Nothing untoward happened during the All Blacks' visit but shortly before kick-off in their quarter-final against Argentina on the Sunday night, with thousands of fans packed into the Fanzone, Christchurch had been rocked by another seriously large earthquake, one measuring 5.5 on the Richter scale.

After the Christchurch parade it was off to Wellington. That evening, with nothing planned, an impromptu team session developed in a hotel room — the players were finally able to relax and share the great adventure that had been the World Cup. The Wellington players could have excused themselves and headed to their homes but they chose to stay. It became one of the special occasions of the whole World Cup campaign.

Graham finally drew the gathering to attention, became quite emotional and delivered a lengthy address. He told the players and the management how much he'd enjoyed their company, reminded them what they had achieved, and thanked them for that — and told them he was finishing coaching the All Blacks.

He'd been asked about his future many times at press conferences during and since the conclusion of the World Cup but had avoided a direct answer. He felt it was right and proper to make the announcement in the presence of the people who mattered most.

The Wellington street parade took substantially longer than it should have because of serious congestion. Often the parade ground to a complete halt, but that didn't matter: the players were delighted to acknowledge the tens of thousands of fans who turned out to cheer them.

Beaver banners appeared in great profusion. He really had become a cult hero, which delighted Graham and the team management because he was a great team member who had been pilloried over one bad performance in Hong Kong.

Graham had utilized Beaver's exceptional qualities of recall when the young player was a regular member of the All Black squad. At trainings, when Graham required the reserve players to be co-ordinated into a meaningful opposition simulating the plays of, say, Australia or South Africa or England, Beaver was put in charge and directed the opposition attack play to perfection. Beaver always got it dead right.

To Graham, Beaver was a classic example of how the rotation policy had developed an extended squad that ultimately allowed the All Blacks to win the World Cup.

Graham learned of two people who, after the team was announced, had premonitions that Beaver would kick the winning goal in the final. Richard Kahui was with him when the team was announced (Kahui being in and Donald out). 'You stay fit, Beaver, because you'll kick the winning goal in the World Cup final.'

'Gee, you talk crap,' was Beaver's response. But it came to pass.

And Kerre Woodham, the personable Newstalk ZB radio host and who is a friend of Raewyn's, said that her mother had a dream that Steve Donald would kick the winning goal in the World Cup final.

The only person who didn't believe he would even have the opportunity to be a World Cup hero was Donald himself. It was just as well Mils Muliaina had finally got Beaver to answer his phone or he would gone off to Bath with a stack of whitebait but no World Cup medal!

The Wellington visit concluded with a parliamentary reception at which Graham, for one of the rare occasions in his term as head coach of the All Blacks, was caught out. With no prior warning, he was advised he would be speaking on behalf of the All Blacks. Graham always prepares himself meticulously for such occasions; impromptu speeches aren't his thing. On this occasion he mumbled a few words, desperately trying to bring his thoughts together. It wasn't, he acknowledged later, his finest moment.

Prime Minister John Key was in buoyant mood; he'd been a staunch supporter of the All Blacks right through. Graham marvels at the way the PM can relate equally comfortably to anyone and everyone. The All Blacks thought he was just great. Why, he'd even 'downed trou' in their changing room to show Dan Carter that he wasn't the only model who looked good in Jockey underwear!

Seeing John Key reminded Graham of a slightly embarrassing moment following the World Cup win. When the Prime Minister entered the changing room to embrace the world champions, he was accompanied by another distinguished-looking individual Graham didn't recognize.

'Who's that with John Key?' Graham asked media man Joe Locke.

'That's the Governor General, Sir Jerry Mateparae.'

'Right.'

Graham went across and introduced himself.

Back home in Auckland, it was time for a truly special celebration for Graham — with his family. He'd scarcely stopped since the final whistle at Eden Park and now finally he could share the moment with Raewyn, sons Matthew (and his wife, Marie) and Andrew, and daughter Catherine (and her husband, Hamish).

It had been Graham's grand plan to bring Raewyn, Matthew, Catherine and Andrew together on the field if, and when, the All Blacks won the final. The intention was laudable. It was wonderful that Graham wanted to share this precious occasion with his family. But the police and security people at Eden Park weren't so sympathetic, and poor Matthew, considered perhaps the most stable of the Henry children, had no sooner stepped on the hallowed turf than he was pounced upon and frog-marched out of the ground, to his embarrassment and Graham's disappointment. Graham tried to remonstrate when he realized what was happening, but no-one was listening initially. In time, common sense prevailed, but the moment was lost.

Raewyn managed to get through the security cordon — an All Black coach's wife plainly holds greater status than his son — and together they did a circuit of the ground, acknowledging the fans.

It was very special for Graham to share this moment with Raewyn after all they'd gone through over more than three decades and particularly after what they, as a family, had had to endure in 2007. Graham felt a lightening of the soul as he completed the circuit of the ground.

Raewyn, who had watched the game in the company of Smithy's wife, Trish, and Shandy's wife, Jan, had thrown up during the first half but managed to hold it together in the second half — although, like every other Kiwi, she had sat rigidly on the edge of her seat for the final 30 minutes, too scared to utter a word. Not so Trish, who had given a couple of nearby spectators a barrel when they started making negative comments about the All Blacks!

Two weeks after the final, by which time he had almost come back to earth, although he was still waking at 4.30 a.m., Graham was asked if he would accept a knighthood.

There had been a lot of speculation that such a title would accompany a World Cup victory but it was suddenly a reality, and Graham was overcome. Before accepting, he discussed the matter with his family, who had endured an emotional roller-coaster ride during his eight years as the head coach of the All Blacks.

Graham had never found it easy to extricate himself from the All Black environment during the long rugby season, when the stresses upon him were substantial, and become instantly relaxed with his wife and family. Some individuals might be able to manage that, he sometimes thought to himself, but he never found it easy. But he did get better at it!

And so it came to pass when the New Year Honours List was revealed that the man who had restored glory and status to the All Blacks and brought euphoria to an entire nation was to become Sir Graham. It was also revealed that Richie McCaw had declined a knighthood.

Graham told a reporter that the title made him feel uncomfortable, but humbled as well. 'When you are involved in a team sport,' he said, 'a lot of people produce those results, not just one person. Rugby is a team game.'

Graham said he understood why Richie had turned down the title. 'He is a young fella and he still has some years ahead of him playing rugby. He would probably feel uncomfortable about having that title, particularly when he is captaining the side. I am sure his time will come.'

At the time of his appointment as All Black coach late in 2003, Graham said to the *New Zealand Herald*, 'We have got to produce a rugby-smart culture because, at the end of the day, brains beats talent. We have to be rugby smart. We have to take the initiative. To do that, you have to produce leaders and decision makers on the field.'

When he signed off in 2011, his team crowned as world champions, all those boxes had been ticked. Along with his fellow coaches, Shag and Smithy, and the management team, with Bert (Gilbert Enoka) as the facilitator, they had introduced that important new culture, made their players more rugby-savvy, and transformed the All Blacks into a team of on-field and off-field leaders and decision makers.

His team had restored the passion and pride in playing for the All Blacks and helped make them aware of their team's amazing legacy, a far cry from the assortment he had inherited eight years earlier that included players who had greater passion for their provinces and their Super teams than the All Blacks.

He is extremely proud of the fact that, in the wake of the World Cup, 11 of the 14 coaches and management team are back in position and only four players have taken off overseas — Brad Thorn and Mils Muliaina (who, respectively, at 37 and 31, are seeking a gentler existence in Ireland and Japan), Stephen Donald (who committed himself to Bath when he wasn't initially wanted for the World Cup) and John Afoa (who for family reasons sought fresh rugby challenges that didn't involve endless travel, in Ulster). He puts this down to the new All Black culture, a learning environment that helps them grow as both rugby players and as people. As Sir Brian Lochore said: 'Better people make better All Blacks.' When you are learning, getting better, are stimulated and want to keep improving, then you want to stay.

Graham wanted this book to be subtitled *Building the Legacy*, which, while entirely appropriate, was deemed by the cover designer to be rather too cumbersome. So *Final Word* it became.

Graham steps down proud of the fact that he has enhanced that All Black legacy by winning 84.9 per cent of the 106 matches he and Shag and Smithy prepared the team for over eight years. In that time they won five Tri-Nations titles, completed three Grand Slams, never lost the Bledisloe Cup, won all 23 tests on end-of-year European tours, humbled the British Lions, and ultimately claimed the World Cup. That is one hell of a record!

So when he reflects on these quite extraordinary achievements, can he reveal a secret formula?

No secrets, he insists, no silver bullets. What makes the current All Blacks great is a marvellous mix of DNA, hard work, ensuring the right people are in place to condition them and prepare them, and the sharing of the leadership (so brilliantly illustrated during the World Cup).

He says New Zealand is blessed with an ideal racial mix. 'When you bring the best Polynesian, Maori and Pakeha players together, you create an on-field explosiveness that isn't matched anywhere else in the world.'

Graham also pinpoints the secondary schools competitions that make New Zealand the best rugby breeding ground in the world. Quality players consistently come through on the schools rugby conveyor belt because the game at schools level is so well structured, highly competitive and well coached throughout the country.

Graham will tell you that because New Zealand teams play the game with the ball in hand, the All Blacks especially, this style is emulated by the young players coming through. Watch a top inter-secondary school match and you'll rarely see the ball kicked, whereas in college games in South Africa, kicks, penalty kicks and drop-kicks abound. But here in New Zealand the emphasis is quite different: it's about running and passing and scoring tries.

Graham's 83 per cent win rate, maintained across four decades, demands huge respect, and so the original outline of this book included a chapter on coaching. Sadly, as the manuscript expanded, it became apparent space would not permit. However, Graham's coaching is so simplistic, his philosophy can be encapsulated in just a few paragraphs:

- Winning rugby is about the control of the advantage line; if you control that, you win the game.
- Winning rugby is about receiving top-quality ball from set pieces, getting it over the advantage line and either scoring tries from those strikes or recycling as quickly as possible and scoring tries from second-phase attacks (which may number 9 or 10 or possibly 12).
- Conversely, your team has to stop the opposition from doing those things, by giving them poor quality set-piece ball and controlling that advantage line. Defence is the backbone that wins games.

- Winning rugby is about having an attack plan from turnover ball, ball kicked to you, or what the opposition give you by their mistakes, or through turnovers at the tackle.
- Every opposition team has basic weaknesses and it's the coach's job to identify these and exploit them. For example, have they got a player we can take advantage of? Maybe a weak-tackling No. 10, a No. 6 who is slow off the side of the scrum, or a right-sided No. 15 who is suspect running right to left because he has no left foot?
- Opposition teams are most likely to be weak at the transition points between the last forward and the first back, either side of the scrum, the rear of the lineout and outside the No. 13, and in behind that first line of defence.
- Make your tackles, treasure possession, and be supremely fit.
- If you can, analyse the referee and be aware of his idiosyncrasies because that can also be helpful.
- Don't boss your players, work with them and involve them in the tactical plan and the decision making; today, it's an 'us' culture rather than the 'you and them' of yesteryear.

If you are ambitious as a coach, you have to push the boundaries. Graham has never been one to coach conservatively for the purpose of remaining secure in the role. 'If you're conservative and trying to decrease the risk, you won't stimulate your players — they won't enjoy the game,' he says. 'Teams playing with confidence, who are stimulated by the way they are playing, do the business. Just like for young kids, enjoyment is the key.'

Graham is proud of the fact that in almost 40 years of coaching, he was never sacked, although he certainly dangled over the precipice in 2007! His advice to coaches is not to worry about defeat: hate it, but adopt a positive push-out-the-boundaries, take-them-on culture. Players expect their coaches to give off the right messages. If keeping your job is uppermost in your mind, it will be perceived that your future is more important than your team's.

His other valuable piece of advice to coaches, particularly those operating at an élite level, is to control your own environment. If you are under pressure, don't read the newspapers, don't listen to the radio and don't watch TV. If you win by 100 then read, listen and watch it all! If you want advice, ask qualified people you respect, but at the end of the day, the buck stops with you.

Graham was looking forward to a more relaxed lifestyle once he completed his All Black commitments, but that hasn't eventuated. Six months on from the World Cup, his diary is busier than it's ever been. The New Zealand Rugby Union has retained him as a coaching mentor, the Argentinian Rugby Union has signed him up to fulfil a similar role with its leading coaches, and he's also mentoring Sport New Zealand's emerging coaches across a wide range of sports.

He is a shareholder of, and an important contributor to, a rugby coaching website, www.therugbysite.com, and has set up, with others (including some All Blacks) a Hong Kong/China/New Zealand import-export company.

When his busy work finally allows, he's looking forward to spending time with his grandchildren — Matthew and Marie's three: Olivia, Finn and Kate; and Catherine and Hamish's two: Sofia and Jake — who are all under five. And Andrew is on the bench waiting to make an impact, which he will!

Graham is grateful for the unconditional support he received from his children Matthew, Catherine and Andrew throughout his rugby coaching career and especially during his eight years with the All Blacks that consumed so much of his time. His brother Brian and sister Carol were also always staunchly behind him.

Both Graham and Raewyn are looking forward to some seriously competitive fishing expeditions. They enjoy fishing because it's relaxing and something they can do as a couple, but Raewyn is a talented angler — she once landed a 35 kg hapuku — so there is always an element of competition when they go out together. Fortunately, unlike death-or-glory rugby matches, fishing competitions are not something that cause Raewyn to throw up!

And Ted's happy— as long as he wins.

Epilogue by Richie McCaw

Graham has been a terrific coach for the All Blacks. As a player you couldn't have asked for anything more in a coach. He has all the attributes necessary to do the job, including that rare ability to change and adapt. If something was not working, he would change it and find something that would work.

He spent hours reviewing videos, analysing, looking for that little something that would likely give his team an edge. He was always looking to add that little bit extra that would give the All Blacks an advantage.

Playing at the top level of the game, you quickly learn that there is not much between the best teams in the world on any given day. That's why that little extra is so vital.

Graham is a master tactician. Not a screamer or a yeller — he doesn't need that; he extracts what he wants in far more subtle ways.

His man-management was superb, especially over the past few years. He had the respect of all the players and knew exactly how to handle each one, both within the team environment and on their own.

I have a close personal relationship with Ted. The more you get to know him, the more you come to appreciate his wonderful, dry sense of humour. I always enjoy his company. I am indebted to him as both a coach and a friend. We will always remain close.

Richie McCaw
April 2012

Graham Henry's coaching record

	Played	Won	Lost	Drawn	% success
Auckland Grammar School	102	95	7	0	93%
Auckland University	98	79	17	2	81%
NZ Secondary Schools	19	17	2	0	89%
Auckland Colts	40	39	1	0	98%
Auckland B	9	6	2	1	67%
Auckland	102	80	22	0	78%
Auckland Blues	39	32	6	1	82%
New Zealand A	3	3	0	0	100%
Wales	34	20	13	1	59%
British Lions	10	7	3	0	70%
All Blacks	106	90	16	0	85%
Totals	562	468	89	5	83%